Education
and the
Information
Society

A CHALLENGE FOR EUROPEAN POLICY

edited by Michael Eraut

CASSELL

Cassell Educational Limited
Villiers House
41/47 Strand
London WC2N 5JE

First published 1991

British Library Cataloguing in Publication Data
Education and the information society: a challenge for
    European policy—(Cassell Council of Europe series).
    1. Europe. Education. Applications of computer systems in
    I. Eraut, Michael
    370.285

ISBN 0–304–32294–6

Phototypeset by Selectmove Ltd
Printed and bound in Great Britain by
Biddles Ltd, Guildford and King's Lynn

CONTENTS

v

CONTENTS

Foreword

THE EUROPE OF THE TWENTY-FOUR

The Council of Europe, with a membership of twenty-four European parliamentary democracies, is the largest of the European political institutions. It represents a total population of some 425 million citizens across the breadth and depth of Europe – from Iceland to Turkey, from Portugal to Norway.

Founded in 1949, the Council of Europe was the first European political organization set up after the Second World War. It stemmed from an idea expressed by Winston Churchill in 1943 that, in addition to the proposed United Nations, regional councils would be required to deal with the problems facing the world after the war. The idea took root and was developed by the leading political figures of the post-war period.

On 5 May 1949 the Statute of the Council of Europe was signed by the ten founding states: Belgium, France, Denmark, Ireland, Italy, Luxembourg, the Netherlands, Norway, Sweden, the United Kingdom. It was unanimously agreed that, to symbolize post-war reconciliation, the headquarters of the organization should be in the French frontier city of Strasbourg, the capital of Alsace.

The aims of the Council are:

- to work for greater European unity;
- to uphold the principles of parliamentary democracy and human rights; and
- to improve living conditions and promote human values.

It also seeks to develop the common features shared by all the peoples of Europe: the 'European dimension' to their lives. Thus although the Council's work is largely carried out through intergovernmental cooperation, the interests of the individual remain its prime concern.

The Council of Europe's Statute declares that each member state must recognize the principle of the rule of law and guarantee its citizens the enjoyment of human rights and fundamental freedoms. Any European state that accepts these democratic principles can apply to become a member. Since 1949 the membership has grown from ten to twenty-four countries, with the accession of Austria, Cyprus, Finland, Germany, Greece, Hungary, Iceland, Liechtenstein, Malta, Portugal, San Marino, Spain, Switzerland and Turkey.

The Council of Europe works in close cooperation with other international organizations such as the United Nations, the European Community and the Organisation for Economic Co-operation and Development. However, the organization's particular role in international cooperation results from three characteristics which distinguish it from these:

- in *structure*, the Council is more than just a purely intergovernmental body: in addition to a Committee of Ministers it has an Assembly composed of members of national parliaments and it involves local authorities and non-governmental organizations in its deliberations;
- in *scope*, the Council covers practically all aspects of European affairs, with the exception of defence;
- in *membership*, the Council includes all the European Community states, a number of 'neutral' and 'non-aligned' countries and other European democracies who share its ideals. It also opens many of its activities to non-member states, thus extending cooperation beyond the 'twenty-four'.*

It is this combination of wide membership, general competence and a flexible structure that give the Council of Europe its unique character. Indeed, as a regional organization it has served as a model for other regional groups of countries in Africa, Asia and Latin America.

---

* Twenty-eight states take part in the Council's work on education and culture – the twenty-four plus Czechoslovakia, the Holy See, Yugoslavia and Poland.

Introduction

This book is about the response of European education systems to the development of an 'information society'. Its source material is the preparatory work, documentation and deliberations of a ministerial conference attended by ministers and senior officials from 27 states that are now parties to the European Cultural Convention. However, the selection and organization of the material has been undertaken with a wider audience in mind. Thus the book summarizes the current thinking, the policies and the practices of these European nations in order to brief future policy-makers and to inform students and practitioners of education.

The Council of Europe's Standing Conference of European Ministers of Education is a biennial event. At its fifteenth session in Helsinki in June 1987 ministers agreed to hold the sixteenth session in Istanbul in 1989 on the theme of 'The Information Society – a challenge for education policies?' This reflected a commitment not only to meet and discuss this theme in two years time but also to devote considerable attention to it during the intervening period. Thus by early 1988 a meeting of senior officials, chaired by Dr Ihsan Sezal from Turkey, the host country, had already agreed upon a format for national reports, asked for relevant case studies and commissioned three expert reports. Abstracts and early drafts of all these documents were discussed during 1988 so that by the end of the year an agenda of issues for discussion had begun to emerge.

The expert reports were commissioned from three professors who between them covered much of the territory the conference wished to discuss. Professor Francis Balle, Rector of the University of Paris VII and also now a member of the French Commission for the Control of Broadcasting, is a sociologist who has written about the role of information in post-industrial society and studied the impact of new media on society and their implications for education. Professor Michael Eraut, Director of the Institute for Continuing and Professional Education at the University of Sussex, has studied the implications of new technologies for the school curriculum, and has a special interest in policy implementation and the in-service education of teachers and other professionals. Professor Gilbert De Landsheere from the University of Liège has a worldwide reputation for his contributions to educational research and teacher education, together with considerable knowledge of several national education systems. He was entrusted, therefore, with the difficult task of writing a synthesis of the National Reports. Given the timetable for preparing conference documents, his report had to be based on early drafts of the reports. However, this had the advantage of allowing the final versions of the National Reports to benefit from his and the other two professors' analyses of the issues. The three expert reports constitute Part 2 of this book.

Given restrictions on the length of the National Reports, it was decided to add five case studies to provide more detailed descriptions of innovations or research of special interest to the conference. These cover: distance education in Turkey; research into computer conferencing as an adjunct to distance education in Denmark; the 'joint licence' procedure for assisting the acquisition of software in France; research into the socio-cultural dimension of the relationship between schools and the media in Italy; and the role of Project Atenea in introducing new information technologies into the Spanish education system. These five case studies comprise Part 3 of this book.

From the end of 1988 work also began on preparing the Conference Discussion Paper. This six-page document went through several versions before the meeting of senior officials was finally satisfied. On the one hand it had to encapsulate within a short space the wide range of issues that had emerged from the planning meetings, the National Reports and the Expert Reports; on the other hand it had to provide the main framework for discussions at the conference itself. The final version was very successful in achieving both these purposes, and it has been used as the organizing scheme for Part 1 of this book.

The National Reports themselves comprise over 200 pages, which makes them too long for inclusion in this book in their current form, although they can be obtained from the Council of Europe in print and on microfilm. Individual reports were restricted in length and therefore had to be selective. So, within the general framework of questions agreed by the meeting of senior officials, each country was free to focus on aspects it considered important and relevant in the light of its own policy and practice. Hence some reports are more theoretical and some more descriptive; some focus only on computers, some give more attention to the media of mass communication; some focus more on future plans, some on past achievements; some give more attention to policy, some to practice; and some specifically address questions of international cooperation. Taken together, however, they provide a substantial body of thinking, policy analysis and evaluation of experience. This has been used as the main basis for Part 1 of this book, which incorporates substantial quotations from National Reports.

What did the conference itself achieve? In political terms, it took the issues up a level and put them firmly on the ministerial agenda. In many countries the period before the conference had been used by education departments as an opportunity to review their policy and practice, with the conference providing a natural climax to this work. Intellectually, the minister's presentations and discussions occupied the territory between the Discussion Paper and the National Reports. Without going into too much detail, ministers were able to expand on the issues in the Discussion Paper and to contribute their own national perspective to the discussion. What emerged was a remarkable degree of agreement on the aims and role of education in the 1990s.

Education should now take a more proactive stance towards changes in society. The new information and communication technologies (abbreviated as NICT in most of the conference documents) should not be rejected but accommodated through a more critical approach based on the fundamental human values of personal choice, equity and the protection of cultural life. In the words of the Finnish Minister of Education, Mr Christoffer Taxell, 'modern technology is a good servant but a poor master'.

There was also evidence that much had been learned from the experience of using educational technology over the past 30 years. More is known about how to plan and introduce educational innovations. Countries are increasingly aware of others' policies and anxious to find out more about their rationales and their impact.

Thus the conference made it possible to discuss where there was agreement and where there was not, and to get an overview of how ministers saw the principal issues. This has enabled a more coherent account to be prepared for Part 1 of this book. Although the Editor takes final responsibility for what is written, his intention is to represent accurately the European view of how education systems should respond to the challenge of the information society. Not only are there excerpts from the National Reports (denoted by the use of quotation marks or indention and reference to the country concerned), but there are also some excerpts from conference presentations and a few citations of additional documents made available at the conference. This allows readers to capture the flavour and to appreciate the quality of the documentation and the discussion.

PART 1

THE CONFERENCE DISCUSSION

CHAPTER 1

Perspectives on the Developing 'Information Society'

Economists and sociologists have identified *information* as the essential feature of production, consumption and exchange in a post-industrial era. This was accepted by the conference as a valid general point about the future, although it recognized that there is considerable disagreement about the relative strength and significance of current trends. Most of the salient characteristics of an information society are transitional, but the problems posed assume somewhat different forms in different economic and cultural contexts. Hence the discussion about the nature of the 'information society' was concerned mainly with assembling a range of perspectives, so that the challenge for education might be more fully understood. Several national reports and ministerial speakers contributed to this process, and the general picture described below would be accepted by most participants as a reasonable summary of their current thinking. A more detailed analysis of some of the issues can be found in the expert report from Professor Balle in Part 2.

1.1 ALTERNATIVE DEFINITIONS OF 'INFORMATION SOCIETY'

Although the expression 'information society' is increasingly to be found in both newspapers and the specialized press, it does not yet have any unequivocal meaning; there are still widespread ambiguities.

The expression has three main meanings:

1. The quantity and rate of distribution of information by all the media with the emphasis on its diffuseness and rapid obsolescence.
2. The quantity of information classifiable, usable and analysable by the new computer technologies, with the emphasis on the theoretical potential of the information and the need for making it more accessible.
3. The central role played by knowledge, particularly knowledge with a well-defined purpose in modern society; knowledge is seen as an important factor in productivity.

These three meanings are combined in various permutations depending on whether the prevalent cultural attitude is one of acceptance or refusal, and correspond to a vast interconnected range of positions in society, intellectual circles and the schools themselves.

In the more intellectual milieu, the concept of information society is a combination of all three aforementioned meanings, and implies an awareness that there is a *process of intellectualization* in modern societies which requires increasing numbers of persons to possess a stock of knowledge enabling them to make creative use of the enormous potential of information. This is being made possible by computing being introduced into all walks of life and by the media playing an ever greater role in the social and cultural environment.

While in many circles, especially schools, there is a common notion that the information concerns exclusively the technological aspects of innovation, there is also a prevalent negative attitude which rejects the whole phenomenon, thus hampering any understanding of the processes which are underway. (Italy)

1.2 THE CHANGING NATURE OF WORK

Present-day society can be described as the 'information

society' and regarded as the product of the technological revolution of the end of the twentieth century, the consequences of which resemble those of the industrial revolution. A gigantic explosion in the volume of knowledge has gone hand in hand with a bewilderingly rapid rise in the speed of communication; the time lag between scientific discoveries or technological innovations and their applications is becoming extremely short. The world's centres of industrial production are shifting with the emergence of newly industrialized countries relying on high technology, particularly the information technologies. The importance of the services sector is growing considerably in the economic structure of Western countries and the increasing use of robotics is leading to the loss of many jobs in production, thus completely transforming the structure of the employment market. (Belgium–French Community)

An increasing proportion of the workforce is involved in creating, processing and transmitting information. New technology enables such work to be undertaken by small groups and individuals who can interact at a distance without having to be co-located. So there are major implications for the way work is organized. Accurate prediction is impossible, but a variety of scenarios have been created to portray possible future developments. For example, it is often suggested that:

Industrial society, characterized by division of labour, centralization, separation between the home and the workplace and a high demand for labour, will gradually give way to the 'information society', the characteristic features of which could be described as the performance of individual tasks by a single person, decentralization, the end of the separation between home and workplace and a low demand for labour (leisure society). (Liechtenstein)

Already an increasing amount of information work is done in the home; and leisure and tourism account for an increasing proportion of the economy. Although it is difficult to predict how far these trends will go, it does seem probable that the pace of change will increase, the pattern of working life will change and the majority of people will change jobs more frequently. This will put a premium on flexibility and on adult education/lifelong learning, a point stressed by the Turkish Minister of Education, Mr Avni Akyol, in his opening speech.

1.3 MASS COMMUNICATION

The penetrating nature of the information carried by the mass media, which makes it possible to reach almost the whole population of Western Europe, has led to visible changes in the habits and behaviour of individuals and society. Radio and television enter homes at all hours every day of the year; the press and publishing houses are extending the range of their products in an effort to adapt to all tastes and special requirements; information networks based on the combined use of telephone lines and television aerials are being set up; computers are entering homes, schools and businesses; individual access to satellite broadcasts is becoming possible and communication via the media is becoming bilateral and interactive.

The falling prices of equipment and services involved in the transmission of information have made access to this category of goods possible for a growing number of people; hence the increasing importance attached to information and the growing emphasis placed on its acquisition. From the points of view of both professional activities and leisure time, the importance of the pictures and sounds received via the media, which are regarded as a major asset in passing on knowledge about today's world and its social, cultural, political, economic and technical aspects, is undeniable.

Moreover, it is becoming more and more important, for the purpose of the orderly integration of individuals into society, that everyone should be able to become, or continue to be, at all times a well-informed citizen in all fields, and that his actions, opinions or decisions should correspond to his potential as a human and social being.

In political terms, it is important for the state to guarantee general access to communications and the 'quality' of the resulting products. This guarantee of quality by no means represents state control over information; on the contrary, the aim is to establish a free market in communications. However, it is important for consumers to be able to choose high-quality products if they wish, duly identified as such and from a known source. (Portugal)

This general acceptance of the positive potential of new information and communication technologies (NICT) was accompanied by strongly expressed reservations about its cultural and civic implications and equality of opportunities. These are amplified in the following sections.

Meanwhile it should be noted that, until recently and perhaps even now, most citizens have failed to grasp 'the overall nature of both current developments and the interdependence between the media, particularly television, and the new computer technologies; and again the relationship between the latter and the more general economic and cultural processes, or the world of knowledge and culture.' (Italy)

1.4 CULTURAL IMPLICATIONS

The new information and communication technologies (NICT) have entered gradually into our culture and our social life, affecting our consciousness, expressions and thought as well as our forms of communication. The subtle, almost clandestine, nature of their influence makes us vulnerable to the new media and threatens our control over our future in quite a different way from the technology-driven changes in the nature of work. Perhaps because the cultural implications of NICT are the most difficult to understand, their discussion gives rise to a succession of hopes and fears. On the positive side:

This mass information society involving increasing communication between people of all cultures will perhaps give rise to a global civilization. Is this not a move towards a more

7

highly developed sense of the universal and greater solidarity between all, and is it not also an opportunity for human groups to be more convivial?

An information society offers favourable conditions for greater openness, mutual knowledge, tolerance and eagerness to understand one another better. It is not a vain hope to expect people to take an interest in their cultural differences and look upon them as an asset.

Like every human reality, however, this coming together and intermingling of individuals and currents of thought are becoming ambiguous. That is why it is all the more important, when taking decisions relating to the education of young people, to consider what underlies the outstanding dignity of every human being, the spiritual dimension guaranteeing everyone a unique and irreplaceable role. (Holy See)

On the negative side there is a major threat to cultural values and social cohesion.

The explosion of information . . . has had many consequences, such as: contraction of the traditional culture and prevalence of the scientific-technological one; the questioning of authority and enormous change in human relations within the family, the school and the place of work; change of mentality and ways of life; and the enormous change in young people's values. The information provided by the mass media on the life styles and values of young people in other countries undermines existing models of conduct and behaviour and at the same time fails to provide a new model. (Cyprus)

Thus there is still a strong fear that young people will be manipulated by the media, although it is now recognized that education cannot assist by resisting or standing aloof. The media are part of the world for which pupils need to be prepared. Nevertheless, there remains a strong threat not to young people in particular but to society as a whole from the cultural domination of externally mediated messages. Small countries and minority languages are particularly vulnerable.

In a small society like Iceland, the recent information revo-

8

lution has caused serious problems concerning Icelandic, as most of the information received is in a foreign language. This includes news in the media, software for computers and information from data banks. The publication of books is expensive because of the limited market, and the same will, of course, be true of the production of television programmes and software. In this respect, Icelanders face grave problems because of the small size of the population and the threat that the loss of mother tongue represents to the independence of a small nation.

One of the measures taken in this connection was to write an ordinance banning the broadcasting of foreign programmes on television without Icelandic sub-titles, with the exception of live broadcasts, where a commentator explains in Icelandic what is happening. (Iceland)

Even this precaution may be partly eroded by the arrival of satellite television.

1.5 THE NEED FOR A PROACTIVE RESPONSE

Throughout the conference, whether technological, economic, cultural or educational issues were being discussed, people sought a middle road between blind resistance to NICT, which would be both undesirable and impracticable, and uncritical acceptance which could be equally dangerous. Passive acceptance of changes brought about by NICT was accentuated by an attitude of cultural and technological determinism, and by the overloading of the mind by a constant flow of information. What was needed was a *proactive* response which, without ignoring current trends and likely developments, brought them under control by making them serve human goals.

The development opportunities opened up by computer technology are so important and so fraught with consequences for society that, in this area, things cannot simply be left to the vagaries of history or supposed objective constraints.

Exploitation of the opportunities provided by this technology and determination to steer clear of the undeniable dangers must be regarded as fundamental duties of society.

The debate on the media and the new technologies is justified mainly by their inherent possibilities and dangers. These possibilities and dangers are unavoidable, and man must develop and control them respectively. If individuals wish to remain active participants in an increasingly computerized society, they must first of all be able to interpret how the numerous developments affect themselves and society. It is only then that the need for new skills to exploit the resources of information technologies makes itself felt. Naturally, it is also necessary to acquire skills in order to be able to use information technology, but this is not sufficient to promote a responsible attitude towards it. (Liechtenstein)

Similarly, the Swedish Minister of Education wrote in his government's 1987 Budget that:

We have reason to be chary of the vision of the future which this perspective ultimately implies. Unreflecting adoption of information technology can have the effect of jeopardizing essential democratic values in society. . . . The key resources of society tomorrow will be knowledge rather than just information. Knowledge does not come into existence until people assimilate and process information and fact. Knowledge presupposes an active approach, characterized by analysis and valuation. Instead of welcoming an anticipated information society, then, members of society have every reason to participate in the development of a knowledge society. The term information indicates a direction to be followed: it is the informant who announces what the uninformed is to be allowed to know. The knowledge society is based on the opposite conception: its aim is to strengthen the possibilities for the individual himself to appraise and value different alternatives. (Sweden)

1.6 EQUALITY OF OPPORTUNITY

A further consequence of this civic perspective, which seeks to safeguard the rights of citizens and to enable them to participate in planning their future, is that people have equal opportunity to acquire the knowledge and skills needed for using NICT. Several countries expressed the fear that more deprived members of our society who currently have little access to equipment and are unfamiliar with the uses of NICT would become yet further disadvantaged.

> The gap is likely to grow wider between the most privileged and those who are less well supported by the socio-cultural environment. Equality of opportunity would become more and more hypothetical despite the huge efforts made to democratize education in the past century.
>
> In the harmful climate created by the demands of what is referred to more and more as 'economic warfare', the increasing difficulty of access to knowledge is likely to be played down and the attention and budget necessary to make up this leeway are unlikely to be granted. The type of education based on the slogan 'give everyone a chance and may the best man win' would be disastrous for the weakest, excluding them from these new societies. (Holy See)

The concerns expressed at the preparatory meetings were succinctly summarized in the Conference Discussion Paper as follows:

> In preparing for the information age, education is presented with many challenges and opportunities. Policies to promote greater social justice and equality of opportunity could be jeopardized if the least privileged members of society are inadequately equipped for a world that depends increasingly on intensive communication by means of the new technologies, as they are now too often left behind in the literacy and numeracy stakes. The knowledge gap must not be allowed to widen. This consideration applies to every category of the population liable to suffer from social or cultural disadvantage

– whether based on poverty, physical disability, national or ethnic background, age, gender or geography. On the other hand, with suitable policies, the NICT could greatly help to bridge such gaps and to build educational equality and solidarity.

Furthermore, equality of access to knowledge and skills relating to the information society, its communication networks and its technologies is essential to democracy. Those without such knowledge will be denied influence over the future developments of a society increasingly affected by technology.

There is a need to counteract the tendency for control to be exercised by information providers over information receivers. Information is, indeed, power, and those who control it can dominate, not to say manipulate, the information society. The challenge for education will be, more than ever, to overcome passive acceptance of information in favour of the active exercise of independent judgement.

CHAPTER 2

Implications for Educational Policies

The gradual development of an information society is giving rise to a number of tensions which need to be resolved in policy and practice. These include:

1. The tensions between past and future, i.e. between traditional culture and new habits and attitudes.
2. The tension between preparing pupils as citizens who will contribute to creating the future and qualifying them for future employment according to externally determined predictions of need.
3. The tension between the formal curriculum of the school and the 'informal curriculum' available outside it.
4. The tensions between teaching pupils about NICT and making the use of NICT part of school life.
5. The tension between responding to vociferous demands from pupils and parents and ensuring equality of access for all pupils.

The Portuguese report summed up the problem as follows:

An education policy appropriate to every social and cultural context must be drawn up with the two-fold objective of adapting the potential of each generation to the foreseeable social trends in the years to come, and at the same time of creating the conditions in which young people can take an active part in influencing and determining the course of this development. Any education policy in an era of far-reaching changes must be turned towards the future while taking account of the present and past, must be compatible with developing trends without abandoning the power to choose which path to follow independently, and must be appropriate in the national context without disregarding the constraints of international interdependence.

The policy issues, on which the achievement of this goal and the interdependence of the above tensions depend, concern what knowledge and skills are acquired in the area of NICT, what is the relationship between schools and NICT outside the school and what is the role of NICT within the school itself. Each of these issues is further discussed below.

2.1 INFORMATION TECHNOLOGY AS PART OF BASIC GENERAL EDUCATION

One conclusion drawn by a number of speakers at the conference was the need to abandon the idea of information technology as a distinct, specialist area of knowledge, at least for educational purposes; and to see it as part of the basic general education of all future citizens.

> In future, every pupil must receive fundamental training in information technology. Such training, however, should not turn pupils into specialists in the field of basic computer technology; rather, they should be helped to recognize that information technology increasingly fulfils the function of a fundamental discipline necessary for other disciplines and subjects.
> Education should also deal with the social effects of the use of micro-electronics on the labour market and on everyday life. Pupils should be enabled to assess the possibilities and limitations of information and communication technologies. (Austria)

As the Scottish Minister of State, Mr Ian Lang, succinctly put it:

> First we have to make sure that our children have a sufficient understanding of the technologies that lie at the heart of the information society. This does not mean necessarily a full technological knowledge for all. But it does mean an understanding of the fundamental principles on which information technology devices actually work. Second we need to make sure that children know about the applications of IT in the outside world and think about and understand the impact that NICT has both upon them as individuals and on the country as a whole. This includes awareness of the extent to which their lives can be influenced by information providers. Then, thirdly, children have to learn how to use the technologies to their own advantage and not let the technology use them.

It was also recognized that proper use of NICT required the same intellectual and personal qualities in both civic and vocational contexts. There need be no tension between vocational and private goals if a range of contexts is used and a stance of critical analysis and personal creativity is maintained.

> The volume of information which is received today through different means, makes it necessary to furnish individuals with elements of critical analysis, selection of information and use of this information in an adequate manner. Only this will allow for a real evaluation of the information. It then becomes a matter of ensuring that citizens can use the new technologies and are familiar with the socio-cultural implications and their possibilities and applications. It is necessary, then, to incorporate these technologies by trying to promote a reflective attitude and a critical analysis of the cultural systems and the values which they are shaping. (Spain)

> Modern man has to develop new ways of thinking and behaviour to enable him to cope with changes and to adjust to them both in private and in vocational life. Education must aim to teach and promote basic abilities, e.g. for communication

and teamwork, so that problems and conflicts can be solved. However, creativity and innovative thinking must also be taught. The ability to cope meaningfully with the increasing amount of information by means of abstract thought processes is to be particularly promoted. (Austria)

Current work and thought patterns are strongly influenced by the new techniques, which call for individual responsibility and initiative, the ability to communicate and cooperate and new general and vocational qualifications. In particular, they increasingly require a capacity for logical and abstract thought. The consequences of the new techniques for communication and understanding must be taken into consideration just as much as their impact on cultural life. The education sector must take up the challenge thrown down in all its fields of activity by the new techniques of information and communication. In so doing, it must not regard its efforts as a mere reaction to this challenge, but make an appropriate contribution to the attainment of the new objectives.

Educational planners must make a critical analysis of the effects of new information and communication techniques and devise courses and teaching methods properly discharged. In the course of this process education must both guarantee compatibility with our cultural heritage and try to prevent people from becoming strangers to each other. (Federal Republic of Germany)

2.2 THE SCHOOL AND THE MASS MEDIA

There was general agreement that schools should avoid both uncritical acceptance of mass media and instinctive rejection. Mass communication has become such an important part of modern society that preparing pupils for this aspect of their future is now an important educational goal. Once more an approach is needed which incorporates both critical analysis and personal creativity.

Schools must compete with external sources of information

which are not pursuing the same educational objectives. Television, in particular, plays an important role in children's lives. It invades their mental horizons, introducing themes which it constantly repeats, and influencing their other activities. But young children are not capable of distancing themselves from what they see on television and do not always distinguish between reality and imagination. Television can only be a cultural instrument when one takes the time to engage in dialogue with the child, and can rapidly become an instrument of cultural impoverishment when the child is left alone in front of the screen.

Schools must play the role of *attentive mediator* between the child and the different media; they must give him a better understanding of the functioning and significance of the media and teach him how to use them. Education about the media means enabling children to learn to use, react to, select, reject, classify, check, interpret and search for information, i.e. to adopt an autonomous and critical attitude towards all types of media.

This process must be begun as early as possible so that, first as an adolescent and then as an adult, individuals can selectively incorporate the messages they receive in the construction of their knowledge, without allowing themselves to be manipulated. This means that they must check the quality and authenticity of these messages and be aware of the culture they transmit. (Belgium – French Community)

As the role of the media is not limited to forming opinions or distributing information, but may also extend to manipulation and deliberate deception, it is necessary to adopt a critical and discerning attitude towards them; it is only in this way that rational relations with the media can be established, making it possible to use them sensibly. Outright rejection of the media cannot be the message of media studies. Instead of responding to harmful uses of the media by prohibition, it is preferable, particularly in schools, to make children and young people capable of analysing, judging and assessing the media by the yardstick of their own personal responsibility towards themselves. (Federal Republic of Germany)

Such a critical approach to the mass media will be difficult to sustain, however, if parents are not also involved in working towards the same objectives, and if schools are not prepared to adopt a similar critical approach to their own internal modes of communication.

2.3 USING NICT IN SCHOOLS AND COLLEGES

Monsieur Jospin, the French Minister of Education, suggested that the information society presented a two-fold challenge to education: 'On the one hand, education has to allow individuals and social groups to control the evolution of the "information society", so that it develops towards a genuine society of communication and culture. On the other hand, education has to be able to take advantage of the possibilities offered by the new communication techniques.' The second requires a strong sense of realism, but at least that is now widely recognized.

> Now that the storm of irrational excitement about the capabilities and potential of the new technological resources has blown over (some people had considered them to be the only effective remedy for many of the schools's shortcomings and the sole channel for teaching innovation), together with the equally simplistic preconception that the introduction of new information technologies into schools threatened the creative capacity and specific nature of school work and constricted students' intellectual abilities and powers of expression, the present situation seems to hold much less conflict. The task ahead is obviously made harder by the fact that a clear understanding of current developments is required if we are to develop an adequate plan obviating the potential risks of implementing and disseminating the new technologies. Such dangers increase where such technologies are misunderstood and misused.
>
> Above all, the method which has been defined as a new 'information and communication orientated educational ap-

proach' must pay equal attention to all sources of information and open the school up to the outside world. The school must be able to achieve the difficult priority aim of teaching much more than mere technical command of the new technologies. (Italy)

This, however, poses the further challenge of how 'to develop the potential of the NICT for enhancing learning about the worldwide physical and cultural environment while, at the same time, fostering the appreciation, understanding and preservation of cultural diversity in a spirit of respect and toleration. The problem is how to benefit from membership of the "global village" created by world communications, without bringing about either the standardization of cultural values or more intensive confrontation and conflict' (Conference Discussion Paper).

While one approach to raising the quality of education is to provide through NICT a wider range of cultural knowledge and learning experiences, another involves the provision of greater support for the learner's own personal inquiry, research and thinking.

In addition to their social and cultural relevance, new technologies offer the possibility of enriching the acquisition of knowledge and attitudes. From the educational perspective, it is interesting to determine the possibilities offered by these technologies in terms of knowledge, analysis and interaction with reality. More specifically, it is a matter of making full use of the possibilities of overcoming repetitive learning and placing emphasis on less trivial aspects: heuristic learning strategies, development of problem solving, new fields of communication and socialization through the media, meaningful learning, education adapted to the individual, acquisition of specific learning processes in specific areas and development of general thought strategies.

These reflections imply changes not only in vocational training specialities in the different branches, but in general education as well. It is necessary to develop capacities for access to and processing of information and problem solving in real situations. In short, it is a matter of taking advantage of the new technologies for the development of human resources. (Spain).

Two final issues remain, both related to the principle of equality of opportunity. One was raised in a vivid speech by the Swedish delegate:

> The methods and content of upper secondary schooling must be developed in such a way so even these young people who are the least motivated for studies are included. Otherwise we will have youngsters who are left behind, left outside. They are the first to be unemployed. Everybody in our societies has the right to get work. That is why everybody also has the right to upper secondary schooling. If you are to win new generations for the ideals of democracy they must know that every one of them will be participating in the life of the society.

The other concerned opportunities for adults, a frequently expressed concern in a conference mainly devoted to education at school level. It is aptly summarized by three searching questions in the Portuguese report:

1. How can adults already employed be better equipped to cope with the far-reaching and rapid changes which are looming ahead?
2. How can the active participation of citizens in a rapidly changing society be harmonized without compromising social cohesion?
3. By what means can individuals and society as a whole be guaranteed access to a growing volume of data essential for autonomous choices and decisions?

CHAPTER 3

Incorporation into the Curriculum

The previous section revealed a remarkable degree of agreement among member states about the educational goals which should guide any policy response to the challenge of the information society. However, while certain policy options are common to several countries, there is also considerable divergence of approach. One obvious reason is the different character of national systems of education, particularly variations in the pattern of secondary schooling and vocational education. Curricular patterns tend to derive from the structure of each system, as well as from historical traditions and cultural expectations. Another reason of possibly even greater importance is the constraint on resources. Not only are there national differences in the overall level of funding for education, but there are also differences in the priority accorded to NICT-related goals. A third reason, often linked with the question of resources and priorities, is that of timing. As later sections will show, the development of trained personnel, quality software and appropriate pedagogic knowledge takes a long time. Hence those countries which are now most advanced in their policy-making and implementation have usually been among the earliest starters, especially in the introduction of microcomputers. Finally there is the innovation strategy itself. This has varied from the introduction of a curriculum change across the whole system, through centrally funded projects working with pilot districts or pilot schools, to decentralized initiatives at school or district level, often backed by some state funding and a local centre of expertise. Some countries have used a combination of these approaches.

This chapter is particularly concerned with how countries are incorporating new NICT-related goals into their school curricula, while the next chapter covers the use of NICT to improve the learning of existing goals. However, this distinction should not be applied too rigidly. To use a computer for learning mathematics also results in some learning about computers. Indeed, some national policies are based on this very principle: many of the goals of learning about computers can be acquired through using computers for learning in the more traditional subjects.

Two further points are relevant to this theme. First, care needs to be taken that a critical approach to NICT is maintained during all forms of usage: for example, the use of film in history and geography should involve some consideration of the selection and representation of information rather than take the producer's viewpoint as necessarily valid. Second, the goals of traditional subjects require modification to take advantage of the new learning opportunities provided by NICT. The use of NICT neither can nor should be regarded as only affecting the means of communication: it also affects the purpose and nature of the message.

Strategies used for incorporating NICT-related goals into the curriculum fall under three main headings:

1. Integrating NICT-related goals into the teaching of existing subjects.
2. Inserting one or two new compulsory subjects into the curriculum taken by all pupils in a given type of school.
3. Adding optional courses.

To these must be added a fourth extra-curricular strategy:

4. Using NICT in school activities which do not form part of the formal curriculum, such as a school magazine, computer club, inter-school links and video competitions.

These strategies are not mutually exclusive and sometimes the overlap makes it difficult to distinguish between them.

3.1 MEDIA EDUCATION

Most national policies treat media education separately from the use of computers, although the two technologies are becoming increasingly interdependent. Three types of goal are commonly advocated:

1. That pupils should have some knowledge and understanding of mass media and their role in society.
2. That pupils should be able to analyse critically media productions and mediated messages.
3. That pupils should be able to use a range of media for their own communication purposes.

The first two of these goals are more commonly found than the third in the compulsory part of the curriculum. Thus in Scotland:

> Media education is intended to enable children and young people to increase their knowledge and critical understanding of the media. In particular they should: know how messages are created; understand the nature and diversity of the mass media; be aware of the technologies involved in media production and distribution; and form and articulate their own responses to the media at a variety of levels.

The Scottish report also identified three distinct approaches to incorporating media education into the curriculum: permeation, inserts, and discrete courses.

> In permeation the study is promoted as part of the normal work of subjects such as English, art or modern studies. Inserts are short free-standing units developed to form part of courses in the main subjects of the curriculum. Finally, discrete courses permit the study of the media to emerge as an entity in its own right, crossing traditional curriculum boundaries.

The commonest strategy appears to involve:

1. A permeation approach in primary and lower secondary schools.
2. Inserts at various levels of secondary education into subjects like native language, social studies and art.
3. Optional courses at the upper secondary level, and also sometimes in lower secondary schools.

The permeation approach is most explicitly formulated by Austria whose 1973 and 1989 decrees both affirmed that:

> Media Education is *not* a specific subject among others but a principle integrated in all subjects of the curriculum, to be applied whenever the opportunity arises. Naturally, some subjects which themselves deal with communication are better suited to media education, but there should be opportunities to analyse and evaluate the media in all subjects.

As the reports from Denmark and the United Kingdom also noted, this approach relies on the discretion and enthusiasm of each individual teacher. Hence there is now a growing tendency to supplement it with more formal requirements. Denmark has just introduced an obligatory 'mass media' topic (about 30 lessons) into the teaching of Danish in the upper secondary school; and England and Wales are incorporating media education objectives into their new curriculum specifications for English.

Although it is still at an early stage of development, the Maltese approach is of considerable interest:

> The primary schools in the private (Church) sector have introduced a textbook and a syllabus on media education. This subject also extends to form 1 and 2 levels in some schools. The introduction of this subject is still in an experimental stage and its up-dating and consolidation will certainly follow.
>
> In the government sector, media education features in the social studies programme, but it is still restricted to certain units of study in particular years. To back up this programme, the Educational Media Centre runs lectures and discussions for secondary school pupils either in the schools themselves or at the centre.

Media education, in the form of communications studies, features as an important unit in a new subject, 'systems of knowledge', which was launched at the sixth form level as part of the university entrance examination requirements (as from 1989). The unit consists of lectures and discussions on the philosophy, history and practice (media) of communications.

The fourth approach is through a series of 13 half-hour television broadcasts carried out by the Educational Media Centre as part of their after-school programmes.

Switzerland also accords considerable priority to media education. Several cantons provide 'detailed methodological suggestions and high quality teaching material, even at primary level', and Geneva and Fribourg have taken the unusual step of introducing media education as a specific subject in lower secondary schools. The Swiss report recognizes, however, that it is the third type of goal, which requires pupils to make their own media productions, that is the least exploited:

> This is because, in particular, it requires enormous amounts of time which schools generally devote to other priorities. Nevertheless, many developments are taking place in introductory media studies courses, in optional courses, where these exist, or in extra-curricular projects set up by some teachers and pupils. Several events organized in Switzerland each year illustrate the vitality of these activities. This applies, for example, to the Zurich 'Videofilmtage', a kind of festival devoted to films made by young people; the number of events of this type is on the increase, but the educational objectives are not always clearly stated. In French-speaking Switzerland the annual 'Ecole et cinéma' event in Lausanne brings together pupils from all regions of Switzerland to present and discuss the films they have produced. 'Ecole et cinéma' also includes a series of very interesting educational workshops (video, montage, animation).

Other extra-curricular activities using new media for expressive purposes are described in the French report: these include school magazines and newspapers and a pupil-produced video prospectus.

These activities can build on a new lower secondary curriculum in which one of the priority objectives is 'the capacity to express oneself and communicate orally, in writing and through visual messages'. Moreover, 'at some point in their secondary school career all pupils must take part in the production of an audiovisual work or film. This will give them a clearer understanding of the process of signification in the world in which they live and act, and will enhance their powers of judgement'.

Optional courses at the upper secondary level were noted in several reports, but rarely described in detail. However, the rationale for the Danish one-year course of four-weekly lessons in films and television knowledge is of particular interest:

Media Understanding

The instruction should develop and create an understanding of the picture media, their language and complexity, so that the pupils can acquire the necessary prerequisite for a critical and conscious attitude towards the media culture which surrounds them. In order to reach this goal, the media instruction must be placed in a historical, political, economic and institutional context.

Independent Media Production

By working with film/video themselves, pupils can learn to understand the special working processes of these media and the possibilities of a shift of consciousness and intensity which living pictures may have. In the course on 'film and television knowledge', half the teaching time is to be spent on independent media production and this part of the instruction has been made as obligatory as the theoretical subject-matter. Thus pupils must sit for an examination both in the theoretical/analytical subject area and in an independently elaborated media production.

Media Experience

Through the interaction between the practical and the analytical media work, it is hoped that pupils will widen their experience of the picture and sound media – and in the long run be able to profit from the possibilities offered by democratization of access to the mass media.

3.2 COMPUTER LITERACY

The term 'computer literacy' is used to denote a basic general education in computing, as distinct from more specialist, advanced or vocational courses. No doubt much that is now classified as specialist will become part of general education during the early part of the twenty-first century, but our concern here is primarily with the next decade. Five main types of goal have been put forward as essential elements in computer literacy.

1. Some knowledge and understanding of computers and their technology.
2. The ability to use a few standard types of software.
3. Some knowledge of computer applications and their use in a variety of contexts.
4. Some knowledge and understanding of the current and future impact of computers upon society.
5. The ability to write some simple computer programs.

The fifth of these goals used to play a dominant role in computing courses but is now accorded less importance as standard types of software have become widely available. Some countries now exclude programming from basic computing courses; but others still consider it essential to the proper understanding of computers.

All five goals can be almost infinitely expanded, and can be extended well beyond the requirements of a basic introductory course. However, their pursuit is limited by a large number of practical constraints. First, there is a shortage of space in the school timetable: to introduce new goals means according lower priority to existing goals. Second, and of even greater importance at present, is the limited access to computing facilities. Although the level of provision varies considerably, there are very few European countries in which access to computing facilities is not still a major constraint. Indeed the magnitude of this constraint, together with concomitant shortages of software and trained personnel, make discussions about the ideal characteristics of a general education in computing seem rather remote from reality.

The optimal use of scarce resources is one reason why several member states have incorporated the goals of computer literacy into the curriculum through introducing a new, compulsory subject – variously called computer literacy, informatics, basic computing or data processing. As noted above, this separate subject approach is only rarely found in media education. Some countries, often through concern for the use of computers as an aid to learning as well as an object for study, have opted for a cross-curricular approach to basic computing; some began with a separate subject approach but are now extending their provision to cover the use of computing in existing subjects as well. Both these approaches guarantee some computer literacy for all pupils.

Other countries, however, have not yet reached that stage. They may offer computer studies only as an option course or only in a proportion of schools. Such partial coverage often signifies an 'experimental project' approach, in which pilot schools are the only participants. The lessons learned from evaluating this experience are then used to inform future policy.

Two interesting examples of compulsory courses in computing as a distinct subject are outlined below.

Belgium – Flemish community

The aims of a 'Computer technology' course for first and second year secondary pupils are that, through experiments in micro-electronics, they should:

> acquire a basic knowledge and understanding of the various elements in data-processing or regulating systems;
>
> analyse simple problems step-by-step and find solutions to them, or at least understand their significance;
>
> learn how to process simple data, using computer technology;

understand the function and various applications of computers and appreciate their inherent and relative importance.

The subsequent data-processing course for third and fourth year pupils aims to:

familiarize children at school, as part of their general education, with the new information technologies, thus increasing their future opportunities;

give pupils basic notions of the use of the new information technologies, prepare them for life in the community and enable them to assess the impact of these new technologies in daily life and the community. They must be taught to think numerically and to look for modular solutions;

introduce principles of programming in a specifically designed setting.

Thus the first year has a strong technology base, with some attention to the logic of data processing and its applications; while the second is focused on applications and social impact, with some attention to programming.

Luxembourg

The course 'Introduction to new information technologies' is taught, to fifth year secondary pupils (age 15), for half a year at high intensity: two or three $1\frac{1}{2}$ hour lessons a week. Only the first three modules are compulsory.

1. *Introduction to the use of computers.* Logo is used for communication with the computer, first in the direct communication mode, and then as a programming language. By this means pupils become familiar with computers, their logic and the functions for their various parts. 'One of the objectives is to show pupils that, by using standard software, it is possible to make computers perform a very wide variety of complex tasks without needing to

program them. To illustrate this function the next two modules introduce the two most commonly used types of software, i.e. word-processing programs and database managers.'

2. *Word processing.* 'Pupils learn to draft a text with the help of appropriate software. They see how it is possible to progress from a very imperfect initial draft to a complete, corrected, restructured, well presented and saveable version. Individually or in groups they create texts which can be put together to make newspapers, brochures, information sheets, etc.'

3. *Database management.* 'At school and in everyday life pupils encounter all kinds of records – mainly of the non-computerized kind. Paper-based files are used to introduce the basic concepts which determine the structure of a database. Later pupils learn to use the basic functions of a database management program: searching, sorting according to various criteria, creation of sub-files and changing file entries. This module also provides an opportunity to teach pupils how to handle the menus of an interactive programme.'

4. *Technical applications.* An example is control technology.

5. *Telematics.* Learning about services such as videotext, telex and telefax. This largely theoretical unit culminates with a visit to a firm to see telematics in use.

This course has a stronger application and 'hands-on' flavour to it than the Belgian course, but gives neither the technology nor the social impact as much attention. The use of Logo in the introduction to computers is unusual. Although San Marino is experimenting with using Prolog as a first computer language, they do not introduce it to pupils until after they have become familiar with word processing and data processing.

Switzerland has an agreed but not binding set of objectives which most cantons have implemented, and Austria, Belgium (French community), Cyprus, Greece and Yugoslavia have also adopted the compulsory separate subject approach to computing at the lower secondary level. Malta will soon be joining them while Finland and Ireland retain optional status for their secondary school computing courses.

The German *Länder* have also reached agreement on the general nature of their introductory computer courses, which range from 30 to 80 hours at lower secondary level. But in Germany, these objectives are intended to be delivered largely through the medium of existing subject areas. Their concept of a basic education in computing is also extremely broad, encompassing all nine of the following objectives:

> analysis of individual experience of information technology;

> instruction in the basic concepts of information technology;

> hands-on instruction in the use of computers and peripheral devices;

> instruction in the possible applications of information technology and how to use them;

> introduction to the use of algorithmic diagrams in problem solving;

> familiarization with the development of electronic data processing;

> instilling awareness of the inherent social and economic effects of the spread of micro-electronics;

> description of the opportunities and dangers inherent in information technology and the establishment of a rational attitude towards it;

> introduction to the problems of protecting privacy and data.

Sweden has incorporated 60–80 hours of basic computing into the teaching of existing subjects at the senior level of compulsory schooling. Their report argues that 'work at the computer should precede more theoretical presentations so as to give pupils a better understanding of information technology and its social impact' and notes that hitherto 'the best progress has been made in teaching word processing, databases and computerized registers'.

Perhaps the most elaborate arrangements for cross-curricular provision are those currently being made in England and Wales, where the benefits of a decade of developing the uses of micro-computers in schools have been incorporated into a new national curriculum. Attainment targets and programmes of study are being established subject by subject; IT-related targets are built into these subject specifications. Science, English and mathematics have already been enacted, and the final report on technology includes a specific component on information technology. The UK report for the conference defined IT capability as including:

1. Familiarity with IT and facility in the use of standard methods of communication between people and IT.
2. Familiarity with and facility in the appropriate applications of IT for activities such as the storage and retrieval of information, the creation and presentation of information, the communication of information and simulation, modelling, monitoring and control.
3. A working understanding of the common principles of the application of IT, such as the nature, properties and structures of information and the nature of information processing and communications.
4. The ability to identify needs or opportunities where the use of IT is appropriate and the ability, individually or as a member of a group, to design and develop appropriate and effective solutions.
5. A general understanding of the range and scope of IT applications and of their social and economic effects on individuals at home, at work and in the community, on the organizations involved, and on society in general.

Although they are presented in a cross-curricular format, some of these goals may be delivered through a specific IT unit if schools so choose. Some at least may adopt the Netherlands approach, whereby those elements which cannot easily be integrated into existing subjects are combined into a subject area called information technology. Another alternative being tried in the UK is an insertion model by which certain subjects 'adopt' one particular aspect of IT capability. Then there is the planned permeation approach of the kind used in France: 'The lower secondary school curriculum is divided into six interdisciplinary subject areas, which are covered simultaneously by all teachers from different angles, the aim being to make pupils aware of the situations and problems of the modern world. One of these themes is information.'

France and the United Kingdom appear to be the only countries making systematic provision of computers at primary level. In France a permeation approach is accompanied by an insert of 50 hours in the last two years of primary school devoted to familiarization with computer culture and computer technology. All parts of the UK have IT-related attainment targets at primary level, and in Scotland the new expectation is that most pupils leaving primary school will be able to use software to:

> draft and present a report on a topic or observations and a piece of imaginative writing;

> create an appropriate datafile structure, enter data and search within the database for information to answer an identified question;

> draw shapes from a given 'paint' menu; draw freehand using a mouse and fill areas in colours or shading patterns; produce a variety of styles of lettering including different fonts and sizes;

> adapt scores of given tunes and change the sound generated using available sound envelopes;

> contribute to the creation of viewdata pages for inclusion in a local system;

> operate a model directly from the keyboard; write a simple program to control an output device and to make a model or device follow a sequence of instructions.

Some countries (e.g. Denmark, Greece, Ireland and the Netherlands) are encouraging the experimental use of computers at primary level, while others have made policy decisions not to do so. Sometimes the reason is financial, but the German *Länder* have agreed to postpone the introduction of computers until the second or third year of secondary school because they believe that 'Pupils must first familiarize themselves with traditional cultural techniques, mastery of which remains essential for everyday life; in addition, these cultural techniques are an essential prerequisite for later experiences with computers.'

3.3 ADVANCED, SPECIALIST AND VOCATIONAL COURSES IN COMPUTER STUDIES

Those countries where pupils enter technical and vocational schools relatively young (aged 13–15) may offer generalist rather than specialist computer literacy courses. As the German report explained: 'for several years to come, technical schools must provide elementary information technology courses, which serve as the basis for all specialized computer studies courses'.

In Luxembourg the general vocational course is a shorter version of the general secondary course. Austria's carefully phased strategy gives more time to vocational students and adapts provision to match an increasing level of specialization with age: 'keyboard mastery in the first year (first grade); mastery of the theoretical foundations of EDP in the second and third years (second and third grades), and, based upon this, an increasing integration of EDP in the various compulsory subjects.'

Where students have already completed a computer literacy course in the lower secondary school, then computer studies in vocational education is more likely to be occupation specific. In Switzerland, objectives in computer studies are specified separately for each occupation; Sweden specifies that such courses should be taught by the vocational training teacher rather than a specialist in computer science. The Dutch delegate argued that 'vocational education in which computer and information technology are not fully integrated is unthinkable'.

Thus computer studies courses of the more advanced kind taught by computer science specialists are most likely to be found as option courses in upper secondary schools, not with a vocational orientation but as a part of a more advanced general education leading to higher education. Some countries (e.g. Sweden and Switzerland) also have a small compulsory element of computer studies at the upper secondary level, while others (e.g. Italy) are building computing into upper secondary courses in science and mathematics.

Norway's pattern of provision is fairly typical of that found in Northern Europe.

> Within the area of study for technical and industrial subjects, and partly the area of study for domestic handicrafts and aesthetic studies, computer technology has been introduced on a large scale. The aim is that the students will learn processes actually used in the world of work, and the use of computer-equipped machine-tools has a key function within the curriculum.
>
> The use of word processing and spreadsheets is introduced in the area of study for commercial and clerical subjects.
>
> In the general area of study an optional course of two hours per week, Informatikk I, has been designed, together with an advanced course (Informatikk II, three hours a week). There is also a two-year foundation course and an advanced one-year course in computer technology. This quite popular three-year course gives the students a basic professional training and meets the requirements for admittance to universities and higher technical institutions.

CHAPTER 4

Using NICT for the Enhancement of Learning and Distance Education

The idea of using new media to enhance teaching and learning arose quite early in this century, then came to prominence during the 1960s when the use of television rapidly expanded and experiments began into computer assisted learning (MacKenzie *et al.*, 1970). Since then different countries have expanded their use of new media at varying rates, according to their national priorities and their financial resources. These developments have had two chief aims:

to enhance the quality of teaching and learning within existing educational establishments; and

to make learning opportunities available to those who find difficulty in gaining access to normal provision through poverty, handicap or distance.

Both these aims were frequently endorsed by conference members.

4.1 THE ENHANCEMENT OF LEARNING WITHIN EXISTING INSTITUTIONS

The long-term goals agreed at the conference were:

1. To realize fully the potential of new media for the enhancement of teaching and learning.
2. To make new media a natural part of school life.
3. To develop within this natural context of use a critical approach consistent with the goals of media education discussed in Section 3.1.

In moving towards these goals it is important to take into account the experience of the past 20 years. Even those countries that have gone furthest in their use of new media still have considerable doubts about how far they have achieved their aims.

In the 1970s, as happened everywhere, the use of the audio-visual media in education was enthusiastically embraced by some teachers and rejected just as emphatically by others. The illusion was fostered that, by themselves, the media were going to improve the quality of education or, on the contrary, take the place of teachers and make schools redundant.

Nearly everywhere there was heavy investment in equipment, and it is not an exaggeration to state that, even in the most isolated corners of the country, schools are in general equipped with various types of audio-visual apparatus. Over the past few years there has been considerable development in the use of video with a correspondingly sharp decline in the use of 16 mm film. There is also renewed interest in 'light audio-visual equipment' which can easily be used in classrooms. However, there have been no recent, comprehensive surveys in Switzerland of classroom equipment from the quantitative point of view (number of different items of equipment, frequency of use, etc.), or the way the media are used (from the qualitative point of view). Consequently, we are obliged to rely on estimates, which are sometimes perhaps a little too optimistic. But many questions need to be answered. Have the media really been made an integral part of communication in schools? This is open to doubt. Very often 'subordinate' or 'subservient' audio-visual materials have been introduced as a kind of concession to modernity; often too, such material is dominant, i.e. it is expected to play an educational role it cannot perform, namely to act as a substitute for the teacher. Audio-visual material is rarely used in an integrated way in partnership with the teacher. One of the possible explanations for this relates to teacher training and the general situation in schools from the educational point of view. The real incorporation of the media into classroom practice requires an educational climate both in structures and in curricula or assessment, and selection criteria involving a conception of the learning and teaching processes which is not always found. Moreover, there is always an element of mistrust of the media, which are associated with relaxation and pleasure, and only secondarily with schools and learning. (Switzerland)

Nevertheless, progress is being made. Changes in the technology are not only making it cheaper, and therefore more available, but also making it more flexible. First there has been a move from live broadcast television to videocassette. Now microcomputers are becoming more available, more powerful and more user-friendly. Soon there will be more rapid and convenient access to both still and moving pictures on compact disc, which will also be interactive. Thus learning activities, which used to be the preserve of the enthusiastic teacher with a special interest in new media, are gradually becoming an accepted part of the ordinary teacher's repertoire: easy to organize rather than difficult, and familiar rather than strange. Eventually, there will be full integration of new media into school life. But how long will it take and how many generations of pupils will suffer from the delay? The answers to these questions depend on implementation policies for hardware, software and teacher education, and on special development projects and programmes: these are discussed in Chapter 5.

In discussing NICT-related goals, Professor Eraut's report (Part 2) distinguishes between (a) the more effective achievement of existing goals through improvements in teaching methods and learning resources and (b) the enabling of new curriculum goals within currently timetabled subjects, which enhance the curriculum and give rise to more adventurous and modern syllabuses. Arguments presented in support of the proposition that use of NICT would improve achievement were that it would bring about improved motivation and retention (Austria, France) and more individualized learning (Sweden). It would also enable pupils to work more independently (France). Several countries indicated that they saw benefits of this kind resulting from the proper use of NICT in the classroom. The importance of the teacher's own personal skills, knowledge and motivation was also repeatedly stressed.

The examples cited of curriculum enhancement through syllabus changes dependent on the use of NICT were very diverse. For example:

> 'In primary schools children put together small databases, say on birds, weather or rivers and so on and so learn how to organize and process information effectively from a very early age.' (UK)

> Use of computers in science courses for logging and/or processing experimental data makes new types of practical work feasible.

> 'The pictures of our planet obtained from geostationary or sun-synchronous satellites give naturalists, geologists and geographers a new way of approaching their discipline and a new way of representing their fields of study which they can no longer ignore.' (France)

> The use in foreign-language and social studies teaching of programmes from foreign television stations both broadens study and brings it right up to date.

> 'In music, IT is increasingly being used to explore new sounds and to create, develop and refine musical ideas. This is especially valuable in helping children with no great musical abilities.' (UK)

The Icelandic report argues for a wider interpretation of the goal of making computers a natural part of school life, making them an 'aid to both teachers and students in the variety of tasks they have to carry out in schools'. This involves four main areas of application:

1. Computers for school administration: among other things, computers are used for recording and processing all data concerning the students and for the computerization of the timetable.
2. Computers in the staffroom or teachers' work rooms: to enable teachers to prepare aids for their lessons.
3. Computers as a teaching aid: it is planned to use computer technology in most subjects, among other things to facilitate the teaching of individuals.
4. Computers for pupils: computers are to be made available to pupils to use in their studies both during the lessons and in their free time. (Iceland)

Both teachers and pupils can use computers as an aid to word processing, data processing and even painting: 'There are some excellent painting packages that allow children to explore and change visual ideas before arriving at something that suits what they want to express. The role of IT is to stimulate and allow exploration. It can never replace, nor is it intended to replace, individual skills and individual creativity' (UK). One further use for teachers and pupils, which may involve both word processing and graphics, is the production of school documents such as magazines, brochures and reports.

Finally, there is the dramatic development noted by Mr Gaetano Adinolfi, Deputy Secretary-General of the Council of Europe, in his opening address:

> The new information technologies also enable transfrontier links to be established between schools. The development of exchanges is an excellent means of getting to know one's neighbours and their languages better. They also permit a new approach to the teaching of history and geography. Moreover, they are a guarantee of better mutual understanding, the basis

of all genuine cooperation.

The combination of computer network links and the exchange of video messages introduces a new dimension to international understanding.

4.2 TEACHING HANDICAPPED CHILDREN

The use of NICT in teaching handicapped children serves two functions. First, it is important to ensure that all children get the same opportunities to know about NICT and use NICT; this may require specially generous provisions for handicapped pupils. Second, there is the increasing use of the computer as a communication aid which can overcome a sensory impairment or motor disability. This exciting new area of development received considerable attention in the French report.

THE DEAF AND HARD OF HEARING

In this area, irrespective of the quality of the software from the educational point of view, computers, with their word-processing capacities, can help the totally deaf child overcome to some extent the problem of self-expression and communication which is an intrinsic part of his handicap.

The Centre Scientifique IBM France has been working on teaching aids to help deaf children master vocalization and speech production. Over the past few years it has equipped about 20 institutes for totally deaf children with voice-processing cards and specially designed software which produces a real time graphic representation on the monitor screen of the sounds made by the handicapped child.

THE BLIND AND PARTIALLY SIGHTED

For a long time young blind people had only limited access to written information but, in computers, they now have a powerful tool to transcribe texts into Braille automatically.

The most recent research has led to the development of a process in which documents are first put through an optical scanner and then memorized, analysed, abridged and printed out on a Braille printer. This equipment can be used by pupils, but also by teachers to prepare lessons for blind pupils and make it possible for them to join in the work of an ordinary class.

CHILDREN WITH SEVERE MOTOR HANDICAPS OR INCAPABLE OF SPEECH

It is probably with these children that the best results have been obtained. For those who can read there are two possibilities when their motor disability prevents them from using the keyboard directly: access to the keyboard via a 'unicorn' device (rod strapped to the head and used to press keys on the keyboard); access to visual symbols via a pneumatic contact. For those who have reached only a pre-verbal stage, computers make it possible, via the means mentioned above, to handle alternative pictographic or symbolic codes (Valençay code, SICOM, Bliss, etc.).

Since the development of equipment and software of this type a few years ago, children have been able to communicate through language with those around them and thus gain access to their common culture. They can also use them for assistance with their school work, or reading and writing, and to control their environment in general.

4.3 DISTANCE EDUCATION

Although distance education has already proved to be one of the most successful applications of NICT, it is still under development. For school age children most countries have traditionally provided (a) radio and television broadcasts for use in the classroom, and (b) children's television to entertain and educate children after school and during their holidays. Children's television is also aimed at pre-school children. Classroom use is rapidly changing from the direct reception of live broadcasts to the more flexible use of cassette recordings. This turns school broadcasting agencies into just another form of publisher. Thus Malta, where broadcasting to schools is a more expensive form of distribution, has replaced school broadcasting by a central video library. However, it still retains its practice of broadcasting educational programmes to children at home after school.

Telescola in Portugal used a more intensive form of distance education to provide the equivalent of the fifth and sixth years of compulsory education for about 60 000 pupils living in very peripheral areas of country or in areas of very low population density.

> Class teaching was backed up by the extensive use of television – about four hours' programmes per day used to be broadcast for these classes throughout the year. The sub-system operated completely separately from the conventional type of education, with no extensive use of the media, provided for all other pupils in the same age group. It had its own teachers, its own teaching materials and even its own form of educational guidance (based on programmed learning with fixed objectives). It also had its own system of organization, administration, etc.

Telescola is now being integrated with the general educational system, but 'without giving up the use of video materials, since the results obtained are in every way comparable with those of other pupils. Apart from this re-integration, the major change was the replacement of broadcast programmes by videocassettes and recorders.' So technically it has ceased to be a distance education system.

It is hoped that 'the flexibility acquired through the substitution of videocassettes for regular television broadcasts will lead to an overall improvement in teacher efficiency. The results obtained will be used to decide whether video recorders should be introduced into all Portuguese schools and, if so, how this should be done, with the benefit of the experience acquired by nearly 3000 teachers over several years.'

The largest distance learning system operation for school age pupils who cannot follow courses in conventional schools is the French Centre National d'Enseignement à Distance (CNED).

This has 80 000 students under 18 and 160 000 enrolled adults. Its courses cover the primary and the secondary curriculum (including preparation for baccalauréat types A–G) and several vocational qualifications.

> Over the past few years, and particularly during the past two years, the CNED has increasingly turned to the new information technologies both to develop new courses designed from the outset with a multi-media approach and to improve existing courses. Radio, audiocassettes and tape recorders have been used for a long time. These have now been joined by videocassettes and switched message networks (Minitel), while in the very near future the list will be extended to microcomputers, interactive audio–videography using the integrated services digital network, universal data readers (pictures, sound and digital information) or CD-ROM, and satellite television. (France)

Most distance learning is directed at adult students. The level ranges from basic literacy to postgraduate courses, though the main focus is often on first degrees for those who missed the opportunity to study immediately after leaving school. The administrative pattern varies from one country to another, and at least five patterns can be discerned:

1. The Norwegian State Institute of Distance Education coordinates and/or commissions work produced in other institutions.
2. Each Finnish institution of higher education arranges open university education separately.
3. Jutland Open University is a joint venture between three Danish institutions.
4. The Open Universities of the Netherlands, Spain and the United Kingdom are specially created national distance learning institutions.
5. Turkey has created a Faculty of Open Education within Anadolu University to provide distance education both to students in Turkey and to Turkish students living abroad (see Case Study 5).

The role of NICT in these institutions is important but should not be over-emphasized:

> The Dutch Open University has decided to place the emphasis on correspondence courses, and to use audio-visual and interactive media only if they contribute something which could not be conveyed or achieved by using written material only. This is in spite of the fact that more extensive use of interactive media is considered desirable to support the Open University students as much as possible. For the immediate future, limitation of media use was nevertheless decided upon because of shortages in manpower, time and money. Another important factor was that study at the Open University should not be restricted to any particular time or place. At the moment most students have only part of the necessary media equipment at their disposal in their homes. Only the audiocassette recorder and the television set are really universally present. For the use of other media, students will have to turn to the study centre for some time to come. Hence the use of media as a supplement to written material is subject to limitations. Media material has to consist of relatively complete units, which are not too small, and which comprise various discrete aspects of subject matter whose connection with the whole course has to be made clear in the programme itself.

The Shelton report from the Council of Europe Parliamentary Assembly noted that 'there has been a considerable surge in initiatives relating to distance education with the advent of direct broadcasting by satellite', a theme discussed at greater length in Chapter 6.

Another possibility mentioned by several countries was the introduction of an interactive element into distance education. The Dutch report implied that this would require equipment which only relatively wealthy students could afford, and the Danish report added that social selection is already an unintended characteristic of distance learning. The poorer students are disadvantaged and therefore the most in need of genuine interaction.

The technologies of first and second generation distance education have had one extremely important advantage:
they have been commonly available and have not as such imposed any bias in the social recruitment of learners. But by giving very low priority to the process of communication, by making communication one-way or very restricted two-way, the result has in fact been a strong social bias in first and second generation distance education. It has mostly appealed to groups of educationally already privileged learners and it has to a certain extent most often 'expelled' the educationally or socially weak learner.

To put it provocatively, *teaching* is the process of structuring and distributing information about certain subjects in the form of printed or broadcast learning material. Communication takes the form of approving/disapproving remarks about the answers given by the students to questions set in the pre-printed assignments. . . .

There is very little communication in the *real* sense of the word between the process of producing and distributing learning material and the process of acquiring the information it provides.

The Danes then develop the arguments that this makes the learning process individual rather than social, and that an interactive element is needed to restore social learning processes. Hence they have been experimenting with distance learning via computer conferencing (see Case Study 1).

Another interesting comment on distance education came from Mr Christoffer Taxell, the Finnish Minister for Education, who noted the administrative inflexibility of traditional educational systems and the partial success of distance learning in overcoming some of the problems. He then put three challenging questions to the conference:

1. Can inflexible administration hinder the creation and development of individual solutions in education? New solutions are found to teaching and technical problems at a rapid rate, but do flexible study opportunities develop

at the same rate?

2. How can we transfer the solutions found within open and multi-form education to conventional higher education and other traditional forms of education and vice versa?

3. How can an effective international network to promote the use of electronic media in education be built and how can we make sure that international cooperation in this field is not too dominated by technology?

REFERENCE

MacKenzie, N., Eraut, M. and Jones, M. (1970). *Teaching and learning: an introduction to new methods and resources in higher education*. Paris: UNESCO.

CHAPTER 5

Approaches to Implementation

Countries have learned a great deal from their attempts to introduce NICT into education during the past decade, which they have judged to have been more successful in some aspects than others. National reports covered four main areas: purchase and distribution of hardware; development, purchase and distribution of software; teacher education, initial and in-service; and research and evaluation. In each of these areas there are important policy issues concerning the level of expenditure, the pacing of implementation and the general innovation strategy; these are discussed in separate sections below. Priority must be given, however, to considering their interrelationship.

In every country experience has shown that programmes in hardware, software and teacher education need to be carefully integrated, and that the balance of expenditure has often been wrong. For example, the Yugoslavian Minister told the conference:

> Our experience has shown that investment in hardware alone cannot give satisfactory results if you do not at the same time ensure that good-quality software and also highly qualified teaching staff are available for this area. Because of this, our information technology equipment in schools is usually under-used and does not produce the expected results. In Yugoslavia, we reckon that the main priority in this field is the development and import of high quality software suitable for

48

specific levels or types of programme. This is a special problem of countries undergoing development, which is the case for Yugoslavia. The second priority in this area is teacher training because the development of modern information technology at schools is hindered by the teachers being uninformed, badly trained or even negatively motivated.

The usual lack of resources also creates a major policy problem:

> The means are inadequate to promote development equally across all the fronts identified as critical – equipment, curriculum (and software) and teacher training – and even less adequate to achieve meaningful progress in each school and university. The policy alternatives range from maximum efficiency involving total concentration of resources on some educational establishments and on some of the fronts, to maximum equity involving total spread, however thin, of resources across all the targets. (Turkey)

Research evidence points towards concentration of resources in order to achieve a 'critical mass' but political pressures are in the direction of equity. Since visibility is important politically, this has reinforced the trend for hardware to be spread too thinly while insufficient attention is paid to software and teacher training.

Several strategies have been used to achieve an integrated and effective programme. One approach is to start with a basic computer literacy course of the kind described in Chapter 3, and then later to spread the use of computers across into other subjects. This strategy, which is well illustrated by the Austrian report, allows a phased introduction of hardware and software into schools, and keeps the range of software and the initial demand for teacher education at a manageable level. However, it does not always coincide with curriculum priorities.

Another approach bypasses the equity problem by decentralization, encouraging different districts and schools to develop different aspects of NICT usage with a combination of local and central funding. Then sharing this experience allows further development in one district to benefit from the pioneering work of others. This has been the approach in the United Kingdom, which is now seeking to consolidate its rich range of local experimentation into a more centralized set of curriculum expectations.

The third approach, usually associated with a strong research and evaluation component, is the special project or programme. This has now been adopted by Portugal and Spain (see Case Study 4). Much useful evidence has resulted from programmes that started earlier in the decade; those of Norway and the Netherlands are described in some detail below.

THE NORWEGIAN PROGRAMME OF ACTION

This programme for the introduction of computer technology in primary and secondary education was launched in 1984 and given top priority for a provisional period of four years. The aims of the Programme of Action were defined in a White Paper to Parliament; and a special Ministerial Task Force was established to coordinate its activities.

> One of the main objectives was to create equal opportunities for all in gaining access to computer development to avoid new class divisions, and particular attention was given to equality of the sexes. Other objectives were to investigate the use of computers as a teaching aid, to consider changes in curriculum and content of teaching, and to stimulate experiments and extend cooperation between various parties in the school community. The programme was also aimed at building up resource centres and qualified personnel as well as encouraging cooperation between the schools and trade and industry. The programme has mainly included projects in a limited number of pilot schools, seminars and courses for teachers and development of software. Although both primary and secondary education were involved, special attention has been paid to vocational branches of the upper secondary school and to special education.
>
> During the initial phase (1984–88) the programme was evaluated in many ways, among others by a group of

OCD examiners. . . . One of the main achievements is considered to be a shift in emphasis in that a growing number of teachers and educationists now are accepting the computer as an important learning aid in education in general. Computers have found their way into schools, and the country has become advanced in developing computer learning materials. The Programme of Action has stimulated more long-term changes and managerial experience which will be important for future school development. The new technology represents a challenge to the teacher's and the school's pedagogical insight and opens the way for innovations regarding teaching approaches. The end of the programme having been reached (1988), a major concern now is distribution of the knowledge and experience gained through the four-year trial period. The national councils for primary and lower secondary education, and for upper secondary education, in cooperation with the counties, have the main responsibility for this task, and the former pilot schools have a central role in this work.

THE DUTCH INFORMATION STIMULATION PLAN (INSP)

The INSP, which received joint support from the Ministries of Economic Affairs and Education, embodied 'a completely new concept in large-scale innovation' – the use of the project model at all levels. 'Not only were the school-based activities designed on a project basis, but the new consultation and implementation structures were to function temporarily as a project, that is until the end of the plan's period.' Most of the early applications were for the acquisition of hardware. But it soon 'became clear that in-service training and software development were necessarily linked to the hardware. So no further projects were started which did not make use of an integrated approach.'

Generally speaking, the goals set by the INSP have been attained. . . . Many teachers have been trained, most schools have a reasonable amount of hardware at their disposal,

51

and a growing store of software is being developed. . . . Where initiatives from business, school boards, schools and government were launched on the same lines as the INSP, better results were achieved than first projected. This is clear from school inspectors' reports based on a complete inventory of the state of affairs in IT education. It appears that far more activities, material and knowledge are available than simply those embodied in the projects introduced into schools by the government.

Three types of follow-up are planned:

Consolidation

This applies to 'those sectors in which the aims have been realized and it is important to maintain the status quo. This is the case, for example, in in-service training for secondary education, and for the introduction of information science in the first stage of secondary education. The means to assure this would be the earmarking of funds and long-term estimates for the replacement of hardware and software.'

Advanced forms of stimulation

For varying reasons, a number of elements only got going at a later stage. For these activities, what is needed is a long period in which to experiment further. The addition of one extra year would be a great help. This is the case for adult education, for the introduction of information science as a compulsory subject in general secondary education, and for the experiments in regional centres for new technologies for vocational education. The setting up of research projects into the applications of IT in education in the so-called experimental schools will take an extra year. Special education will be served partly by a catching-up operation linked to primary education. Pilot projects on applied hardware for a number of types of sensory or motor handicaps will continue.

Modified approach

In a few instances it has been shown that the original aims of the approach thought out in the INSP were not the most practical or the most attainable. This was a good lesson. This has led to a change of course in the last year and a half. In these cases it is desirable to lengthen the project period, so that the new approach is given a chance to prove its worth.

This is the case for software development, for higher vocational education and the teacher training colleges, and for primary education. For higher vocational education and the teacher training colleges the spear-point strategy was decided upon in 1986. This meant that the existing knowledge in the institutes was concentrated, and forged into a large professionally run project in combination with expertise from certain sectors of trade and industry.

Primary education has also made a hesitant start to employing a broader strategy, which arose because of pressure from the schools themselves. This has now been taken up by political circles. This means that schools may send their teachers on courses and that they are then eligible to receive hardware.

[In summary], the INSP may be considered a success, not only because a good number of the operational goals have been realized, but particularly because of the impact the plan has had in the eyes of society and in a quantitative and qualitative sense. The absolute necessity of introducing computers into education and learning about them has become far more generally accepted. Many teachers already use them and will be followed in turn by their colleagues. The government's budget and school boards' budgets show that funds have been earmarked for the continuation of these activities. That is a good result.

Yet this good result is precisely what gives us reason for concern about the future of the use of IT in education.

This concern involves two questions:

1. Can we prevent teachers and hardware suffering a

shortage of materials? That is to say: will we be able in the long term to keep producing lesson materials and trained teachers? The present situation as regards software development and initial training courses gives reason for concern.

2. Will we be successful in continuing to convince decision-makers, parliament and educational organizations that the intellectual and financial input into IT education is worthwhile? A lot of money is tied up in IT, and the educational budget is constantly under pressure of the constant need for economies. For vocational education it will be easy to show the benefits. It will be more difficult for secondary and other educational establishments to provide convincing evidence.

Great expectations are always the most vulnerable, so whether the achievements of the INSP can be sustained in the long run remains to be seen.

5.1 HARDWARE ISSUES

Apart from the general recognition that too much attention had been given to hardware and the more technological aspects of innovation, there was relatively little discussion of hardware problems. Perhaps this was because some countries, such as France, had already made massive investments in hardware, while others were still troubled by the financial difficulty of making any substantial progress towards equipping schools not involved in pilot projects. Several countries with information technology as a new subject in their curriculum reported their current level of equipment. Austria now has seven PC work stations plus one BTX work station in every high school for courses in computer studies and varying percentages of schools with additional computers for subject teaching: 64 per cent for physics, 30 per cent for chemistry, 15 per cent for geometry. Denmark reports an average of 15 work stations in upper secondary schools, and a somewhat lower average in primary schools.

Most schools have a computer room with 10 to 15 computers in a network, in clusters of four or, less often, standing alone. In addition, depending on the numbers available, there will be some mobile work stations and also a few mostly small computers permanently deployed in physics and chemistry laboratories. The computer room and the mobile work stations are at the disposal of all subjects and make for an environment that is easily adaptable to a range of specific applications.

Machine counts can be deceptive because equipment may not be in constant use. Lack of software or of trained teachers may reduce utilization, as can lack of technical support or proper maintenance. In Italy, for example, 32 per cent of computers are out of order. Inflexible management also limits the time for which pupils have access to computers. Significantly, only Sweden provided data on pupil access times:

> The following figures show average computer time inputs for various fields at the 25 schools, together with minimum and maximum time inputs:

> | | |
> |---|---|
> | Distribution and clerical | 53 hours (5–150) |
> | Economics | 54 hours (10–215) |
> | Liberal arts | 10 hours (0–20) |
> | Social science | 14 hours (3–30) |
> | Natural science | 24 hours (4–40) |
> | Technology (3 or 4 years) | 38 hours (0–60) |
> | Building and construction | 5 hours (0–15) |
> | Electro-telecommunications | 69 hours (10–380) |
> | Motor engineering | 8 hours (0–30) |
> | Metalwork | 34 hours (0–100) |

Hardware policy also involves a series of difficult compromises. Governments naturally prefer indigenous manufacture but this may not always be the cheapest form of provision. Where software is developed in-country, standardization helps to reduce costs and ensure maximum use. But when software is imported, compatible machines are needed to run it; so a range of equipment is necessary.

A further problem in vocational education is compatibility with business use outside education. Finally, there is the historic effect of special deals with computer companies or gifts from the local community. These often sabotage attempts at standardization, and may also have implications for equity.

Nevertheless, there are some general principles which should govern the selection of school computers:

> A low price per work station is the prerequisite for the equipment of a majority of schools with a sufficient number of devices; one has to take into account what elements are included in the system;

> Reliable repair services located in the vicinity of the school must be ensured;

> The product line should be available over several years so that a step-by-step equipment progression with compatible devices is possible;

> The architecture and standard operating systems of computers should be designed with an eye to expandability;

> The maintenance of existing programs and the development of new and better programs by software manufacturers should be guaranteed in the long run, including with regard to their utilization with different hardware;

> Schools should have the possibility of acquiring low cost standard programs – above all including site licences, i.e. one licence to cover all machines in the classroom.
>
> (Bund–Länder Commission, 1989)

5.2 SOFTWARE AND MATERIALS DEVELOPMENT

Rather more attention was given to the perceived shortage of educational computer software than to other types of material. The principal problem is not in supporting computer literacy courses, because these can use software already available in the commercial sector, such as word-processing, database and spreadsheet packages. Indeed, increasing use is being made of these 'generic tools' in other areas of the curriculum. The problem lies in all those other potential subject-specific applications of computers which require software designed for specific topics and useful only to schools. Many countries reported that it was unrealistic to expect this task to be undertaken by teachers in their spare time, as this had created a rash of programs of very low quality. But the size of the market was still too small for a wholly commercial approach. The key questions were 'What kinds of software should be given priority?' and 'How can governments increase the supply of software of acceptable quality?'

The first question, concerning the priority to be given to different kinds of software by a national programme of development, was addressed in some detail by the Swedish report, using a typology based on *frequency of use* (many lessons or few) and the *role of the user* (active or passive). This is shown in Figure 1.

Figure 1 should be looked upon as an aid to evaluating a computer application. Is it pedagogically reasonable and is it economically justifiable to invest in drill and practice programs in education? This software is expensive for the school as it is developed for a limited part of the curriculum and it has to be updated continuously in order to contain current knowledge.

In many parts of the world, software is produced that can provide a complete education in a whole phase, in the curriculum or in a course. This computer application is shown in the square at the top left of Figure 1. The design is often built on questions and answers mixed with some isolated exercises. Sometimes they contain possibilities for the instructor to measure the performance of the pupil. This instructional software (courseware) is designed to replace the teacher in such a way as to offer an economical education that can easily be distributed. Swedish policy is not to use such applications in education.

Lessonware (the square at the bottom right of Figure 1) can be of special value, because it could make special training

FREQUENCY OF USE

Courseware (often in the form of instructional programs)	**Tool programs** (e.g. word processing, tools for simulation, CAE programs, expert system shells, databases)

Many lessons or occasions in education

Drill and practice	**Lessonware** (often in the form of a field of knowledge)

Few lessons or occasions in education

ROLE OF THE USER: Passive   Active

Figure 1   Classification of educational software.

58

possible. Such training might otherwise be impossible to provide. An example is a computer program that shows different chemical reactions or the effects of different kinds of radioactive emissions.

In order to use lessonware programs, computers must be in different places all over the school. This means that lessonware could indeed be of great value for education, but its use is most expensive, because the software is expensive to produce and a large number of computers is required.

Software that gives the user great freedom and that can be used in many ways is usually called tool programs. These programs give the user opportunities and facilities but demand great user competence. For most teachers there could be a need for a double competence: in the first place to handle the program, and secondly competence in using it in a pedagogical way when teaching.

The efforts in the Educational Software Group at the Ministry of Education have to a great extent been devoted to increasing knowledge about experience with the use of different tool programs. This development work has shown that new working forms in school and new methods have to be developed in the future to make full use of these computer applications.

Finally, the experience of the Educational Software Group is that attention should be focused mainly on different kinds of tool programs and secondly on developing some lessonware of special interest. Drill and practice programmes that constrain the freedom of the pupil could be pedagogically justified in some special situations. Courseware has no place in central plans for education in Sweden.

Another point raised was the cultural specificity of much educational material. Apart from the obvious factor of language, the report from Portugal argued

the need for each teaching aid to be matched as closely as possible in cultural terms with the target group for which it has been specifically designed. This obviously makes it difficult to transfer teaching materials directly between different cultural contexts, whether social, linguistic or geographical. In this field it is more sensible to adopt a cooperative production or co-production strategy than simply to translate or adapt products from an external source.

The degree of cultural specificity is also likely to vary according to the subject and the extent to which pedagogic strategies have been incorporated into the material or left for the teacher to decide. Thus coursework is less transferable than lessonware or tool programs. There remains the problem raised by several national reports of how to increase the currently inadequate supply. This was introduced at the conference by the Icelandic delegate in the following terms:

> Past experience has shown that the commercial market cannot be counted on. It is therefore inevitable that if a part of the money already spent on educational hardware is not to go down the drain, authorities will have to subsidize software production. The market for educational software is relatively small, and it is important to find ways to increase its size. One way is to promote standardization in hardware, so that as many systems as possible can use all high-quality software produced. An endeavour should also be made to make translation and adaptation of software from one language to another as easy as possible. To reach this goal more intensive European cooperation could make a significant difference. As far as cooperation between different countries is concerned, there could be organized co-production such as is already underway in the Nordic countries.
>
> Apart from steps to increase the production of quality software by official funding and cooperation between countries, national authorities also have to promote the reviewing and evaluation of all educational material produced and supply schools and teachers with reliable information on its quality. Such information should also be available through European or even international cooperation.
>
> The third kind of input authorities have to make to increase the supply of quality software, so that the potential of the information technology to improve education will be

realized, is to ensure that software development and the use of computers in schools is more closely integrated with the general curriculum development.

One aspect of the question of how to increase the availability of these materials for teaching has not been mentioned and that is copyright. National authorities will have to make an all out effort to solve the problem copyright rules pose in most countries, regarding software, audio-visual material and educational media programmes. In this field international cooperation is essential.

The copyright issue was raised by several countries, and an innovative French approach to the problem is described in Case Study 2. This is based on the concept of a 'joint licence' between government and publishers to ensure a supply of agreed items of software for schools. Detailed descriptions of government support for software development were also provided by Spain (see Case Study 4) and the Netherlands.

As far as courseware development is concerned, we have learnt from our mistakes. This wisdom has been incorporated into the four departure points which form the basis of the POCO project running at the moment and set the guidelines for further activities.

1. Taking the market into consideration must be the basis of any initiative. This means that:
    - When deciding which programs are to be made, the characteristics of market demand must be taken into consideration. Form and content should be adjusted accordingly.
    - Schools will not get the programs for free as a result of the subsidy for development costs. They will have to pay for them. In that sense they will get used to the fact that this is a new expenditure factor.
    - Educational publishers will be brought into the project as far as possible and from the very beginning, that is, when specifications and marketing are decided upon. This may result in a design determined by the publisher. The

publisher will, as always, run a certain risk, although it is a shared risk in this instance since the government has also invested.

2. We realize that software is expensive, more expensive than the usual run of teaching materials and aids which have to be bought for educational purposes. This means that we cannot expect the publishers to make the investment in software provision all on their own. The government has given temporary assistance through projects like POCO and Courseware Midden Nederland, in which a part of the development costs has been financed by the government.

3. The government is aware of the lack of knowledge prevalent in the field of courseware development. Few people are good at it. Publishers cannot put teams to work at will. We have therefore tried to put the little talent we have together in large-scale projects, whereby a pool of people can be drawn upon. At the same time attempts are being made to retrain teachers to become courseware makers and to keep them for projects in the field of IT and education.

4. The final point involves the nature of the demands made on the program which we have instigated. From sheer necessity (because of market demands and in relation to the fact that the making of courseware is complicated) we have set ourselves the task of making programs in which user-friendliness is the first concern. There are two sides to this – the content side and the organizational side:
   - As far as content is concerned, programs should relate to everyday situations, with repeatable learning contents. In this way frequent usage is promoted.
   - The program must be easy to work in class. It should not need a *tour de force* on the part of the teacher to get it working and to get the pupils working with it.

The development of audio-visual materials raises some rather different issues. There was concern to retain the major contribution made by national broadcasting agencies, but also to benefit from the wider access opportunities which could be available via satellite. However, these and other audio-visual materials were so numerous in some countries that it was difficult for teachers to find the most appropriate materials for their needs. Newer types of resource, such as video disk, were more like computer software – with not too many titles as yet and a market that is still very small because of the price and scarcity of hardware.

5.3 TEACHER EDUCATION

Teacher education was the theme of the previous Standing Conference of European Ministers of Education, which met in Helsinki in 1987. It is now given increasing prominence in national policies for introducing NICT into education. As the Belgian (French Community) report acknowledged: 'It is very difficult to incorporate computer technology into everyday educational practices in such a way that it really supports the teaching approach adopted by the teacher. The problem areas concern attitudes, technological competence and the production of educational software corresponding as closely as possible to individual needs.' Both the teacher and the technology have to adapt to each other – an easier task, some argued, for new teachers than for their older colleagues. That was seen both as a more difficult and as a longer-term process:

> The retraining of teachers in computer studies has been very pressing. Many courses have been organized for both primary and secondary school teachers so that, now, at least a part of the teaching force has received some training in the use of computers. However, it is probably not possible to make plans for the use of computers as a normal part of school life for a good few years to come. There would have to be a radical change in the teaching methods and the organization of school work, and it is unlikely that teachers, who have been in the profession for years, are likely to change radically the methods they have adopted. Therefore, it is essential to

emphasize the use of computers in the training of teachers, so that teachers begin to look upon information and computer technology as a natural part of every individual's education and training. (Iceland)

Some countries reported that compulsory computer studies courses were now included in initial training, as well as courses in audio-visual education. Others reported progress in this direction. Media education was rarely a compulsory component of initial training but was often available as an option.

The conference gave more attention to the more difficult task of in-service training, though largely at the policy level. Given some of the difficulties mentioned above, it is perhaps surprising that little attention was given to the effectiveness of what was provided – a topic pursued in Professor Eraut's report in Part 2. Since a wide range of approaches has been used, it ought to be possible to learn from the diversity of experience in different countries.

Perhaps the most comprehensive programme of in-service education has been that of Denmark, who were able to report that 'by the end of 1987 most teachers had some familiarity with computers and their use in an educational context'. This was followed by details of their programme for upper secondary schools.

All teachers will receive a 20-hour course locally, usually at their own schools. After that they will be given a regional course of 40 hours. At this stage some differentiation of course content takes place according to the subjects taught by the individual teacher. Finally, 200-hour courses are given to three teachers from each school, typically a science teacher, a teacher of social studies and a modern languages teacher. In these courses great emphasis is laid on the use of computers in specific subjects.

By the end of 1987 more than 90 per cent of all upper secondary teachers had completed a 20-hour and a 40-hour course, and more than half of the 200-hour courses had been held, the last being scheduled to take place in early 1989.

Luxembourg made a greater distinction between basic training and advanced training, both taught at a university centre:

> Basic training is organised in the form of 4, 8 or 16 hour modules, which take place partly during working hours and partly outside the school timetable. The aim of these seminars is to provide technical training to all teachers and initiate educational projects in existing subject areas. Advanced training is designed for teachers who will be teaching computer studies in upper secondary classes. Its total length is 600 hours, i.e one year's training. Teacher trainers are also recruited from among teachers who have followed a course of this type.

Belgium set up and used computers in education centres at its five French-speaking universities; other countries used universities for specialist diploma courses in computers in education but not for basic training.

The problem for many countries is the quantity of basic training required. So more radical solutions involving distance education are now being explored. Mr Daniel Coens, the Minister for Education for the Flemish Community in Belgium, described their new two-stage training strategy to the conference.

> In the first stage, basic training in the new technologies should be given by way of distance education, supported by written materials. The new information technologies' aim and place in the information society are studied together with their incorporation into didactics. In this context, we must make sure that all subject disciplines go through the same stage, as each of them still forms a classic assimilation pattern in education (formal as well as informal). In this way, the integration into subjects – so much wanted – will come within the range of possibility.
>
> In the second stage, individually directed support should be given to each participant enrolled in the course during practice sessions organized in teacher-training centres. Practice sessions are a must, as they offer the opportunity to make use of a great variety of facilities that enable participants to put into practice

the theories that have been taught, to get an answer to any questions that might arise and to make a creative contribution through contacts with colleagues, tutors or instructors. A 'double-session' system is needed here: one kind of session to be devoted to general principles, the other more specifically to the various subject disciplines and didactics.

The Netherlands, Norway and Turkey also referred to the use of distance education for teacher training. The logic of using the NICT to teach about the NICT was extended by others to include the use of video records of good practice as resources for both initial and in-service training.

Training in media education is also developing, though not with the same priority. Norway and Switzerland reported good coverage in some districts only, and in several other countries training is largely confined to especially enthusiastic teachers. France, however, has developed a network of provision by a most original approach:

> The Centre de Liaison de l'Enseignement et des Moyens d'Information (CLEMI) runs training courses for teachers with the participation of journalists and media representatives. These teachers are organized into a network which covers the whole of France, and they, in their turn, run practical courses in their own regions (under the authority of local education officials). This structure enables a fairly small team to maintain relations with classes and schools throughout France. CLEMI courses are tailor-made to meet specific demands. They may last from three days to four weeks. They may be very general (knowledge of the media and their use in the classroom) or very specific (media and resources, school radio stations, etc.), depending on their target groups.

Austria is another country which gives high priority to media education and its report provided one of the few accounts of the pedagogic principles involved:

- In the first place teachers should be allowed to engage in media education on the basis of their own independent learning experiences and only in the second place on that of the study of relevant information.

- Working out projects and putting them into practice is, in addition to the teacher's own learning experience, the most effective form of further training. The greatest part of the learning effect is attributable to discussions about the topic in question.
- Theoretical reflection should primarily be reflection on one's own learning and planning.
- Stabilization and dissemination of media education work can best be achieved through positive experience of successful work and subsequent discussion.
- Training should take account of school reality and should not necessarily presuppose radical changes.
- Training should not require from teachers an extensive study of theoretical models or intensive preparation.

Similar pedagogic principles were put forward by Spain (see Case Study 4) and Portugal, where the Minerva project is seen 'as a stimulus towards permanent, searching reappraisal of the teaching process in its essential features (whether or not it is based on the new technologies)'.

Consequently teacher training has high priority in the Portuguese strategy for the introduction of the new information technologies into education. The basic aim of this training is to establish a climate conducive to self-motivation among teaching staff in the study of the appropriate educational use of the new technologies. This implies a forward looking attitude and the sharing of experiences and ideas. In this way training solidly based on purely educational motivations will encourage an approach to the use of the new technologies with built-in defence mechanisms against alienation – and the transmisson of this approach; similarly, the approach will be put into practice in such a way as to avoid the dangers which are inevitably associated with it (for example, the exacerbation of individualism) and to enhance the positive potential of the new technologies as the mediators of certain social values, by encouraging team work, respect for the rules of courtesy and mutual assistance. (Portugal)

Finally, one should note that it is not only the classroom teachers who need training.

> The shortage of teacher trainers with appropriate experience is especially acute, and their training should be a priority. The training of head-teachers is also urgent, given the crucial importance of their attitude in determining the success or failure of innovation. Their training should take account of the application of NICT to school management. (Conference Discussion Paper)

5.4 RESEARCH AND EVALUATION

During the 1950s many countries made enormous efforts to introduce NICT into schools in order to keep pace with developments in wider society and to show that schools also could and should make use of NICT. The political imperative was to get something happening quickly that was visible. Hence heavy investments are planned for the future. The conference agreed that it is now urgent to learn from the experience of the 1980s and to collect evidence of its impact on teachers and pupils. As the Conference Discussion Paper noted:

> Very little is known about the effects of this spending, especially in meaningful cost–benefit terms. What has been accomplished? What has been successful? The results of policies should be constantly researched and evaluated, particularly with a view to determining future policy options. It may be increasingly hard to justify continued high-level expenditure if effectiveness remains in doubt and priorities unclear. Likewise, scientific research is needed on the effects of the NICT and the media in education, young people's media tastes, learning materials, etc.

Accordingly, the Luxembourg Minister of Education, Mr Marc Fischbach, called for the exchange of information on how countries are currently evaluating their programmes in order to develop appropriate evaluation strategies for the future. But only Norway and Sweden reported evaluations of nationwide programmes (rather than pilot projects where evaluation was often a built-in component). Norway's Programme of Action (reported at the beginning of Section 5) was externally evaluated by the OECD (OECD/CERI, 1987), and is now subject to ongoing evaluation by the International Movement Towards Educational Change (IMTEC). Sweden, with its strong tradition of educational research, sponsored several related studies which together give an accurate picture of the situation in 1988. For example, their account of the use of computers in senior-level schools includes the following findings:

- All schools are making plans which closely follow the syllabus, underlining that work at the computer should precede more theoretical presentations so as to give pupils a better understanding of information technology and its social impact.
- The best progress has been made in teaching word processing, databases and computerized registers.
- The schools are equipped with a computer room, which in most cases has eight computers. Teaching is often organized in such a way that there are not more than two pupils at the same computer.
- Most schools have one teacher who has completed 10 weeks' INSET and serves in a back-up capacity. A clear majority of these 'resource persons' are mathematics and science teachers, but the number of social subjects teachers involved is growing.
- Teacher attitudes towards computer science are predominantly positive on the part of mathematics and science teachers and vary in the case of social subjects teachers. Only a few teachers are downright negative.

Several countries, including Sweden, reported research programmes which will give future policy a stronger empirical base than has been possible hitherto. The Netherlands report is of particular interest here for its explicit discussion of the planned relationship between research and policy.

To learn more about the possible effects of interactive media in education, but also of the difficulties that will be met, a number of research projects are to be conducted in the Netherlands. A leading principle is that in the short term the emphasis must be on careful investigation, while steps towards implementation should be postponed until after some years, when more definite conclusions about interactive media in education become available. A policy paper setting out these intentions was presented to representatives of education and later to Parliament. In both circles the plans were welcomed. Implementation of this policy was started at the beginning of 1987. A number of projects have been launched. Among these are projects on the educational use of videotext, on-line use of a geographical database in general secondary education, the use of interactive video in primary education, initial teacher training and in-service training. More are in the process of development.

To ensure that educationists are associated with developments in government policy regarding interactive media, all plans for projects are discussed with a group of representatives of education. In this way it is hoped to keep educational circles informed about progress with interactive media, while at the same time advantage can be taken of available knowledge in this field.

Attention was also drawn to the need for more basic research to deepen our understanding of learning and of schools as educational institutions. The Swiss Minister argued that: 'An important place is given to research, as much pedagogic as fundamental, for research is the key to success in the long term. Indeed, there are many fields to investigate ahead, in particular that which concerns the psychology and pedagogy of learning and the true influence of the new technologies upon this.' An excellent Italian research programme into the relationship between schools and the media is reported in Case Study 3 in Part 3.

As the Greek delegate noted, research is an important area for European cooperation, and a much more scientific description and analysis is needed in order to distinguish between universal and more specifically national factors.

Besides the investment required to implement NICT and media in education, of utmost importance is the constant evaluation of the results of the policies made, having always in mind the future policy options. So research is needed on all the interrelated subjects, such as the effects of NICT and media, the reactions of the young people and the quality and usefulness of the learning materials. But the first priority lies in detailed and methodic recording of the problems, differences and capabilities which exist in the European region. This will allow: (a) the proper planning of the priorities which should be made concerning NICT and media in the various educational levels, and (b) the production of material which will meet the needs of European society as a whole.

REFERENCES

Bund–Länder Commission for Educational Planning and Research Promotion (1989). *Overall concept for education in information technology.* Federal Republic of Germany.

OECD/CERI (1987). *The introduction of computers in schools: the Norwegian experience.* Examiners' report. Paris: OECD.

CHAPTER 6

European Cooperation

It was natural for European cooperation to appear on the agenda of a conference which itself provided an excellent example of the process. Moreover, it was more than a token appearance. The use of NICT in education has proved to be an area where all countries see an important role for European collaboration and wish to strengthen it further. Delegates repeatedly stressed the need for countries to learn from each other's experience in this field.

The documentation for the conference included a single volume of reports on European cooperation on education in 1987 and 1988 from UNESCO, OECD, the Council of Europe, the European Community, the Nordic Council of Ministers and the European Free Trade Association. Successful cooperation was also mentioned in many of the national reports. The work of the Nordic Council of Ministers is of special interest for its emphasis on collaboration in software development.

A joint software group, with a secretariat in Copenhagen, comes under the Nordic Council of Ministers. Nordic co-operation on information technology in the school sector is making rapid strides. Since January 1986, funds have been awarded for activities comprising information exchange between the Nordic countries, work on a Nordic software description standard, a catalogue of current research and development work in the Nordic area, work on agreements and copyright questions, and teacher education, for example.

The software group of the Nordic Council of Ministers publishes a journal, *Nytt om data i skolan*, containing articles on particular themes from all the Nordic countries. The annual Nordic software design courses have been appreciated by teachers and financial support has been awarded for the further development of several draft programs. Courses and workshops on optical media, dynamic simulation, expert systems in teaching, communication and tele-teaching, information databases in the school sector and CAD/CAM are included in this venture, together with international exchange. Nordic cooperation also includes development work aimed at investigating the educational advantages/applications of computer networking. (Sweden)

This collaboration is now extending beyond Scandinavia, as Norway offered a course in 1988 on design of pedagogical software within the Council of Europe's Teacher Bursaries Scheme. They also reported that 'a special agreement has been concluded concerning the access to software developed under the Scottish Microelectronics Development Programme, and similar agreements with other centres abroad are being considered'.

The Irish delegation draw attention to the benefits they received from projects sponsored by the European Community:

The Department is attempting through active participation in projects organized and aided by the European Commission to complement its own research and development activities and to enhance its development programme through sharing of experience with its European colleagues. Ireland is participating therefore in three projects, in the present action programme, i.e.

1. Models for Transfer of Software Project no. 102.
2. Classroom Uses of Databases in Science Project no. 109.
3. Prolog and Knowledge Bases in Schools Project no. 124.

Project no. 102 has chosen the biology shell developed under the Department of Education research programme as a prototype for further study across different countries.

Several countries stressed the need for the co-production of software, the exchange of information on materials evaluation, the sharing of research findings and collaboration over copyright. However, the issue given greatest attention at the conference itself was collaboration in distance education. This followed a report and recommendations from the Parliamentary Assembly of the Council of Europe, which was presented to the conference by Sir William Shelton. The report described existing cooperation in distance education; noted the transformation of the situation by the advent of direct broadcasting by satellite and, in particular, the launching by the European Space Agency (ESA) of the experimental Olympus satellite covering approximately the member states of the Council of Europe with nine hours daily dedicated to distance learning programmes; then recommended that the Committee of Ministers:

1. Invite governments to create in the framework of the Council of Europe a Board for Distance Teaching in Europe, possibly on the basis of an Open Partial Agreement.

2. Initiate and promote intergovernmental cooperation on distance teaching, on the multilateral co-production of distance education material and on the interaction of distance-teaching developments with ongoing traditional teaching in schools and universities.

3. Give encouragement to moves towards a European open university network based on cooperation between distance teaching universities in all European countries.

4. Encourage the necessary legal harmonization to facilitate credit transfer and also the harmonization of copyright regarding course transfers between educational institutions in different countries.

5. Promote the more general use of satellite technology for distance education and encourage networking among universities and scientific institutions in post-academic courses and areas of advanced technology (for example medicine).

6. Invite broadcasters to collaborate more closely with educational bodies on the production and transmission of suitable educational programmes.

7. Encourage the exchange of information on developments in this field.

Although the conference was not required to pass judgement on this initiative, it was warmly welcomed by a number of delegates.

Finally, there was some discussion of issues relating to the transfer between countries of technology and know-how, on which the general view was that expressed by the Conference Resolution:

> To reduce the social and economic imbalances between European countries, the products and experience of the countries which have gone furthest in such development should benefit the others without diverting them from their own aims and purposes or threatening their cultural identity. In this regard, cooperation on the transfer of educational technology and expertise through the appropriate organizations and institutions should be strengthened.

PART 2

EXPERT REPORTS

CHAPTER 1

The Information Society, Schools and the Media

Francis Balle

1.1 SUMMARY

THE POST-INDUSTRIAL SOCIETY FINALLY IDENTIFIED

The 1960s saw the newspapers' age-old monopoly of information destroyed by radio and television. There has since been a growing diversity of types of media expression and interaction between them, whereas for a long time the media had been relatively independent of each other. This symbolized the transition from an industrial society to an 'informatics' or information-processing society. The determining factor has been the creation, processing and transmitting of information, which is now central to the activity of modern societies. As a result, the number of information-related jobs has grown rapidly, while the number of industrial jobs created has decreased. Thus, the cultural and social as well as the economic environments have been altered.

The salient features of the new era are (a) the ever increasing number and diversity of available media; (b) wider personal and selective access to networks, programmes and services; and (c) the abolition of frontiers between many media.

For the individual, this has meant emancipation from previous limits to communication and from the constraints of time and space. Yet despite advances in new information and communication technologies (NICT), educational systems are inadequate and often poorly adapted to the new developments, and the result is under-educated and unprepared citizens. Knowledge of NICT is becoming essential and computer illiteracy will place people in a position of inferiority. Already, large companies have spent an enormous amount of money retraining their employees in information technology.

THE REALITIES AND ILLUSIONS OF THE INFORMATION SOCIETY

Communication in all its forms is considered the new panacea. But is it truly a new frontier or merely a misguided illusion? The paradox of the media is that they enslave at the same time as they liberate. While the media help to overcome the limitations imposed by distance, they also refer individuals back to themselves, to the limits of a just-conquered freedom, which may turn out to be illusory because of lack of imagination, lack of time or money, or lack of ability to maintain personal contact.

Communication has now become the privileged vantage point from which society questions itself about such ideas as how technology influences social order, how training matches employment, etc. Economically it is a constantly shifting but growing sector which requires adaptability. It challenges education by inviting people to rediscover the importance of intelligent discipline and by requiring new relations between the world of school and the world of work.

Selective interactive telecommunications will now tend to progress faster than unidirectional broadcasting (like television) since they allow for more freedom of choice and less imposition. The abundance of the media in general and the development of interactivity will allow people to choose the programmes or services they want, rather than suffering the messages chosen for them by publishers or broadcasters.

THE MEDIA AND THE SCHOOL: DIVISION OF LABOUR OR COMPETITION?

What conclusions can be drawn from a brief overview of the attempts from 1950 to 1980 to use radio and television for educational purposes? On the negative side, it may be said that the use of television in schools has failed to fulfil its promise, a trend that led many to abandon the experiment. On the positive side, there have been some benefits, though not those that were expected. As a result, the experiment has been continued, but in a quite different direction from before.

These results may be attributed to either excessive optimism or excessive pessimism. On the negative side, schools viewed television or radio as mere tools without integrating them enough into the classroom or making productive use of their potential. Instead, lessons were merely given in front of a camera or a microphone. Schools did not learn to make use of the intrinsic capacities of media resources and made no effort to adapt teaching to include them. On the optimistic side, some expected the media to compensate for all the weaknesses and shortcomings of the schools. In essence, some wanted the television to become the school.

The conflict between schools and the media resulted from the fact that both were suffering from delusions of grandeur and sought exclusive control over thought and culture. Each mistakenly believed that one day it would be able to monopolize the education of children. Today, the two recognize their dependence on each other. The media arouse curiosity about matters which can often be comprehended only by means of the tools provided by schools.

The growth of collaboration between schools and the media may be attributed both to the impact of new technology beginning in 1979–80 and to less ambitious goals on both sides. The advent of new technology has had three main results: (a) a record rate of media growth since 1980; (b) a realm of communications that has been extended to range from the most detailed and microscopic to the most general and large scale; and (c) improved individual and selective access to all kinds of information and communication.

In addition, both the schools and the media have set their sights lower in relation to each other. No longer is television seen as the source of all power and prestige – the answer to everything – that should take over schools. For their part, schools have discovered that they do not have an educational monopoly over children. The stage has now been reached when each may be able to concentrate on what it does best, on fulfilling its appropriate role.

However, we must beware of two myths: first, that more information means more democracy, whereas information is only of value to those who have learned to use it and constitutes power only for those who, having understood or interpreted it, have the means to take advantage of it. Second, that universal communication heralds universal brotherhood and the recon-ciliation of mankind, whereas in fact it is the community which precedes communication and not the reverse; even if communi-cation may eventually reinforce the community.

The formal education system will have difficulty in responding to the demand for increasing numbers with ever higher qualific-ations and for a form of teaching that matches the needs of life-long learning – at once personalized and on a massive scale. However, the new technologies may provide an answer in the form of remote teaching systems, telematics services, etc., which allow individual and selective access to knowledge. Once more, knowledge can only benefit from cooperation between education and NICT.

CONCLUSION: THE NEW RELATIONSHIP BETWEEN SCHOOLS AND THE MEDIA

The real issue today is how to develop the most productive and harmonious relationship between education and the media. The future lies in the stocking and supply of selected audio–visual products to be used in a local educational context. Informatics will give access to a multiplicity of sources of culture and education. The school's role will be not so much rearranging the flow of images as commenting on values. Undoubtedly, education will be radically transformed with regard to curriculum, methods and aims, a challenge which should be seized.

1.2 THE POST-INDUSTRIAL SOCIETY FINALLY IDENTIFIED

THE SHOCK OF THE 1960s

Although 1960 was a key date in the information world, the shock it brought was not understood for what it was. 1960 meant first and foremost the end of the monopoly of the daily paper, which lost its role as exclusive master over information. Radio and television came into their own. At the same time, the press began to gear down. Diversification of formulas and a broader range of tones and ambitions gave rise to mutual borrowing and influence between genres which had long been alien to one another. But the change did not stop there. Indeed, much more was needed before the reign of the media could take hold. The decisive factor was the role of mediator which journalists finally assumed, spontaneously or deliberately, between, on the one hand, their readers and, on the other, the actors or authors of current events, or the established representatives of arts and sciences. In a word, journalists had to succeed in embodying statutorily the words addressed by society to itself about itself; and, to that end, a thorough shake-out of the roles of the three media – written press, radio and television – and their distribution was required.

By virtue of their vast and unnumbered readership, the first born of the 'mass media', the great dailies gave the journalist an unprecedented social status. The information journals, dailies first followed by weeklies – the former almost always eclectic and the latter still only rarely specialized – gradually extended their empire over new social classes in search of standardized entertainment and distinctive signs of the *Zeitgeist* (the press began to divide itself into a press of exchanges, a group-specific press, an elite press, a women's press, a children's and adolescents' press, a single-theme press, an escapist press, a militants' press, etc). Marketing specialists everywhere were guided by the same principle, namely that the search for 'pure targets' was the price the press now had to pay for its continued growth. Their good fortune was further boosted by the fact that progress in printing techniques favoured the application of their recipes: micro-publishing allowed the publication at low cost of papers with editions of only a few thousand.

Until the 1960s, the roles of radio, television and the press were clearly demarcated. The advent of radio in the 1920s and that of television between 1945 and 1955 scarcely encroached on the predominance of the dailies. The co-existence of the three media was based much more on division of labour than on competition. The preserve of the press was information, while radio 'specialized' in music and variety and television opted for feature films. Only in the field of information did the distribution of roles always remain true to the maxim that radio announces the event, television shows it and the press explains it. Under this arrangement, the press obviously came off best.

In 1960 came the upheaval. In the United States, the first sign appeared with the victory of John Kennedy over Richard Nixon in the presidential election. All the political analysts of the time attributed this victory to John Kennedy's superior performance on television. In 1961, at the time of the closing events of the Algerian war, it was France's turn to discover the formidable power of the radio. The appeals launched by General de Gaulle to soldiers in the Algerian *djebels* with their transistor radios rapidly took on an emotional and political force with which no written account could have competed. Only then did journalists and newspaper readers fully comprehend the merits of the transistor radio and the capacities of television: thenceforth, news feature programmes on radio and television proliferated, successfully complementing the necessarily superficial information in the newspapers and thus enabling the new media to compete with the major dailies.

INFORMATION AT THE HEART OF OUR SOCIETIES

An information-based economy

This media explosion–implosion is not an isolated phenomenon. In truth, it is to be seen as the symbol of a change in society's identity: the transition from an industrial society to what we call the 'informatics society' today. The emergence of this new type

84

of society dates back to the years 1956–7, and the first place to be affected by it was the United States.

In 1956, for the first time in the history of an industrialized country, the number of white-collar workers – technicians, managers, civil servants, office workers – exceeded that of so-called blue-collar workers. For the first time, industrial America was giving way to a new society in which a majority of Americans was no longer employed in the production of consumer goods and equipment but in the production of information.

The following year marked the beginning of a total information revolution: the launch of *Sputnik* by the Soviets in early October was the technological catalyst for which a society increasingly dependent on information had been waiting. For the real and poorly understood importance of *Sputnik* was not that it was the start of the conquest of space, but that it ushered in the era of global communication via satellite. It is plain that the transformation of the earth by satellites into what Marshall McLuhan called 'a global village' was not immediately perceived. Contrary to what is sometimes still believed, the major effect of the satellite era has been not so much the opening up of space but the focusing of earth upon itself.

It is always difficult to grasp and define that which is in the process of happening. The most far-sighted thinkers of the age are no exceptions. The first to dub this new age the *post-industrial* society was Daniel Bell, a sociologist at the University of Harvard. A close analysis of this post-industrial society clearly demonstrates that it is nothing less than the 'informatics' society. The criterion always adopted to describe the structure of a society – the number of employees absorbed by the various sectors of the economy – is perfectly operative here: the number of information-related jobs has grown continuously. Whereas in 1950, only 17 per cent of Americans performed activities directly connected with information, this percentage now stands at over 60 per cent. In a study commissioned by the American Department of Commerce, an information expert, Dr Marc Porat, classified all occupational activities and parts of activities in the information sector, in the industrial production sector and in all other sectors. He inventoried 440 occupations distributed over 201 industrial enterprises. He proceeded by identifying from among these occupations those directly related to information, in order to work out what proportion of the GNP they accounted for. To clear the ground, he began by drawing up a list of unequivocally information-linked occupations. This enabled him to isolate a first occupational category, which he called the primary information sector. The job of this sector is to produce and distribute information equipment or supply specific information services to the community, encompassing activities as diverse as the manufacture of telecommunications equipment and computers, printing, the mass media, advertising, accounting, teaching, management, certain financial activities and insurance. In 1967, 25.1 per cent of the American GNP came from this primary information sector. The economic contribution of people employed to supply information to the companies they work for (what Marc Porat calls the secondary information sector) stood at 21.1 per cent of GNP. According to a more recent study by David Birch, these sectors' share of economic activity has been growing continuously: this study has shown that of some 20 million jobs created between 1970 and 1980, only 5 per cent were industrial jobs and almost 90 per cent related to information, the transmission of knowledge or the services sector.

Today, almost all specialized occupations call upon the services of people linked to information in one way or another: lawyers, teachers, engineers, programmers, systems analysts, doctors, architects, librarians, journalists, etc. It is true, in a way, that an industrial worker, for instance a fitter or machine operator, is supposed to be perfectly informed about the task he or she is performing, but what distinguishes occupations adapted to the informatics or information-processing society from the others is that the object is no longer simply to assimilate information but essentially to create and transmit it. Today, it is clear that the main strategic resource is the acquisition and distribution of knowledge. Nowadays, we mass-produce information as we began to mass-produce cars only yesterday. The financial capital held by a number of individuals is no longer the determining strategic element in the successful creation or management of an enterprise. That element is knowledge and, if possible, knowledge held by all. Noyce, co-founder in 1968 of Intel Corporation, a company which enjoys a strong reputation on the market today, made statements in this connection which leave no room for doubt: unlike the steel industry, the automobile industry and others, he explained, the semi-conductor industry had never been an oligopoly. On the contrary, it was an industry which was able to make more intense use of grey matter resources than of financial capital.

The transition from the industrial society to the informatics society

It is clear that the transition from an industrial society to an informatics or information-processing society could not take place on the economic level only. This change in the kinds of jobs held by the majority of the population of the so-called industrialized countries has plainly meant a change in both human relations as a whole and the *Weltanschauung* adopted by this society. During the agricultural period, what counted was the interaction between man and nature. In the industrial society, man is doing battle with a nature that is already tamed. In our informatics society, it is in exchanges between people that the vital stakes are played for. This is reflected by a geometric progression in person-to-person transactions: direct interpersonal communications, telephone calls, signing of cheques, etc.

The most characteristic and determining feature of the informatics society was no doubt the speed with which it altered our cultural environment and our habits of mind. Indeed, the pace of change will go on gathering speed while communication technology keeps on cutting down the time it takes to transmit information. For a letter sent by post to reach its addressee takes two days; today, if an electronic transmission procedure is used, the letter reaches him or her in several seconds. To give another example, the day a shot was fired at President Lincoln, the news reached the four corners of the United States mainly by telegraph. But as the country was not yet linked up with England, it took five days for word of the event to reach London. The extent to which times have changed is evident from the fact that the day a shot was fired at President Reagan, a correspondent of the London *Spectator* typing a story just a stone's throw from the scene of the incident heard the news by telephone from his editor in Britain, who had just seen images of the assassination attempt, televised immediately after the event.

The creation, processing and transportation of information are at the very heart of modern society. Out of the combination of technologies such as telephone, computer and television, an information and communications system has come into being which is capable of transmitting data and allowing instantaneous interactions between the human being and the computer. Moreover, for the first time in the history of society, the economy is based on a key resource which is not only renewable by man at will but capable of generating itself, to the point where we are in danger of being submerged. Almost 10 000 scientific articles are published every day. Scientific and technological information is growing at a rate of 13 per cent a year; in other words, it is doubling in volume every five and a half years. This increase should reach 40 per cent a year with the appearance of new, more powerful computer systems and a growing scientific population.

The change that will revolutionize office work will affect the place of work even more than the nature of it. Thanks to terminals and word processors linked up to an office several kilometres away, tomorrow's secretaries will almost everywhere choose to work at home. And not only secretaries, but all those whose job is to generate, prepare and distribute information, for instance in industry, banking or insurance.

The computer and knowledge

The problem is this: we are undoubtedly buried in information but we are terribly lacking in knowledge. In the United States, the verdict is damning. The Carnegie Council of Policy Studies recently stated that, given the inadequacy of public education, approximately a third of young people were under-educated, under-employed, under-adapted and therefore incapable of making their way in American society. It is, alas, not hard to imagine where lack of basic knowledge and ignorance of information-processing techniques are in danger of leading us. In the informatics society, to be without this knowledge would be tantamount to trying to pinpoint a book in a heap piled at random, or in the collections of the Library of Congress without the use of a catalogue, a list or an index . . . or even the help of a librarian. In other words, anyone who does not know how to use a computer will immediately be placed in a position of inferiority.

Whether or not we use computers in our jobs, the main thing is to become familiar with and acquire a knowledge of computing, as this new technology is bound to flood the entire world of work. A further, already foreseeable consequence of the rapid change that is emerging is that no one will be able to pursue the same occupation for all his or her working life, even if that occupation is directly related to informatics. The change in the offing will force us constantly to renew our skills. Already today, major private enterprises devote huge sums every year to retraining and training of their staff.

On all sides then, the computer is invading our lives, changing our human relations and our relationship with the world. One day, no doubt, Steve Jobs, co-founder of Apple Computers, will be proved right in his assertion that we have to help create a fashion so that everyone will want a computer of his or her own. This may seem ambitious, but we should not overlook the lesson of the past: when cars were first built, people bought them for pleasure. Today, entirely different considerations lead us to acquire one: reasonable fuel consumption and ease of transport. Nowadays, we buy personal computers for pleasure. Cars have become indispensable because half a century ago we 'decided' that our economy was to be based on the automobile. Everything indicates that the computer will follow the same progression: from an object acquired to satisfy man's desire for technological novelty, it will become a fundamental need of the citizen, something he or she cannot imagine doing without unless there is a radical change of civilization.

A DIFFERENT ATTITUDE TO COMMUNICATION
TECHNOLOGY

The possibility of picturing together the subjects and objects of each communication allows us to consider present realities differently, as the absolute influence of the obsessions and prejudices of the moment – both in the commerce of ideas in general and in news coverage in particular – is eroded. The range of possible modes of communication also leads to a clearer apprehension of the media thanks to the distinction, for a given society, between the potential of the available technology and the use people decide to make of it.

Furthermore, a diagnosis of the communications system, its institutions and the activities over which they preside, confers the right to judge the social order itself. Not only does it allow a better evaluation of the use made of technological capabilities and a clearer view of the way in which institutions live up to their promises and the trust placed in them; above all, it enables a society to consider the opportunities offered it and the concomitant dangers which threaten it from the point of view of personal and political freedom.

The interactionist mode of thought as applied to the world of communications justifies a preliminary question: what possibilities do technologies taken as a whole provide for each of us, whether we wish to express our thoughts or gain access to the expression of the thoughts of others? The salient feature of recent developments is, at least in the wealthiest democracies, undoubtedly the ever-increasing abundance of available media. Every year, they grow more numerous and more varied. The book and the newspaper have long ceased to be the only 'autonomous' media: with the videogram, the video recorder and the video disk player, animated images with sound are now as accessible to everyone as are printed documents.

Thanks to cables and satellites, means of broadcasting in the strict sense, from the transmitter to a multitude of receivers, are now being thrust towards two extremes – the smallest communities on the one hand and the entire planet on the other

90

– along the path opened up by Marconi in 1896. The result is narrowcasting at one extreme and broadcasting at the other. The media no longer transmit only sound but also images, graphics, texts or data. Diversification and proliferation of techniques is also happening in the world of two-way communications, inaugurated by Graham Bell's telephone in 1876. Thanks to the unexpected marriage of telephone, television and computer, we now have not only the possibility of a long distance conversation between two people, but also of the exchange between several people, thousands of kilometres apart, of all kinds of texts or images, fixed or animated, with or without sound – a form of exchange hardly imaginable on that scale at the start of the 1980s.

The second salient feature, striking even by its technical potential alone, is individual access to networks on request. Until recently, users of programmes or services transmitted by networks were prisoners of the pattern set up by broadcasters: only messages imprinted on autonomous or 'off-line' data carriers, such as books, disks or videocassettes, were permanently available. Now existing equipment enables anyone to have access by mere request, whenever he or she wishes, to all kinds of services transmitted via Hertzian waves or cables, thanks to the existence of networks and possibly their links with satellites. Thus, videography in both its versions, broadcast teletext or interactive videotext, is constantly accessible to everyone, just like newspaper or pre-recorded cassette.

Thirdly, progress in communication technologies long separate from one another is marked by their gradual convergence. Each medium – press, telecommunications and cinema, radio and television and finally teleinformatics with its cluster of services – was, from its birth, a particular universe with its own equipment and professionals, its own arrangements and assignments. In an initial phase, the mere fact of bringing one technology closer to another brought about relative improvements. For instance, 1944 saw the convergence of radio and the tape recorder, 1952, that of television and the video recorder, 1964 that of television and the satellite and 1978 that of the video disk and informatics. Sometimes, it was the association of two different technologies that gave rise to a new medium: the telephone and informatics gave rise to teleinformatics in 1964; Hertzian broadcasting and the computer to the Antiope teletext system in 1979; finally, informatics and telecommunications to interactive videotext in 1984. Henceforth, simultaneous developments in informatics and telecommunications enable us to envisage the transmission of all signals in digitalized form by a single network with one- or two-way transmission. The *réseau numérique avec intégration de services* (RNIS, digital network with integrated services) already gives an intimation of this future network, free of the barriers which still exist today between broadcasting, cablecasting and telecommunications or, in other words, between Hertzian broadcasting, cable radio and television and physical and non-physical telephone channels.

The proliferation of equipment, new access-on-demand devices and the removal of barriers between some media: what could this three-fold technological development mean for the individual? In other words, what are its most foreseeable implications for each of the representatives of the society experiencing it; for the conditions of one's exchanges with others and the meaning one assigns to them; for one's perception of one's place in the various social universes in which one finds oneself, whether of free will or of necessity?

In an initial phase, the development of communication technologies is interpreted by everyone as a *two-fold emancipation*: on the one hand, emancipation from the limited nature of exchanges with his or her fellows; on the other, emancipation from the multiple servitudes of distance in time and space.

Emancipation, first of all, with regard to limitations. The abundance of opinions, information and works put into circulation and pooled by the media has become at once a reality and an ideal. Thanks to technology, people 'communicate' with one another more and more. And every day, the number of those who consider this possibility of communicating to be the greatest privilege of their age grows a little larger. It is impossible to separate 'communication' as recreation and as the expression of a desire, an opportunity which it would be not only a pity but also a sin to forgo: the *sine qua non* of all progress, including that of freedom for all and for each individual.

Emancipation, next, from another constraint: that of distance.

Thanks to recording techniques, time and space are becoming less and less of an obstacle to the exchange of ideas, to 'communication' between people via the multiple expressions of their thought. Thus, the media provide a possibility of disproving ever more easily and more effectively the once adamantine law that people's interest in things, people or events is directly proportional to their nearness to home. Thanks to the wonders of technology, the number of transactions between human beings no longer varies in inverse proportion to the distance between them. Indifferent to the constraints of distance, telecommunication today, easy and efficient, more varied and less expensive than ever, not only allows a remote presence; it also becomes an instrument of remote action through 'interactive' services such as teleshopping or remote booking.

This plethora and multiplicity of new media has at least one major consequence from the point of view of the citizen's relationship with the media: an increase in individual and selective access to all kinds of programmes and services. Domestic video equipment – video recorders, video cameras, compact disks, VCDs and ICDs (video-compact disks and interactive compact disks) – which has recently appeared provides for the image, animated and accompanied by sound, all the access, recording and processing facilities which were previously the prerogative of sound and for centuries before that were associated exclusively with text.

While these new autonomous media have been spreading among the public, equipment has been in place for several years which enables everyone to gain access on request to all kinds of services, be they audio-visual programmes, information or training services, interactive or otherwise. Linked to transmission networks, this equipment provides the same possibilities of individual and selective access as do a newspaper or a pre-recorded cassette.

It is to the cluster of services accessible on request that we refer when we speak of 'teleinformatics' (remote data-processing) and 'videocommunications'. Teleinformatics is the range of information or training services, in the form of texts or graphics, produced by links set up between computers and means of transmission. 'Telematics' (télématique), a word coined by Alain Minc and Simon Nora in 1978, is only one part of teleinformatics: that which concerns uses for private individuals rather than organizations. 'Videocommunications' refers to the entire cluster of services or audio-visual programmes accessible on request as a result of links set up between the resources of broadcasting and those of telecommunications.

Society as a whole can thus benefit from selective and individual access to information, something which only recently was the prerogative of large companies.

1.3 THE REALITIES AND ILLUSIONS OF THE INFORMATION SOCIETY

Communication, in all its forms, is therefore the new panacea. But should we necessarily welcome its long-awaited reign, now it has finally dawned? A panacea for some, for others communication is merely a slogan. There are two types of fears. The first is that communication, with the possibilities provided by the new media to communicate 'within one's own four walls', might create a society of monadic, compartmentalized individuals who would end up losing contact with their fellows. In other words, is not the freedom created by the new media in danger of turning into the very opposite? Secondly, as they cause their forerunners to gear down, will the new media create new jobs tomorrow or, as with other economic activities, lead to the elimination of more jobs than can be easily replaced by the emergence of new occupations?

Technology is ambivalent: it enslaves and emancipates at the same time. At the very moment when the media seem to be triumphing over certain forms of servitude, they open the way to unexpected hazards, forcing the individual back on him or herself, to the outer limits of a joyously and almost rashly conquered freedom. This is not because individual choices are sometimes illusory, the apparently different objects being, in reality, similar or equivalent, nor yet because these choices are not really free; but, more profoundly, because they are in danger of being constricted by lack of imagination still more than by lack of time or money. With whom does one 'communicate' when one can communicate with the whole world? What should we look at when we can look at anything? What should we record and preserve when we can record everything? When communication techniques conceal behind their promises the inevitable limits, those of the force of circumstances or the human will, the freedom they offer is merely an illusion. Abundance then becomes a genuine form of poverty, wretched and tragic.

By a similar irony, the conquest of distance may mean a defeat for communication. Telecommunication as a whole is marked by ambivalence: it is at once liberating and oppressive. Since the first electric telegraph in 1937, the men of Prometheus's civilization have been tirelessly seeking the realization of an immemorial dream, that of ubiquity. Even before the rise of the new media, the history of the telephone and radio and television bear this out. Today, it is not only words that can be transmitted over distances, but also images, statistical data and instructions. Telecommuting, for example, is put forward as a convenience; its effectiveness is nevertheless inevitably restricted by the impossibility of personal exchanges, and the feeling it gives the individual of living in a kind of 'info-bubble' appeals to some more than others. 'Remote presence' comes up against the same limitations and harbours similar dangers: telephone and videophone do not merely provide a way of breaking the feeling of separation from another; they also constitute a convenient *Ersatz*, a way of escaping contact with others or a variously successful compensation for encounters people fear to seek lest they should fail or prove elusive.

Such is indeed the paradox of the media: they throw man back on himself, while at the same time opening up remote access to the words, actions or works of others. Telecommunication, easier and more varied than ever, has given birth to the utopia of universal acquaintance and communication of each with all. And the dream of a universal and liberating communication nurtures, in the same proportion, the obsession with useless knowledge and abortive exchanges with our fellows.

These reflections prompt a preliminary remark: if we consider both technical possibilities and the uses made of them, we realize that two-way telecommunication has brought about a spectacular advance in comparison to that heralded by one-way television broadcasting. In the breach opened up by telephone and computer, two-way data and image exchanges seem destined for a particularly glorious future thanks to videocommunications and teleinformatics. Progress of one-way broadcasting media, those which suggest comparison with a watering-can rose of varying diameter, for instance local cable-television networks or direct or semi-direct television broadcasting systems, is moving much more slowly. Hence the emphasis on exchanges rather than activities relating to 'publication' proper. It is as if two-way communications were suddenly taking their revenge on vertical communications which came down from the heights of the social edifice, as if the new rise in communication in all its forms was the long-awaited compensatory response to the tyranny of the 'mass media', the privileged instruments of publication activities.

Moreover, some of the techniques which have developed in recent years – micro-publishing (publishing of books or news-papers with limited circulation), the possibilities for individuals to record sound or images, pre-recorded videocassettes and video disks, remote information of numerous small groups – are based exclusively on a convergence of interests, concerns or freely selected objectives.

The price of growth for all media lies in diversification or specialization, whether of the themes they deal with or in the audiences they address. While making possible this development towards 'micro-media', technology at the same time provides the individual with the possibility of selecting his or her group relations or social allegiances, objective affiliations and subjective references. Thus, associative exchange is gradually taking over from exchange between colleagues, the propagation of social causes from that of social identities. Of these identities, those imposed upon us are giving way to those we choose. This is not the too hastily proclaimed victory of specialized media over mass media, but the result of an abundance offered simultaneously by both: the possibility for each individual to choose a club in preference to a corporation, a voluntary association in preference to imposed collegiality, informal networks in preference to formal organizations.

Thus, the order of any media-rich society will henceforth follow this two-fold trend, under the influence of the combined effects of technologies and the utopias they inspire: on the one hand, a preference for telecommunications rather than television broadcasting; on the other, the possibility more liberally offered to each individual to choose social attachments other than those imposed upon him or her. There is a two-fold tendency, or rather additional possibilities given to people to express themselves or gain access to the words and works of others. Among media, the new does not replace the old, but rather opens up for it the way to a more brilliant career. The law in this case is that of all or nothing, plenitude or poverty, for everyone.

For societies that plump for plenitude, the question is therefore one of choosing the respective proportions the various communication activities are to take on. The image civilization? Hegemony of television over mind? The main point lies elsewhere: it lies in the use made by each individual of the various available methods and modes of 'communication'. For a given social area, it lies in the way in which people's time and trust are apportioned between the various versions of exchange, propagation and publication.

Each communication activity has a significance of its own, and the value set upon it is more a function of morality than of sociology. Exchange, be it collegial or associative, always concerns interests or centres of interest common to its protagonists: in the first case, it asserts a collectivity that already exists; in the second it can, in particular cases, give rise to a collectivity before going on to reinforce the links between its members. Propagation-related activities are different from exchange inasmuch as they are directed towards anonymous audiences whose contours are less well-defined. Their significance differs considerably depending on whether the source of the messages appears to its recipients as a personal mediator or a mere interface. Propagation of an identity institutionalizes groups hitherto condemned to interpersonal relations only; it establishes them by transposing them from a latent to a patent state. Propagation of a cause is more an exercise in popularization, conversion or persuasion, performed on a group which it also helps to institute.

Finally, publication activities have other virtues and other limits with regard to the collectivity and its constituent members. Its law is that of the addressees, who always have the last word. Hence the plurality of its ambitions: to inform, popularize, create. But hence also its perpetual temptation to give way to fashions and hobbyhorses on the basis of conceptions associated with the dominant trends of the moment.

We see then that over-development of the media is not in itself a matter for fear. The new media superimpose themselves on the old without obliterating them, thereby providing new prospects without eliminating any. It is in the mastery and intelligence of their use that the true problem lies.

Neither El Dorado nor decoy, communication is, a few years short of the year 2000, the privileged platform from which society asks itself questions about itself, its present and its future – more exactly, about the way technologies are influencing the social order and, by the same token, about the way training matches up with employment, the way we learn to master today's sciences and the prospects for their future use. Communication today is not a sector of activity like any other: it is a shifting landscape in which jobs and training are invented on a day-to-day basis. And the unknown, as we know, gives rise to fears and anxiety. Let us speak plainly: we know that in future, activities other than communications will come to resemble more and more those which are generated by communications, requiring of the majority at once acquired skills and a considerable ability to adapt. There is therefore no reason why communication sectors should give rise to more fears than others.

It is true that the manifold jobs in communications borrow from the most demanding and universal intellectual disciplines: observation of facts, explanation of events, understanding of situations. No one can forecast what the tools and ambitions, the means and ends of communications will be tomorrow. In terms of employment, the audio-visual media and information services are probably more promising than is often thought. And communication in the service of institutions, in-house or directed towards the outside world, is doubtless still more so.

More than other activities, communication invites people to rediscover the importance of intellectual disciplines with the help of general education. It also establishes new relations between the world of school and the corporate world. Thus it brings the school as a training ground face to face with its responsibilities. At what precise stage are these relations between the media and school today?

1.4 THE MEDIA AND THE SCHOOL: DIVISION OF LABOUR OR COMPETITION?

THE AGE OF SUSPICION

The age of communications is here and no one can fail to realize it. We are thus witnessing today the end of a misunderstanding which for years caused the media and the education system to take opposing sides. Each claimed for too long to have the monopoly of what Montaigne called 'L'institution des enfants', that is to say not only their education but also their upbringing in the broadest sense of the word.

The largely free and open market has given journalism its seal of approval. There has therefore been a great temptation for a number of journalists to take themselves for teachers. 'We journalists', wrote Jean Schwoebel, 'are the primary school teachers of the twentieth century': to identify journalism with the teaching profession is as disastrous today as the identification of journalists with 'publicists' or men of letters was in Balzac's day. The underlying cause of this identification in our age is a convergence between the way journalists and teachers describe their respective vocations. Their polemics go back to the challenge of the school by the media in the 1960s.

The advent of the popular press at the end of the nineteenth century did not impinge on the world of childhood. Newspapers therefore did not appear to jeopardize the family's influence, which had been exclusive for too long. For the same reasons, the emergence of radio in the 1920s also failed to cause anxiety among parents or the teaching profession. Television, on the other hand, was very quickly perceived as a challenge to their influence. To many people, the threat it represented was all the greater because it appeared to fill the vacuum suddenly left by the breakdown of the family structure. A German survey from 1954, referred to by Jean Cazeneuve (in *La Société de l'ubiquité*, p. 157), showed that two-thirds of a very large sample of the population claimed to remain at home more often since acquiring a television set. Moreover, 'the percentage of people giving this reply was particularly high among . . . those . . . with primary education and among blue collar workers'. All these observations point in the same direction. None the less, no one of them provides a basis for determining the respective shares of parents and television in the 'socialization' of children. As W. A. Belson comments in *The Impact of Television*, the introduction of television into a family very probably leads to a reduction in exchanges between the family members, and the time they spend together watching television is by no means a measure of the quality of their relations.

The media in general and television in particular can have a different effect on the family, by presenting a particular image of family life which reinforces to varying degrees the role of each family member. But the confrontation does not go very deep.

The rivalry between school and the media is becoming increasingly shriller and more emotional. The list of the education profession's grievances against the whole range of media is a long one. They are all drawn from traditional anti-media polemics. It is claimed that the media often give the illusion of knowledge: someone who reads the newspapers or who watches television a lot can easily and immediately acquire what Louis Porcher calls 'un savoir en miettes' (piecemeal knowledge), knowledge which is not remotely in keeping with the canons of scientific rigour and learning. The culture served up by the media is like a harlequin coat, a patchwork culture made up of lots of little pieces, 'a mosaic culture' to borrow Abraham Moles' expression, which, unlike learning in the academic sense, which generally progresses from the general to the particular, does the exact opposite. By the same token, the idea of the media as vehicles of a civilization given over to mass production and mass consumption, confirming the victory of objects, has enjoyed much currency. Equally widespread is the idea that the media propagate a mass culture that is daily gaining ground on the culture we call 'classical'.

The point here is less to list the grievances harboured by education against the media than to identify the reasons behind such a violent diatribe and this 'excommunication' of the media to which the media are responding today by accusing schools of taking refuge in a ghetto and hiding from real life.

We find the answer clearly expressed in the words of a primary school teacher recorded by Claude Brémond in the course of a survey carried out among Catholic teachers in the state system in 1964, the words of the school master of a small village in Brittany: 'It is not my job to bring instant gratification. I am the schoolmaster in my grey smock with my stick of chalk, I am still the "Third Republic" school master. How can I compete with the alluring, enticing and immediately satisfying properties of television?' This apologia betrays perfectly the reasons for this indictment of the media; the school is defending its monopoly of culture; it is defending a realm which sees itself assailed by an enemy from without.

The school was not long able to ignore the gauntlet thrown down by television. Television, the flagship of the media, had infinitely more 'firing power' than the family, the popular press and radio. School and television do not merely perceive each other as rivals in the transmission of culture. Both also stake a claim to possession of 'true culture'. The media are thus arraigned by the school on two counts: firstly as purveyors of culture and secondly as creators of a culture doomed to mediocrity, conformism and kitsch. At the same time, the school is excommunicated by the media, in whose eyes it is to be blamed for remaining indifferent to the advent of the new culture born of their explosion.

Teachers have often answered the growing counter-offensive with their opponent's own weapons: under the pretext of cosmo-politanism or in order to follow their pupils' interests more closely, they have pleaded for the adoption in schools of the media's most tried and tested methods. At the same time, the media men have sometimes been tempted to liken their vocation to that of professional educators, perhaps impatient to supplant them once and for all or merely ambitious to inherit at last a long coveted prestige.

Indubitably, journalists and teachers can justly claim that they are subject to the same requirements: personal probity and intellectual rigour. However, the main point is elsewhere: it lies in the confusion, fostered by converging claims, between their respective tasks or vocations, and, more particularly, the confusion which has set in between information concerning topical debates or events and civic instruction addressed to future citizens. Why indeed should not the media fulfil the promises which sometimes seem to leave schools paralysed, promises of equality and emancipation in the face of the various and sometimes combined disadvantages of birth and ignorance?

In a democracy, journalism and education have two different vocations. To take one for the other is to forget that topical events do not occupy the same place in the world of school as in that of the information media: for schools they are merely one possible illustration which may be used to provoke or exercise thought; for the media they are the necessary point of departure. The journalist begins with current events and moves towards what makes them intelligible, striving to overcome his or her readers' misapprehensions; the teacher introduces his or her pupils to intellectual disciplines, both of observation of facts and of formal analysis. Although they sometimes travel the same road, they do so in opposite directions: the media arouse curiosity about matters which can often be comprehended only by means of the tools provided by schools.

To perceive journalism and education as interchangeable is also to forget that the popular media, press no less than radio and television, constitute a 'parallel' school – a place of education after school or parallel to it – only to the extent that these purveyors of information respond to expectations, interests or curiosities which have already been aroused at school or elsewhere, in the course of other social exchanges, for instance within the family.

Surveys all point in the same direction: people watch on television and read in the papers what they have learnt to appreciate and understand elsewhere, by other means at some time in the past. This explains why the media, rather than working towards greater equality, reproduce and accentuate inequalities in relation to 'culture'. This is the reality behind the maxim that people get the papers or programmes they deserve.

THE REASONS FOR A MOVE TOWARDS COOPERATION SINCE 1980

Why has the question of school–media relations been formulated differently since the years 1978–80? Why have educational authorities and the people behind the media been giving the impression since the dawn of the 1980s – not only on the old continent but also in the New World and Japan – of being confronted with the same challenges and the same difficulties, of having to fight the same battle and therefore having to enter into more fruitful relations?

Use of the media by schools from 1950 to 1980

What conclusions can we draw from a very rapid purview of the attempts made by schools between 1950 and 1970 to use the resources of radio or television? To simplify a little, we may state that, at worst, the introduction of television into schools proved a failure. It did not achieve its self-appointed goals. Television's foray into schools was accordingly dubbed a failure and, in most cases, the experiment was abandoned.

At best, the use of the media by schools did produce some results assessed as positive, but they were not at all those which were expected. The experiment was therefore pursued nevertheless, but in a totally different direction from the one envisaged at the outset. Whether we take the Italian Tele Scuola, operative between 1958 and 1972, Tele-Niger, which ran from 1964 to 1971, the experiment conducted under the Kennedy administration between 1964 and 1973 and directed towards American Samoa, or school television in France, the result was, invariably, something of a fiasco.

The reasons for these failures are not hard to find. Firstly, schools used television and radio as a mere medium, a mere instrument, denying it the right to teach in its own way. It

103

was 'school on TV', as Henri Dieuzede pointed out. School was conducted before the eye of a camera, or before a microphone in the case of radio. Consequently the instrument was robbed of all its intrinsic capacity. No effort was made to adapt teaching methods or to use the instrument imaginatively. School still had the first and last word. This excess of mistrust on the part of the school was countered by another equally pernicious attitude, namely what we might call an excess of optimism: the media were expected to do everything, both what schools could not do and what they no longer wished to do. Television or radio was there to attenuate the inadequacies of the school, make up for its shortcomings or its failings. In such cases, it was no longer school on television, it was television acting as school and taking its place.

In both cases, relations between television and school reached deadlock. In the first case, the uselessness of television was patently obvious: it added nothing to what the school was capable of providing by itself. In this respect, it could even be said that it did not bear comparison: a televised lesson can never be as rich or as pedagogically successful as a lesson given by a teacher who is well acquainted with the class, knows how to take it, etc. In the other case, excessive expectations which could never be fulfilled only served to broaden the disillusionment brought about by so instrumental a use of this 'magic box', as many perceived television to be.

Reasons for the change

The reasons why things appear to have changed are, firstly, the technological shock which began in 1979–80 and, secondly, the fact that both sides have become more modest.

As we have seen, the progress of the media today is marked by three phenomena: firstly, since 1980, the rate of media growth has reached an all-time high; secondly, communications are rushing headlong towards the infinitely small and the infinitely large; thirdly, substantial progress is being made in individual and selective access to all sorts of information or all sorts of communications. At the same time, gone are the days when

104

television was spoken of as all-powerful and the source of all prestige, when it was expected to do everything, to play the school's role and take its place. School for its part has also acknowledged that it is not the only factor in children's education and upbringing.

The real question today is no longer whether school or media will finally win out in the struggle for the monopoly transmission of knowledge, but rather where the true role of each of these two institutions lies. On what is the true legitimacy of each of these institutions based? Whence does each derive its authority? The true question is neither what television does to children, nor whether television will take over from the school; it is how the various media can perform in conjunction with the school the tasks over which the school long believed it had a monopoly. At the same time, we must ask ourselves how the school can direct what it does best towards scattered audiences, the very ones addressed by the media and which do not necessarily have anything to do with the school as an institution.

INFORMATION GAMES AND WHAT IS AT STAKE

Information is not the key to democracy

For the media to play an effective educational role in cooperation with the school, they must enjoy a degree of credence in the eyes of public opinion. This credence is somewhat undermined by a number of clichés which, in the final analysis, always serve other interests than information and knowledge. These are the same clichés or the same dominant representations which are used to justify, today as in the past, the right of certain people to tell the media what they must do and journalists what they must say, so that media and journalists may enjoy the only freedom they deserve and individual readers or viewers can receive the gospel, that of the state.

The first of these clichés, which cannot fail to institute precisely what it claims to remove, is the idea that information is the key to democracy and that one and the other necessarily progress or regress together. Thus, the information organs, invested with the role of a 'fourth power', are alleged to be the best allies of democracy and participation by the citizens in the management of matters which concern them. Since 1945, teachers and journalists, politicians and ordinary citizens have been tirelessly repeating on both sides of the Atlantic, at the United Nations or at UNESCO, that, on the day when the citizens finally have access to 'full and objective' information, democracy cannot fail to triumph. This idea has particularly caught on, since it lends itself to every imaginable embellishment: thus, from an equivalence between information and democracy, it is easy to derive the assimilation of knowledge to power.

It is doubtless true that the citizens will exercise their responsibilities happily provided they are kept informed in as valid a way as possible of matters pertaining to the common interest. It is equally true, however, that by disseminating news and passing on their assessment of it, the media nurture the citizens' judgement and influence their opinions and behaviour with regard to everyone's concerns. Finally, no one can deny that information today is more plentiful and perhaps also more comprehensive, and that it circulates better, more quickly and in larger quantities than in the past: its network is in the course of becoming planet-wide with intercontinental routes, transnational axes and local links.

This seemingly irrefutable evidence comes up against other truths, already mentioned above, the very obviousness of which perhaps serves them ill: information is only of value to an individual if he or she has learned to use it. It has no significance except in relation to the person who propagates it. And it constitutes power only for one who, having understood or interpreted it, has the means to take advantage of it to administrate things differently. 'People watch on television and read in the papers what they have learned to appreciate and understand elsewhere, by other means, at some time in the past.'

Communication machines are not a panacea

Another piece of conventional wisdom which has come under fire recently is the importance attached in our technology-mad societies to the mirages and multiple ambiguities of what is customarily called the reign of communications. Local radios, cable and satellite television, videocassettes or video disks and domestic information services – the advent of new media to join the old ones which are still operative nurtures the most extravagant hopes among engineers and sociologists or philosophers, equally converted to divination. Both groups see the wonders of technology as heralding universal communication, the day when anyone can finally have access to anyone else or to anything anytime from anywhere and in any imaginable way: brotherhood through electronics, the reconciliation of mankind thanks to communicating machines. They envisage the providential liberation of the television viewer thanks to cassettes, cables and 'interactivity'.

By their extravagances, those who dream of the global village are accessories to the idea that, thanks to the feats of interactivity, the media will do for the better tomorrow what their precursors, which still operate on a one-way basis, long did for the worse. It is difficult to put forward even the slightest objection to this idea, which is very widespread. The one possible objection is altogether too obvious. However powerful the new media are, whether or not they are capable of setting up two-way communications with images rather than just with speech as in the past, what can they really do to counteract the decline of solidarity and certain forms of social interaction? As technologies, why should they necessarily participate in the reconstitution of a social fabric torn apart by interest-group egoisms or ideological conflicts?

Undoubtedly, images will circulate on a two-way basis tomorrow as words and printed matter do today. But the professional optimists confuse community and communication. What they forget or affect to forget is that communication is the expression of a will, of a will to be or live together, which almost invariably pre-exists it. In one sense, it is the community which precedes communication and not the reverse, even if communication may eventually reinforce the community. What good is a telephone without an address book? What good are 'communication' machines, if, before they use them, people have not been taught to live together, to speak to one another, to listen

107

to one another and always to respect others without ever ceasing to combat what they believe to be their errors?

THE SCHOOL CHALLENGED BY THE TELEMATICS SOCIETY

The role of telematic distributing services

Microsystems, for individual production and distribution, and the megasystem, based on satellites, are now altering the media to the point where the question of their relationship with school can no longer be formulated in the old terms of school television. Unlike school television, the satellite, although it broadcasts direct, does not aim at the user *per se* but at institutional groups, not only school-based but also in the field of continuing education (local or company centres, etc.). Used in this way, a satellite channel can transfer day and night a quantity of messages so great that, to begin with, it would probably exceed the amount of teaching material produced. Advantage could be taken of stocks of films, or rather sequences, borrowed from the *répertoire internationale du documentaire et de la fiction* (international documentary and fiction inventory), which we imagine would provide cultural support. Only afterwards would the satellite distribute educational products.

Those who have clearly understood that the satellite is being considered here purely as a distribution service, that it is by no means a pedagogical institution but a tool which can be used for exchanges between teachers, users and production institutions, will understand equally clearly that the project's main aim is to give initiative and autonomy back to local groups by virtue of the added support the satellite will provide and, in a more general way, through expected developments in telematics.

It is here that the school may feel threatened: from all points on the political spectrum, a single objective is being proclaimed: an increase in the number of people holding a *baccalauréat* and promotion of a form of teaching matching the demands of continuous training, at once personalized and on a massive scale. It is fairly safe to assume that the education system as it is now will have difficulty in providing a suitable response. Creation of posts and construction of establishments is not enough to solve the dual problem of developing initial and in-service training.

New technologies do indeed allow another approach. It is symptomatic, for example, that in the face of highly diverse requirements and the scattered nature of target audiences, more and more training agents are thinking about remote teaching. In France, out of 76 universities, 21 have remote teaching systems for a total of over 25 000 students (i.e. the equivalent of a large university). The University of Provence, for instance, offers its home students a DEUGSSM (Diplôme d'Etudes Universitaire Général Sciences des Structures et de la Matière – general university diploma in structures and material sciences). In spite of the material difficulties which sometimes arise (performance of experiments at home, for example), this type of activity is proving a great success, especially as electronic distribution also provides a means of helping students in difficulties. After trying out telephone consultation services, in 1983, the teaching team envisaged setting up a videotext service to solve a number of problems inherent in long-distance teaching, particularly the need for personalized assistance.

A further example of the success of these new types of 'media–academia link-up', the telematics service installed at the Centre Universitaire Sud de Calcul de Montpellier (CNUSC) comprises a distribution service, a physics and chemistry dictionary accessible by multi-criterion sorting, revision multiple choice questions and correct answers to problems. This service is managed from Marseille, but may be operated from any terminal linked to a telephone. Anyone willing to pay the communications costs could manage it from Colombia (demonstrations were given there in 1985). A major computer centre such as the CNUSC has the advantage of being rarely out of commission and operating round the clock 365 days a year, a veritable godsend for working students who often have to study very late at night, and a service with which university computer centres without telematics cannot hope to compete.

It is obviously in the telematic distribution service that student–teacher (and student–student) interactivity takes place. Each student has an electronic mail box in the department's distribution system and can put questions to the teachers in charge of the course when he or she so wishes. Students can also communicate with fellow students by means of the students' directory. They sometimes discover in this way that they have neighbours following the same course. Self-assessment by multiple-choice questions on Minitel meets a real self-evaluation need and provides a way of supplementing training given.

There is obvious interest both in France and abroad in this remote teaching of experimental sciences and the telematics service, of which the University of Provence has so far been the sole pioneer. These two experiments will, in all probability, be followed by others. Their interest is plain: through remote teaching, it is already possible to provide those who wish to retrain in a given sector (preparation for a competitive examination for example) without taking a university degree with course modules which they attend as external students. However, the timing of these courses depends on the university's timetable. For obvious reasons of infrastructure and organization, it is not feasible to offer training or even planning *à la carte*. Nevertheless, this is the direction in which the Ministry has been guiding continuous training through the 'Appel de projets système de formation multi-média individualisés' (call for personalized individualized multi-media training system projects).

The idea is to promote a flexible training system by breaking down the constraints of the traditional system and introducing individual access, self-training equipment using all the resources of technology, local or remote assistance, participants' meetings and validation of knowledge acquired. Moreover, these 'pedagogical products' will lend themselves to study within the framework of a training 'market', industrialization and even export.

If we compare these aims with remote teaching as practised abroad and with the experiment of the University of Provence, we cannot but be struck by the convergence of the objectives pursued; their relevance today is further borne out by the recent creation of the Multimedia Foundation. We may also wonder whether, for France, university-level remote teaching could not be a solution for a wider public than the strictly university-based audience, for example those undergoing continuing training at university level.

Teaching modules made up of written course material, exercise diskettes for use on a microprocessor and packages containing practical exercises and audio-visual documents are solutions which are bound to catch on sooner or later. The opportunity to study at home under the guidance of high-quality teachers and to attend the university or meeting centres for periods of time to exchange experiences and learn how to work in a team is a profitable solution for everyone. The development of communication techniques enables us to imagine a way of monitoring remote work, provided that each student is equipped with a microcomputer linked up to a minitel.

In huge sectors, the transmission of knowledge can and does take place via all the new media referred to above. Communication is no longer the preserve of a privileged few: by proliferating, diversifying themselves and making the most of the technological revolutions triggered by informatics, the media have made possible something that, only 30 years ago, would have seemed fantastic: individual and selective access to knowledge. With the new media, each person can select his or her own learning pace and what to learn; no one can lay down *ex cathedra* what he or she has to know. Thus it is clear that there is no longer room for any sort of feeling of rivalry between the media (with television in the vanguard) and school: today, knowledge cannot fail to benefit from cooperation between the two, and technical progress has by itself succeeded in making obsolete the old contrast between 'traditional knowledge' and 'knowledge associated with real life'. Never again will the relationship between the school and the media revert to the type of misunderstanding which gave us 'school television'.

1.5 CONCLUSION

Each of the ills of knowledge observed today seems to be matched by an appropriate remedy. The remedy for the massive backlog may be a form of basic education multiplied by the most powerful vectors of Hertzian broadcasting and – why not? – satellites. At the other extreme, at the very peak of knowledge, where individual memories fall short, the answer may be data banks (both the mental power of a battery of calculating machines and the global ubiquity of teleinformatics). Between these extremes, satellites can also convey a whole range of channels suited to all levels of education in the light of local needs, low population density and shortages of teaching staff.

The real question today is therefore how we can develop these media–school relations.

If we acknowledge the difficulty of gaining access to audio-visual production, at least that which seems to be the indispensable accompaniment to textual documentation, we shall come to the conclusion that the only possible future lies in the stocking and supply of increasingly relevant and carefully chosen audio-visual products. These messages will no longer be broadcasts of films but documentary elements to be inserted into a local educational context. The contents we hope to see are, as we know, very much bound up with the data carriers, that is to say methods of storage, the present prototypes of which are the video recorder and audio-visual disks.

A particular type of author-producer will have to be mobilized, one who combines the dual vocation of teacher and creator of images, a dual vocation which is favoured by neither of the institutions (university or television) nor by any market, with the exception of a few rare publishing and broadcasting companies bold enough to see it as a still fragile chance for development in the more distant future.

The essential point remains: what is this debate, which pits the civilization of the written word against the civilization of the image, all about? Firstly, it provides a preliminary definition of the mode of culture and, secondly, it entails a pedagogical debate on the image as a vehicle for information.

To stick to the prosaic, namely the second point, it could be observed that the image has always been just as much part of human culture as language and that there is therefore nothing so contemporary about it. As regards its effectiveness in conveying contents, I shall not launch into any sophisticated arguments here.

I hope I am not straying too far from common sense in suggesting that the image is better suited to descriptive disciplines, just as sound has proved helpful in the learning of languages. However, as we approach the realms of thought or abstraction (in connection with the exact sciences, legal or philosophical concepts, etc.), it is necessary to discard representations. We thus dispense with a spurious in-depth debate on the image and move on to discuss audio-visual systems.

Marshall McLuhan was bold enough to say that when the child left its television screen to go to school, it could only regress. This assertion is indignantly rebutted by many teachers, who hold up the school as an antidote to television, which they see as incapable of creating order in the mind and as a perpetrator of the notorious mosaic culture as defined by Abraham Moles. It is possible to point out ways of differentiating this flow of images and rearranging it into more coherent units; however, there may still be unusable or even undesirable programmes. At this point, I feel bound to express my view about the essential role of the school. As I see it, it is not so much a question of leaving it to the school to put ideas back into order as of entrusting it with the infinitely more difficult and important task of *commenting on values*.

Many children experience another formative environment and freer supplementary activities outside school, less restricted by the administration of learning and based on a much wider range of inspirations and inclinations. We cannot expect the school to do everything, nor should we stake everything on learning. Informatics allows us to envisage a multiplicity of sources of culture and education.

Thus, even for someone who has no knowledge of computers, all that is needed to use the computer as a machine for processing information – that is storing, listing and connecting contents – is an understanding of the directions for use of a program; the effect of informatics on teaching is therefore crucial and looks very much like the automation of an industry. We can foresee a probable revolution which will affect intellectual work as profoundly as the industrial revolution changed the physical dimensions of human labour. We shall then observe a total upheaval in the functions of knowledge upstream of the contents of our learning. Teaching is bound to be transformed as a result, in three different respects: in its curricula, its methods and its aims.

Even more than has been the case with the mass media – whose influence on teaching has been marginal – the influence of informatics may well go right to the heart of education. In the face of the threats of proliferating media and changes in access to information and knowledge – made possible by computer technology – our advice is to attack rather than retreat. To fight evil with evil, and with its own weapons. This amounts to asking teachers not only to catch up with the enemy but to beat it on its own ground!

The Information Society and Education

Gilbert De Landsheere

2.1 SUMMARY

This chapter is intended to provide a personal synthesis of the National Reports. Two main areas of focus emerge; one is the question of how to teach students critical and autonomous judgement with regard to the mass media, and the other is how best to use new information and communication technology (NICT) and the media for educational purposes. Although there are differences of approach among countries and varying attitudes and value judgements about the use of NICT in the classroom, most agree that NICT, when used for the purpose of education, will be a useful tool. Yet the process of introducing NICT and media in schools has not been sufficiently evaluated, despite the fact that the media have become a vital aspect of society.

INFORMATION

This section makes the distinction between providing education in the enlightened use of information, using information technology for teaching and learning, and teaching about information technology. Each aspect is discussed in turn. For the first, after rehearsing the different levels of cognition – from simple

perception to the higher cognitive processes of analysis, evaluation, and synthesis – the author shows that all education should
help bring pupils closer to the goal of learning to react intelligently
to information. Most of the national reports agree that this should
be a task for all fields of learning, and not any particular one. For the
other two aspects, the conclusion is that while teaching information
technology (computer culture and specialist knowledge and skills)
has gained a secure foothold in school curricula, particularly at the
secondary and higher levels, the computer as a teaching aid is still
far from establishing itself, since the necessary 'critical mass' of
computers, software and trained teaching staff has nowhere been
reached.

The poor quality of educational software is also mentioned.
Because of increasing illicit copying of software, there is little hope
that commercial companies will continue large-scale investment
in this area. Only the establishment of public services producing
software on a national or regional scale and working in close
collaboration with similar services in other countries will enable
this hurdle to be cleared.

DEFINITION OF THE INFORMATION SOCIETY

One fear related to NICT is that young people will be overwhelmed
or manipulated by over-information. In this case, it is especially the
underprivileged who will be affected if information technology
becomes a factor in 'economic warfare'. Differences in receptivity
inherent in social and cultural differences and between generations
must be respected when working with NICT. It must be kept in
mind that an information society must also remain a humanistic
one in which all benefit from technological advances.

Among the conventional forms of media, the press was the first
to be introduced in the classroom to teach students about current
events. This represented an opening up of schools to the outside
world and soon included radio, TV, film, and videos. Countries
such as the United Kingdom are now facilitating more educational
programmes through public service broadcasting.

The author cites NICT's capacity to facilitate worldwide communication. Translated into educational terms, this suggests that

young people will have more exposure to world problems, different cultures, etc. The hoped for result is a deepening of reflection about and knowledge of other peoples. In order to serve both individual and societal interests, several NICT-related objectives are suggested: teach pupils the capacity to synthesize what they hear and see in the media; develop and exercise critical faculties; preserve cultural heritage and distinctions; teach discrimination and judgement in choosing media resources; offer equal educational opportunity for all; teach self-expression.

Education should also aim to combat the mindlessness and other negative aspects of the media. For example, Austria suggests making constructive use of the media by helping students to become discerning media consumers, to find meaning in their experience with media, and to exercise creativity by producing their own media projects.

NICT: A NEW FOCUS OF KNOWLEDGE

As of yet, there are few data available on the results of large-scale application of NICT in education. Such data will eventually be useful in evaluating the effectiveness of NICT teaching. In the meantime, there are lessons to be learned from older teaching methods with media materials.

Computers and information technology will have several effects on teaching methods, both because of the vast amount of data made available and because of the increasing need for proper education in putting the information to intelligent use. A key factor in teaching with NICT is encouraging active interaction with the material and especially between teacher and student, rather than passive intake and rote memorization. When applied successfully, NICT will transform traditional didactic teaching into a lively and more involved process. Teachers will have more freedom to experiment with teaching methods and be able to allow for more personalization in the classroom.

For educational reform to occur, adequate teacher training programmes must be established. Increasingly, governments are requiring that future teachers take at least an introductory course in computer literacy. Yet even among the trainers themselves there exists the difficulty of keeping abreast of the most recent developments.

Some countries have taken steps to provide in-service training for teachers, especially in computer science, to keep them up to date with the latest NICT techniques. Some have even experimented with televised distance education programmes. Unfortunately, such training usually consists of short courses focused on the technology itself rather than on its implications for teaching methods.

NICT AT THE SERVICE OF TEACHING AND LEARNING

A further educational result of mass information media is the founding of open universities, designed to offer education to all adults, who may design their own courses and progress at their own pace. Open universities also serve as a testing ground for adult education methods as well as for educational applications of information technology.

NICT has also greatly contributed to distance learning through television and radio broadcasts, cassettes and computers, and now allows for much more interactivity between student and teacher. Education of the disabled has also been improved with technological advances and computer-assisted learning.

COPYRIGHT

Copyright violations have become an increasing concern for both the authors of software programs and the schools that use them. Steps must be taken to regulate copying and prevent further pirating of materials.

2.2 INTRODUCTION

It is now widely acknowledged that many young people devote more time to watching television than to their education and that radio, television, newspapers and magazines often occupy more of adults' time than their occupational activities do.

In response to this situation, two ideas are emerging: the need to equip the young and the less young to cope with this bombardment from the media, and the possibility for formal education of deriving some advantage from the parallel education system offered by the media. Equipping ultimately amounts to enabling people to understand the operation of the media and to judge them critically on the basis of high-minded values. Opening up the education system to the flood of information outside simply means opening it on to the world and on to the realities of life.

While there is a unanimous desire to prepare people for life, the various national reports reveal fairly considerable differences of approach between countries or autonomous regions towards institutional measures. In some cases media education is a major part of the curriculum, while in others it is far less formalized and may even be left to the collective responsibility of a school's teachers as a whole. Sometimes it is also made available to adults as part of adult education schemes, while sometimes there is no sign at all of any such arrangement.

Attitudes and value judgements regarding extracurricular information also vary. Some parents and teachers almost regard the penetration of information and media messages into schools as a type of pollution, or at any rate as a form of expression lacking any artistic value.[1] Nevertheless, certain comments encountered in the national reports, though marginal, do suggest that such negative reactions are very much on the decline. There is little doubt that young people learn a great deal through the media and are influenced by them in their interests, attitudes and values. However, the process has never been evaluated with any reasonable degree of rigour, and this is a serious deficiency.

Nothing can alter the fact that new information and communication technology (NICT) is finding its way into schools, where its presence is bound to be increasingly felt. One of the surest facts in educational psychology is that learning has no real prospect of

---

[1] A 1982 UNESCO (Grünwald Symposium) report emphasizes the need to strike a new balance between the education system and the communications system, which tend to ignore or even oppose each other.

success unless it is founded on the learner's own experience and problems. By attempting to exclude the media, education would be blacking out a vital aspect of life.

Should media education be general or specialized? There is a clear trend towards a general education based, in the most favourable cases, on active participation. Creating media messages is surely the best means of understanding them. However, this remark needs to be substantially qualified with regard to information technology, to which several countries devoted the bulk of their reports. A movement in favour of imparting a general knowledge of information technology is clearly emerging in secondary education, but it is difficult to judge whether it already carries as much weight as the technical approach.

Agreement is virtually unanimous that NICT can improve teaching methods and the content of a large number of subject areas. So far, however, hopes have often been dashed. Only rarely have curricula been revised in the light of the new opportunities and, above all, inadequate provision has been made for the necessary teacher training. The more progress is made, the more the key importance of this factor is recognized – and the more complicated the situation appears.

Even though many trainee primary school teachers are given a general introduction to information technology, the benefit of this may well be jeopardized by the lack of opportunity to use high-quality teaching software in practice. Moreover, the falling birth rate often restricts the scope available to young teachers. Courses and seminars for teachers already in post are provided almost everywhere, but their relevance is still far from established. The action really needed in order to alter teaching approaches in a significant way does not yet appear to have been identified.

Here lies the major priority for educationists, for there is a danger that microcomputers will end up gathering dust on the shelves alongside audio-visual material. Effective ways of providing meaningful in-service training for teachers must therefore be sought as a matter of urgency. The next stage is to seek ways of reaching at least a critical mass of trained teachers, which means several million teachers for the Council of Europe member states as a whole.

However the education system is organized, it cannot do its job all by itself. Not only should all the parties concerned support its efforts – hence the need for family training (cf. UNESCO, 1982) – but the media themselves should shoulder a major share of responsibility. Here, too, the obstacles to be overcome are enormous, since quite apart from the economic interests involved, particularly where advertising holds sway, the dynamics of the mass media are largely incompatible with the principal objectives of education. José Vidal-Beneyto summed up this antithesis very graphically at the beginning of the preparations for the sixteenth Session of the Standing Conference by postulating that the communication society is based on three main principles: emphasis on bad news rather than on constructive or positive aspects; repetition, particularly in advertising and publicity, rather than innovation; a preference for the immediate and the ephemeral, rather than the durable and the well-established.

Education has a duty to take up all these challenges as the twenty-first century draws near. If used properly, NICT can contribute to this effort, and probably in a decisive fashion.

2.3 INFORMATION

What distinguishes the traditional media – the press, radio, etc. – from the new ones is the role of the computer, which, thanks to digitalization, can store, process, shape, select, transmit, interpret and even (heuristically) create information.[2] In fact, there are now few media in which the computer does not play a part; hence Francis Balle's remark that information technology exerts a unifying influence on the media, blurring the boundaries between them.

The most promising future prospects for education lie in the possibility of combining the media and information technology, for some extraordinary opportunities are thereby emerging for

[2]On the complex nature of information, the selectivity of its representations, its ideological power, its agenda-setting functions and its amplification of the dominant discourse, see, *inter alia*, the report by Masterman (1986).

truly interactive education (Switzerland).

The ubiquitous nature of the computer in the new media context, for which it is increasingly playing a subordinate but essential role as conveyor, classifier, translator and 'processor', has led some to equate it, or even the entire NICT sector, with a medium in itself. This close partnership between computers and media accounts for the Federal Republic of Germany's view that media education also includes computers. It is surely wrong, however, to go as far as the report on a European workshop held in Prague in 1987, at the European Information Centre for Further Education of Teachers, which, according to a UNESCO document of May 1988, states: 'Computers is here used as a shorthand term for the range of new technologies of information and communication available for classroom use' (UNESCO, 1988, p. 9). It is now several years since P. Schaeffer (1984, p. 56) pointed out that only by a questionable extension of the meaning of the term could information technology as such be equated with a mass communication medium.

It may readily be understood why information technology (equipment, teaching, application, budgets) occupies a significant or even exclusive place in many of the national reports, although as a result the means of production or transmission has been accorded more importance than the product itself. In fact, over and beyond the problems raised by the adequate equipping of schools with hardware and software, a clear distinction between three different aspects should be made, at least for teaching purposes:

a study of the problems involved in teaching information technology;

a study of the problems of using information technology for teaching and learning;

a study of ways of providing education in the enlightened use of information.

The first aspect concerns the definition of a specific teaching technique forming part of a wider teaching methodology. The second aspect comprises two elements: (a) independent learning;

and (b) the use of computers as educational aids, which teachers and pupils must learn to use, with the interaction between skills and processing (in this case, teaching skills and courseware quality) once again being of decisive importance. The third and final aspect concerns the daily lives of children and adults, at almost every waking hour, at least for those who live in what is commonly called the information society.

EDUCATION IN THE ENLIGHTENED USE OF INFORMATION[3]

Information is not an isolated phenomenon

Unlike artistic experience, information does not stand in isolation. Whether intentionally or otherwise, it has the effect of stimulating a learning process whose implementation, nature or impact should ideally be controlled by the receiver. It is, of course, possible for a wide variety of resources and devices to be deployed by transmitters to maximize the chances of their message making an impact. Manipulation techniques have even been developed for the purpose of reducing the receiver's free will. The French report quotes Liliane Lurcat who, in this context, describes the restrictive effect of the passive, uncritical and one-way relationship between a fascinated viewer and television. The result is a process of learning by impregnation, characterized by the learner's unawareness. As the Liechtenstein report notes, all ability to think may disappear.

In normal conditions, an individual's reaction to the receipt of an item of information is situated somewhere along a continuum ranging from nought to the most sophisticated use of his or her critical faculties. Nought corresponds to a situation where an item of information reaches the individual (e.g. film star X has been selected for a particular part) and is understood by him or her (simple cognition), but is not memorized. In this case, information is by no means synonymous with knowledge, a matter to which the Turkish report devotes an interesting discussion.

[3]On the media education question see also the important work by Masterman (1988).

Simple memorization – which might be described as a mechanical process – goes a little further. Many do not proceed beyond this point and indeed sometimes boast of having amassed a parrot-like store of knowledge ('nothing more than unintelligent ingestion'). At the next stage the information stored is applied in an uncritical fashion. The use of such-and-such a product is advised, such-and-such a course of action is recommended, and these suggestions are unquestioningly acted upon as soon as the opportunity arises. These three initial stages are characteristic of the lower cognitive processes.

The situation is entirely different when the individual analyses the information and holds it up against the criteria of truthfulness, honesty and usefulness – in other words, when he or she examines it critically and evaluates it. Such a process, which depends initially on analysis, may be followed by synthesis. This becomes creativity in the event of the production of a new structure, either in absolute terms or in relation to earlier productions by the same individual. Analysis, evaluation, synthesis and creativity are the 'noble' operations, the higher cognitive processes.

This is the context of an important passage of the Swedish report, which mentions that Sweden has not completely and unreservedly accepted the existence of the information society as an established fact. The report goes on to say that 'unreflecting adoption of information technology can have the effect of jeopardizing essential democratic values in our society' and that 'the key resource of society tomorrow will be knowledge rather than just information . . . The term information indicates a direction to be followed: it is the informant who announces what the uninformed is to be allowed to know. The knowledge society is based on the opposite conception: its aim is to strengthen the possibilities for the individual himself to appraise and evaluate different alternatives.'

The report of Belgium (French community) displays the same fundamental concern when it stresses that reliable and objective information requires, apart from lucidity and non-conformism, a sound knowledge of social mechanisms and a good command of communication processes and information techniques. Ideally, young people should be persuaded to subscribe to 'an internationalist code of ethics, making them sensitive to the need for solidarity among all human beings'(French Belgium). All media education should include the passing on of values.

Such is the background to educational schemes and programmes intended to teach the intelligent and enlightened use of the information which the media lavish upon us – indeed in such profusion as to entail the risk of disinformation. The individual, having access to a virtually unlimited amount of practical, technical, scientific and cultural information, is in danger of embarking on an increasingly erratic process of information gathering. Pigasse (1981, p. 17) writes that this surfeit of information may well in the end lead to under-information. He describes this as the 'interference phenomenon', whereby the influx of unwanted information paralyses electronic communication systems.

One aspect often overlooked in connection with the use of information is the transition to action. It should always be remembered that knowledge means not only being acquainted with facts but also being able to act on the basis of the information and theoretical knowledge acquired.

The educational challenge

It would be wrong to think that specific exercises, such as a critical examination of the press, are sufficient for the purpose of learning to react intelligently to information. In fact the entire educational process should, from the earliest age, help to bring the pupil closer to this goal, and hence all aspects of teaching methodology are involved. The task is all the more tricky as pupils spend a considerable amount of their time in receiving information from out-of-school sources which do not pursue the same objectives as school education. Television in particular, if watched undiscerningly, can become an instrument of 'cultural impoverishment' (French Belgium).

Just as pupils are very poorly prepared to make proper use of freedom and democracy if they have never experienced anything but the authoritarian imposition of knowledge, technical skills and life skills, so they will, unless taught day-in day-out how to lead an active and effective life in the information society, run the risk of becoming seriously alienated. The importance latterly accorded to metacognitive processes is fully justified: pupils (and their teachers) should indeed constantly question their knowledge (and therefore, in particular, their information) and learn to apply validity-, sufficiency- and logic-testing strategies to arguments, inferences, conclusions, etc.

The idea that education in the proper use of information should be a task for all fields of learning, and not any particular one, emerges from most of the national reports. It is worth emphasizing here that this education cannot be authoritarian or coercive without defeating its very purpose.

THE USE OF INFORMATION TECHNOLOGY FOR TEACHING AND LEARNING PURPOSES

It is unlikely that teaching will ever cease completely to be a collective activity. The problem is not, therefore, to provide an individual teacher for every pupil, but to identify forms of group education whose efficiency is comparable to that attained in the ideal situation of individual tutoring. Current research has shown that this is possible (see Bloom, 1986).

A teacher, faced by his or her group or class, should act as the conductor of an orchestra whose instruments are the various teaching resources: lecture-type teaching alternating with independent study, class work alternating with work in small groups or individual work, use of textbooks or other reference works and of the entire range of conventional audio-visual aids, exploration of the environment, the possibility of meetings with educators other than the class teacher, computer-assisted learning and so on. As the list shows, the computer is but one instrument in a large orchestra, an instrument whose proper place cannot yet be assessed. One thing seems sure: it will not occupy this place unless it fits functionally into the current educational process. Ideally, each pupil should be able to use a computer whenever he or she feels the need to do so and with the same facility that he or she would consult a textbook or use some other kind of teaching material.

An initial requirement can thus be seen: the need for an adequate number of immediately available computers. Even on the minimum assumption of 20 minutes' use per pupil per day,[4] it is clear that even the countries which are at present the most advanced will not have enough computers by the year 2000. It can be calculated, on the basis of a recent CERI publication (OECD/CERI, 1988), that there are approximately nine microcomputers in each secondary school in a group of 11 Council of Europe member states (Austria, Denmark, France, the Federal Republic of Germany, Iceland, Ireland, the Netherlands, Norway, Portugal, Sweden and the United Kingdom). The computers are usually grouped together in one room, which is scarcely calculated to facilitate their use for purposes other than computer science.

The problem is not confined to hardware. The CERI report stresses that, with the exception of technical schools, no teaching establishments, whether primary or secondary, seem as yet to have attained the 'critical mass' of computers, software and properly trained teaching staff.

In the present circumstances, even if a sufficient quantity of educational software did exist, it is far from certain that teachers would make the best use of it at the right moment. As is surely known, tried and tested techniques of individualized teaching have existed ever since the early twentieth century and are explained to trainee teachers, but are scarcely ever put into practice.

The poor quality of educational software is also a long-standing problem. The development and testing of complex software conforming to demanding psychological and educational standards is costly. With illicit copying further aggravating the situation (the Yugoslav report speaks of a black market in software), there is not much hope that commercial companies will invest on a large scale in this area. ('We cannot expect the publishers to make the investment in software provision all on their own' – Netherlands.) Only the establishment of public services producing software on a national or regional scale and working in close collaboration with similar services in other countries will enable this hurdle to be cleared. International collaboration should not, however, obscure the fact that the introduction of information technology into education raises specific problems in each country and that

[4]This is the hypothesis advanced by Melmed (1983).

local solutions are essential, if only for linguistic reasons (e.g. Greece, Iceland).

The San Marino report makes an important comment with regard to software: much software is based on 'programmed teaching'. But many teachers do not readily accept predetermined learning programmes. Similar observations in other countries suggest that basic software which allows wide scope for flexible intervention by teachers will often be more readily accepted and used.

The overall picture is far from satisfactory, which explains the present stagnation in many countries. Disappointment is acute when miracles fail to happen. Now that the irrational stage is over, the situation appears less favourable. A study begun by the Italian Ministry of Education in 1984 has revealed a disturbing symptom, namely a low rate of use of computers installed in schools (32 per cent were, incidentally, unusable at the time of the survey). In 1985, another Italian study showed that only 70 per cent of the equipment available was being used.

Again in 1985, a report by the General Inspectorate of the French Ministry of National Education showed that despite the growth in the number of computers available, actual classroom use of microcomputers had remained stable or even decreased (OECD/CERI). This finding should, of course, be updated and supplemented. A point particularly worthy of note is that in Scotland, where teacher training has been given special attention, the computer is now securely established in schools.

From a rather more distant viewpoint, the present overall situation may be described as follows. Secondary schools have, so far, been in a considerably better position than primary schools, several countries still being unsure of the wisdom of making computers available to children of less than 12 years of age.

Where primary schools do possess computers, they have been used, especially to begin with, to provide pupils with drill and practice programs or to introduce pupils to the Logo environment, for which there has developed a real craze. The situation is changing in both respects. First, program quality is gradually improving, and the use of word-processing software and the use, and even constitution, of databases are increasing. Second, interest in the

Logo environment seems to be decreasing, sometimes markedly in certain countries (notably the United Kingdom). In general and technical secondary education, the information technology aspect predominates, in the form of general information technology or the systematic study of this technology. At this level of schooling, the computer is still relatively little used in most countries in subject teaching.

A clear distinction needs to be made between the use of computers *per se* and the use thereof as information-technology tools such as word-processing programs, spreadsheets, database managers, graphics systems or programs controlling turtles and various other robots, not forgetting electronic mail.

The publication of school newspapers, together with information exchanges which sometimes assume an intercontinental dimension, is giving a new lease of life to one of the principal instruments of active teaching. Moreover, the creation by pupils of databases in various fields tackled by them is of major educational value. On the other hand, the role of interactive video disks has not yet been defined.

Beyond these considerations, one thing is certain: schools must initiate their pupils in the use of computers as early as possible, without in any way trying to turn each one into a computer scientist. Experience shows that an intelligent introduction to the use of computers can be effected from primary school onwards, starting either with a technique such as word processing, or with a brief initiation in the Logo environment or similar constructivist approaches.

TEACHING INFORMATION TECHNOLOGY

Many leading experts feel that anything more than a superficial knowledge of information technology is of use only to those who intend to make a career in this field. For others, the use of computers would involve no more specialized knowledge than the average motorist has of mechanics, electricity or – as will soon be the case – information technology. For example, the United Kingdom report speaks of a scale of objectives to be attained in education in information technology and micro-electronics.

The principle of a certain computer 'acculturation' for all seems to be increasingly widely accepted in the light of the expanding role of computers in practically all walks of life. In most cases, this process takes place during secondary education.

In the broadest terms, this involves imparting a computer culture not only in the form of specialist knowledge and skills, but also as a new way of thinking. 'Information technology is a faculty or force that is totally permeating concrete and abstract reality and creating new conceptions, new forms of interpretation, new ways of management and new insights into our lifestyle' (G. Secchi, Italy). Clearly, the teaching of information technology as a specific subject contributes not only to the above-mentioned psychological development; its use as a tool for other subjects also plays a major part.

Clearly, information-technology teaching has already gained a secure foothold in school curricula, particularly at the secondary and higher levels, while the computer as a teaching aid is still far from establishing itself.

2.4 DEFINITION OF THE INFORMATION SOCIETY

Professor Balle's report (Chapter 1) examines the nature of the information society in depth. From this point of view, the value of the national reports resides in their choice of what aspects they regard as the most noteworthy ones.

At the more general level, the Holy See expresses a fear and a hope. The fear is that young people will be manipulated by over-information, a danger which threatens the most deprived in particular, for they are less well supported by the socio-cultural environment. Moreover, a type of education designed to allow the 'best' to win in 'economic warfare' is a serious threat for those most at risk. The hope is that increasing communication between people will develop a greater sense of the universal and greater interest in cultural differences: 'when taking decisions relating to the education of young people, it is important to consider what underlies the outstanding dignity of every human being.'

All the reports agree on the salient features of what might be called the physical properties of contemporary information: its mass, its multiplicity of form, its speed and its transnational nature.

The French report emphasizes the extent to which present-day information disregards all national boundaries, while Portugal notes 'a universalization of the interdependence of nations'. This trend will not, however, efface the differences in receptivity inherent in social and cultural differences or, quite simply, the generation gap (Turkey).

The influx of international information which, in some countries, accompanies an influx of foreign visitors – whether business people or tourists – is causing considerable changes in families and schools and at workplaces, particularly in the case of countries which, like Cyprus, were until recently fairly isolated. Attitudes and lifestyles are transformed and enormous adjustments are occurring in values, especially among young people. Surely it could hardly be otherwise, as the information explosion is simultaneously affecting intellectual life (NICT is a potential amplifier of human intelligence – Spain), the law, politics, economics, the arts, leisure activities, etc. Greece predicts that the very structure of society will be modified.

The report by the Federal Republic of Germany points to three particular indicators of the advent of the information society:

- The constant expansion of the 'production' of information or knowledge (said to be doubling every five or six years at present).
- The permanent increase in the proportion of the active population involved in the production, processing and transmission of information (in the Federal Republic of Germany the information sector now accounts for one job out of every two).
- The boom in information technology markets and the supply of related services (by the end of the twentieth century 70 per cent of the whole active population are likely to be directly concerned by NICT).

As already mentioned, it is by no means certain that the arrival

131

of an information society like the one currently emerging heralds a more human or humanitarian society (Sweden). It is evident that technical progress does not automatically lead to an enhanced quality of life (Liechtenstein). The battle to be waged in order to ensure that it does should be viewed as one of society's fundamental tasks. It is but one more chapter in the long and painful struggle for the achievement of a truly humanistic democracy.

Amid all this conjecture, one thing is certain: the emergence of the information society is not questioned by a single country.

Technically speaking, the concept of information denotes the signs and coded messages sent by a transmitter (source) to a receiver (see McBride, 1986, p. 260). The press, radio and television constitute what can already be termed the conventional sources of information.

The Swiss report states that in its main connotation the term 'information' is virtually confined to 'modern information' (new technologies). This relegates an important aspect of information – the written word – to the background. The report also underlines the difficulty of obtaining a reasonably clear and comprehensive picture of the situation, especially since many aspects are still at the planning stage or are no more than wishful thinking. The Italian report points to another restriction placed on the meaning of the term 'information society', namely the tendency of some to consider its technological aspects only. The report also notes that negative attitudes towards the mass media and NIT are as prevalent among young teachers with little motivation or ability as among their older colleagues.

The Swiss report analyses the role of the media (particularly, the audio-visual media) in education. This role is three-fold:

1. A teaching aid that is:
   - 'subordinate' (introduced as a concession to modernity),
   - 'dominant' (expected to play an educational role – as a substitute for the teacher – which it cannot perform) or
   - 'an integrated partner'.
2. A subject of study or an academic discipline: media studies, semiology, appraisal of information, etc.

3. A means of expression: perhaps the most fruitful and least exploited aspect.

THE 'CONVENTIONAL' MEDIA

The press in schools

The press was first introduced into schools by teachers who wished to bring a current affairs element into their lessons or had discovered some scientific, historical or literary information in the press which could be of educational value. Such initiatives did not always meet with the approval of the authorities, because of the possible political tendentiousness of the press.

The contribution that can be made by a judicious use of the press in schools is now much more fully recognized and defined thanks to awareness of the advent of the information society. Various systematic schemes have ensued, such as Actuel Quarto in Belgium (press file on major events and current issues) and Krant in de Klas (The press in the classroom) in the Netherlands.[5]

In 1985, the Council of Europe and the Association Région, Presse, Enseignement, Jeunesse (ARPEJ) organized a colloquium entirely devoted to 'The press in school' (Gerbex, 1985). This meeting not only gave rise to a description of the situation and major initiatives taken in the different countries, but also showed, first, the civic importance of education for and through the press – freedom, democracy, pluralism of expression – and, second, identified the major questions involved. The creation of a European club for the press in school was proposed on that occasion.

The entry of the press into schools represents not so much a technological innovation as a change in educational attitudes. The school is no longer a sterile environment protected from current events and the disturbing questions they often raise, but is opening up to the outside world.

In 1986, the Council of Europe organized a teachers' seminar on the theme 'Mass media education in primary schools'. Particular attention was paid to the press: the report of the meeting brings out

---

[5]General information on the press in schools can be found in Amidei (1984).

well the main aspects of the educational use of the press (Bevort, 1986).

School education now includes a growing technological element in the shape of the audio-visual media. This element is sometimes exclusive, when it merely involves the use of equipment (overhead projectors, language laboratories, etc.), and sometimes partial when information is received from outside sources. Most European countries set up educational audio-visual centres after the Second World War, with common types of equipment finding their way into almost all schools. The relative remoteness of these origins may explain the modest place occupied by the 'conventional' media (radio, cinema, television and so on) in the national reports.

School radio

School radio made its appearance in the late 1920s, shortly after the large-scale penetration of the European market by radio. The general impression emerging from the national reports is one of dwindling importance for this medium, although it can sometimes develop, as in Switzerland, into a broader form of educational radio which, among other things, tackles media education. In Malta, radio is giving way to television, but is continuing to cater for adult education.

Cinema

Cinema entered the classroom very early on, as a considerable body of literature attests. However, its use has remained very restricted in scope. It has mainly been used to give complete lessons (for example, films on venereal disease) or to supplement and illustrate a teacher's instruction (geographical films, etc.). Having come into use at a time when lessons were of the *ex cathedra* type, films were themselves sources of one-way information, which also explains the decline in the use of the traditional films in schools. Critical study of the cinema, on the other hand, is still strongly established.[6]

[6]Abundant information on this subject can be found in UNESCO (1987).

Although school film libraries or similar services exist in most, if not all, countries, they receive scant mention in the reports. Norway refers to a State Film Board, which is in fact a resource centre from which schools can borrow films, video recordings and other audio-visual material.

Masterman (1986) comments that wherever media studies treat the media as popular art forms, there is a tendency to give priority to study of the cinema (the seventh art). The fall in cinema audiences is, however, well-known in many countries (despite a countertrend in some, notably the Federal Republic of Germany and Luxembourg, as far as young cinema-goers are concerned). At no other time in its history has the cinema had less claim to be recognized as a truly popular art. The bias in its favour seems to be depriving television and press studies of the place they deserve. At the colloquium on 'The cinema and audio-visual aids in education systems in Europe: the educational and cultural stakes', held at the Council of Europe in November 1988, the participants addressed a number of recommendations to the sixteenth session of the Standing Conference of European Ministers of Education of the Council of Europe based on the consideration that 'audio-visual language, through the film and television media, today constitutes the main instrument for mass information, education and culture'. Among these recommendations is the wish to set up a university network and a European Centre given over to initiation to audio-visual language and education in the film and audio-visual media (Council of Europe, CDCC, MED-16-HF-48).

School television

The boom in school television occurred during the 1960s. Following a honeymoon period during which some basic mistakes were made, owing to the lack of fundamental didactic training on the part of many producers, enthusiasm began to wane here too. However, the subsequent success of several full-scale educational series, such as 'Sesame Street', should be mentioned. A series of Italian television broadcasts intended to improve literacy ('It's never too late') also proved successful. Another interesting development is the increasing importance attached by Switzerland to media education in television programmes for schools.

The introduction of video recorders was a decisive advance, as it enabled teachers to record selected programmes and use them whenever they best suited classroom needs. This point is well illustrated by Malta, which, after making intensive use of school radio, is now switching over to massive use of video recorders. Every school is being supplied with them. A central video library run by the Educational Media Centre will provide software. Television will continue to provide home study programmes after school for one hour a day to a wide age group (3–18 years).

In Turkey, one channel will be used exclusively for educational television.

In French-speaking Belgium, where schools are also equipped with video recorders, only about 7 per cent of pupils now watch school television live.

A sub-system of primary education (fifth and sixth years) has for many years been operating through the Portuguese Telescola, broadcasting four hours a day to some 60 000 pupils in thinly populated parts of the country. The pupils' results are comparable to those of other pupils. Some modifications have been made, and the sub-system is now integrated into the general system and greater flexibility has been introduced into teaching methods with the use of videocassettes and recorders.

Apart from programmes specially produced for schools, television channels broadcast a large amount of material of considerable educational value, concerning either the media themselves or the more conventional aspects of school curricula. Masterman (1986, pp. 6 and 7) cites the outstanding contribution made to Channel 4, in the United Kingdom, by an educational liaison officer responsible for organizing the use of an ever-growing number of open, informal educational programmes, which are neither aimed at a narrowly defined group of learners nor centred on specific study programmes. The officer's department issues sets of companion material, conducts periodic phone-ins, supervises the distribution of a magazine whose readership numbered 180 000 in 1986, facilitates the copying of programmes for educational purposes and arranges various follow-up activities (exhibitions, lectures, meetings between producers and viewers, etc.).

More generally, policy in the United Kingdom seems exemplary in so far as it requires all television broadcasting authorities to provide an element of public service broadcasting, notably educational programmes. Decisions as to content of programmes rest entirely with the broadcasting authorities themselves.

In this connection, the United Kingdom report mentions an impressive number of hours per year:

Adult education/continuing education

BBC 1	154 hours
BBC 2	121 hours
ITV	156 hours
Channel 4	390 hours (plus open college transmissions)

Schools TV per year

BBC 2	500 hours
Channel 4	375 hours

It therefore seems that the future of educational television has already been largely mapped out.

On the educational aspects of an active television input at primary school, see the report by Bevort (1987) mentioned in the context of the press in school.

INFORMATION TECHNOLOGY

With the arrival of ever cheaper and more efficient microcomputers on the scene, the educational world in all its branches – general, technical and vocational – was unable to ignore the fact that all productive sectors have undergone an information technology invasion. Huge problems were posed by the need to provide schools with hardware and to produce appropriate courseware, and these problems are still largely unsolved. The same applies to the retraining of teaching staff. Nor is sufficient account being taken of the significant improvements which computers will undergo in the coming years, particularly as far as image and sound quality is concerned.

The report of the OECD Centre for Educational Research and Innovation (CERI) makes a clear distinction between information technology and data communication.

> The two technologies that are being studied in the context of the CERI's work are informatics and data transmission. By informatics is meant either a stand-alone computer or a terminal with its various software packages for computer-assisted instruction (CAI), word processing, spreadsheets, database management and graphics systems, a computer used in multimedia configurations, i.e. hooked up to slide viewers, videotape recorders or video disks, or computer-controlled teaching aids such as turtles or other types of robot. By data transmission is meant either the linking up of computers in a local network within a school or university, or a hook up with outside networks via a computer or terminal (e.g. videotext) so as to be able to access databases, interface with other systems and hook up to distance-learning systems.

THE NEW MEDIA

These are interactive media which combine audio-visual elements with computers, such as interactive video disks, or telecommunications–computer combinations. Under the heading of new information technology UNESCO generally includes computers, optical fibres, information and communications satellites, video recordings and so on.

As the Netherlands report points out, none of the countries concerned seems to have a clear-cut overall view of what these new media will mean for schools. It is possible that the ever-expanding range of computer tools (word processing, automatic data search programs, computerized dictionaries, writing monitoring programs, etc.) will be the first to prove of effective value to schools.

EDUCATIONAL OBJECTIVES

It is assumed that the new technologies extend an individual's capacities by increasing his or her ability to reflect on a logical, abstract world and hence embrace much broader and deeper problems than previously. The individual must, however, link these forces, both new and old, with those of other people by first of all communicating with them, an act which has been made very much easier (Federal Republic of Germany).

Education needs to pursue a set of NICT-related objectives in order to serve the interests of individuals as well as society as a whole:

teaching individuals to interpret the media, i.e. enabling them to analyse the organization of messages according to the type of medium and express these analyses verbally (France);

teaching pupils to use NICT intelligently;

teaching people to select media according to specific objectives;

developing people's critical faculties and enabling them to exercise them independently;

learning to distil the significant from the insignificant (UK);

making it understood that for one single ephemeral reality, there is a multitude of different representations possible which are not the exact reproduction of the whole of reality and with which it should not be confused (Council of Europe, 1986);

ensuring compatibility with the cultural heritage;

offering equal educational opportunities throughout the country and to all groups of inhabitants – different generations, men and women, the disabled, different ethnic groups, immigrants and so on;

offering equal educational opportunities whatever academic orientation is chosen – general, scientific, literary, vocational, technical or artistic;

teaching self-expression with the help of the media;

collaborating with families, firms, employers and employees;

139

inculcating a holistic approach to information, so that it is always viewed within its broad philosophical, political and social context;

enhancing the effectiveness of education for the more highly gifted;

enabling children and young people to analyse, judge and evaluate the media in the light of their personal responsibility towards themselves.

This kind of education is all the more important as it will frequently have a marked effect on academic perfomance and emotional equilibrium (Federal Republic of Germany).

The Federal Republic of Germany considers that media education as a whole should also serve to transmit values. 'It should not only cultivate a sense of judgement but also educate and strengthen moral and social behaviour. It ought not to decrease the possibility of satisfying individual needs and interests'.[7] These targets cannot all be met by school education alone.

On the negative side, education should:

counter the unthinking use of the media;

prevent people from becoming alienated from themselves;

avoid any blurring of the boundary between reality and fiction, a phenomenon which the sophistication of present-day media can quite easily bring about in psychologically weak individuals (confusion leading to the adoption of similar attitudes towards real and fictitious situations – France);

counter the yearning for permanent, instantaneous entertainment;

combat the feeling of insecurity in the face of powerful, ubiquitous media, as well as the escapism that such media can engender;

---

[7]Bund-Länder-Kommission für Bildungsplanung und Forschungsforderung. Materialien zur Bildungsplanung. Heft 16. Gesamtkonzept für die informationstechnische Bildung, p. 30.

more generally, allay all ungrounded fears of NICT;

prevent the influx of foreign-language information and films from jeopardizing the national language, a special danger for smaller countries (Iceland);

check the decline in creativity;

combat apathy;

counter the impression that 'quality' spells 'boredom';

campaign against vulgarity and bad taste.

A difficult question arises in connection with the last two items. Should media education include the presentation of poor-quality or downright obscene programmes? The Danish authorities' response to objections by teachers and parents is that students must be able to tell good from bad and should not therefore be restricted to a study of 'cleaned-up' programmes but, on the contrary, should examine the various products of mass communication as made available in everyday life.

Media education should also provide a new form of linguistic expression. No media education can exist without language education. A language used solely for processing and transmitting data can be just as important as the language used for complex human communication (with all its ambiguities, ironies and paradoxes). For that reason the various forms of communication should be studied and used so that whichever one is most suitable at a given time can be chosen (Federal Republic of Germany).[8]

On the subject of objectives, two examples of national positions are worth quoting. In 1973 Austria issued a decree on media education. In the course of time, such education has become increasingly clearly differentiated from measures concerning the traditional audio-visual media. The objectives set are:

to awaken pupils' critical awareness of communication phenomena, so as to turn them into discerning media consumers (critical-mindedness);

[8]*Op. cit.* note 7, p. 33.

141

to help each pupil individually to develop his or her intellectual, affective and linguistic capacities;

to enable pupils to understand and experience meaningfully the structure, means of presentation and effects of the media;

to teach pupils to act creatively in the media field, benefiting from and successfully completing their creative projects.

These objectives should be pursued in all subject areas rather than within one new subject area.

In Denmark the cornerstones of media education are as follows:

understanding the media, their language and complexity, a prerequisite for a critical and conscious attitude towards media culture (this training should be placed in its historical, political, economic and institutional context);

independent media production (by producing films, videos, etc. themselves, students can much better appreciate the nature of the media; one-half of the media studies timetable is devoted to this activity, and examinations cover this practical aspect to the same extent as the theoretical part).

One further aim is to equip students to benefit from democratized access to the mass media.

On a more fundamental level (Masterman, 1986), media education should:

- Convey an understanding of the principle of non-transparency: the media do not simply depict reality as if they were a window opened upon it; they represent it in the light of political, commercial and personal concerns which pupils must learn to detect.
- Explain media rhetoric, i.e. the techniques used by the media to construct meaning: the selection of sounds and images, situations, narrative structures and so on. This involves learning how to 'deconstruct' messages and get beneath their surface.
- Show how to identify ideologies. The media give but a

selective and partial view of reality, even though this may seem true, national and authentic. Any distortions are not innocent; in particular, values are constantly at stake.

- Show how to identify the various interests being served by the images and ideas put forward.

In compulsory education, these aims are pursued indirectly in that they do not constitute a separate subject but are expected to be pursued in all subjects.

As already mentioned, an introduction to the media may form a separate subject. The canton of Fribourg in Switzerland has a highly detailed curriculum for the pre-specialization period of education. General objectives are accompanied by a list of more specific goals to be attained at each level (first-year introductory phase and second and third-year consolidation phase). These specific objectives are set, for knowledge and skills alike.

In the upper secondary schools of most cantons there are either specific courses in (or viewings of) cinematographic works or option courses in the production of Super 8 or video films. Again, in Switzerland, the panorama project is being launched, which will invite children to put together the photographic memory of the country (about 19 000 slides).

Opération Jeunes-Téléspectateurs-Actifs, a scheme carried out in France between 1979 and 1982, is another example of the measures taken to achieve some of the objectives listed. Using a video recorder, teachers look with their pupils (aged between 3 and 14) at programmes already seen at home and then discuss them with the pupils (the CIRTEs – Integrated Educational Resources and Technology Centres – have taken over this task). Still in France, the 'Plan vidéo collège' is more specifically based on a critical analysis of images and on the production of images which may be combined with the written and spoken word as a means of enhancement.

Malta has adopted a broader approach, having recently introduced a course entitled 'Systems of knowledge' in the final year of upper secondary level, which will count as part of the university entrance examination. The course covers the philosophy, history and practice of communication.

2.5 NICT: A NEW FOCUS OF KNOWLEDGE

EFFECTS ON EDUCATION POLICY

The objectives which most countries wish to achieve have just been explained. The dominant concern is to implement an educational policy appropriate to national society without disregarding the requirements of international interdependence. This interdependence is, of course, primarily of an economic, scientific and military nature, but it is also cultural in that if any culture were nowadays to shut itself completely off from others it would soon become anachronistic because of the phenomenon of universalization closely linked with the information explosion. Guaranteeing the 'right of free access to the products of other cultures' (Portugal) is now more than ever a duty of democrats.

It is also a democratic act to 'guarantee individuals as well as society as a whole access to a growing volume of data essential to their autonomy of choice and decision-making' (Portugal). Balle refers to the danger of the 'electronic gulag' – a very real danger, as George Orwell so eloquently predicted. It is not therefore just education policy but policy as a whole that is at stake: the choice of whether or not to live democratically. It is clear that all the countries concerned are deeply aware of this dilemma.

Consequently, over and above the range of specific objectives assigned to it, education will have the fundamental task of creating an awareness of the significance of life's problems and the existence of information resources capable of providing solutions to them. In short, the aim is to encourage each individual to obtain the requisite information in order to satisfy his or her *own* needs rather than those of potential exploiters.

As the Portuguese report clearly puts it, caution should be exercised with regard to commercial manipulations which 'give educational administrators and teachers illusions of "progress" and "modernity" that have little to do with an effective reform of education'. Clearly, 'for there to be a significant improvement in the quality of teaching through the use of educational technology, considerable resources (including time) must first be devoted to training the authors, designers and producers of teaching materials, and the future users of these products' (Portugal).

All countries are aware of the scale of expenditure needed to equip schools adequately. France, Great Britain and others set an early example by launching large-scale planned initiatives in this field.

The report of Flemish Belgium lists the four major policy options available regarding the acquisition of hardware and software and, possibly, the use which may be made thereof in the classroom:

1. A fully decentralized policy, leaving all the initiative to schools or even to individual teachers. Teachers and school principals displayed such initiative when low-cost equipment, such as small film projectors, tape recorders or the earliest microcomputers, first came on to the market. The outcome is well-known. On the plus side, some useful experience of self-instruction was gained by a number of interested teachers, who have since become fully conversant with information technology. The minus side includes an amateurish approach to educational software, whose quality has suffered and continues to suffer from the inadequacy of the material acquired, and from a lack of training and enthusiasm on the part of teachers. Moreover, incompatibility between software packages has created notorious problems.

2. A wholly centralized policy (e.g. Greece). The advantages of unified action are obvious. However, matters soon become complex in countries like Belgium, where there are a multiplicity of organizing bodies.

3. A policy which is initially centralized but accords increasing freedom of action to the 'grass roots'. This system, which is the one that reflects most fully the principle of adapting educational arrangements to prevailing circumstances, combines the advantages of general unity (particularly with regard to items of equipment and hence their compatibility) with all the positive aspects of an environment-friendly approach.

Some of the reports show clear signs of a trend in this direction, which is probably the one that will prevail in the medium or long term.

4. A decentralized policy with limited centralization in certain areas. This is the approach used in Great Britain and Norway, where it has proved its worth.

The choice between the third and fourth options is directly connected with the whole history of education systems: France and Great Britain offer sharply contrasting examples in this regard.

Whoever the decision-making authority may be, it has in its turn a choice between two policies (OECD/CERI):

'sectoral' policy, which usually concentrates resources on technical and vocational training;

'global' policy, directed simultaneously at all levels of education, with computer science, computer awareness and computer-assisted teaching and learning as differential objectives.

A general trend towards the second policy is discernible. Once again, however, there are differences of approach: either resources are scattered among all schools or, as in Norway, efforts are provisionally concentrated on experimental schools. In addition, Norway has launched a major programme of different activities at national and regional levels. This will enable a choice to be made of the most suitable strategies for implementing the programme of education in new information technology.

It is important to note that little is still known about the implications of the large-scale application of NICT to education. Some isolated aspects have emerged haphazardly, but sufficient experimental data are not yet available to permit the real effects of NICT to be gauged (Spain). This point is of fundamental significance, for it does seem that only large-scale experimental research projects, coordinated on a Europe-wide basis, offer any real chance of obtaining in good time the data that will be required if far-reaching educational reforms are not to be embarked upon virtually blindfold.

This is also a matter of general policy, particularly since many

146

European countries are still seriously lacking in educational research institutions or services or networks.

EFFECTS ON COURSE CONTENT

It is generally felt that not only the content of all branches of education, whether general, technical or artistic, would be modified – albeit it to varying degrees – under the influence of NICT: all those taking part in a UNESCO workshop in 1986 on the question of mass media and education acknowledged that the audio-visual media were also powerful teaching agents and would constitute a curriculum parallel to the academic one.

A mastery of oral, written and graphic means of expression and, of course, an understanding of the messages thus transmitted have everywhere become necessary. In France, new subjects and sectors are appearing, such as an information technology option or a cinema/audio-visual option, in upper secondary schools: a senior technician's certificate in the audio-visual media has also been instituted, while in lower secondary schools one of the six interdisciplinary themes to be covered by all teachers, from different angles, is information. Examples abound of the place being occupied by information and communication technology in various subjects. Mother-tongue and modern-language teaching is, of course, a prime area. But equally striking is the broadening of approach towards such subjects as history, geography and civics, which are increasingly benefiting from the availability of well-stocked data and information banks whose universalization can open up young citizens' horizons to an extraordinary extent.

To sum up, what needs to be done is not to start from scratch again but to reconcile old yet still valid learning processes with the inescapable new ones (Federal Republic of Germany).

Mass media education is tending to spread throughout school education (France, indeed, is starting at the nursery school stage), and teachers frequently appear to enjoy a large degree of autonomy in this regard. The specific courses or schemes to be observed in several countries are not replacing the partnership with the various subject areas, but supplementing it. In Malta, a textbook on the media is being distributed in Church-run primary schools on an experimental basis. In Norwegian schools, media education is integrated into the teaching of the various subjects, particularly the mother tongue, but it may also be covered in greater depth on an option course of 2–3 hours a week at secondary level. In Denmark, systematic instruction in the mass media became compulsory in upper secondary schools on 1 August 1988.

Other countries are less advanced. In Finland, interest in media education has rekindled in recent years. It includes both electrical and graphic communication. Depending on the school and teacher, the content and method of media education vary greatly in Finland. Similarly, in contemplating future prospects for its school system, Liechtenstein is debating the place that the media should occupy. According to a new Swiss regulation on recognition of secondary school leaving certificates, pupils are required to have taken an information technology course, whatever the type of certificate.

On the specific question of the introduction of computers into schools, the general conclusions reached by OECD/CERI (August 1988) seem appropriate. Firstly, microcomputers may influence classroom management (group work, increased communication among pupils and between teachers and pupils, etc.) in all disciplines. Secondly, four changes may be expected:

- The introduction of new technology-related subjects, beginning with computer awareness and computer-aided design.
- Changes in the cognitive content of traditional activities: the mechanization of calculation means that in the teaching of mathematics more time can be spent on understanding the concepts involved; with the task of rewriting eliminated, more emphasis can be placed on researching ideas, organizing a text and so on. Metacognition has a greater part to play in learning.
- The emergence of new activities and topics in existing subjects (quantitative analysis in the social sciences, computer-assisted composition in music, etc.).
- Increased use of exploration, discovery and model construction in learning processes.

EFFECTS ON TEACHING METHODS

Computers can enable types of education to be developed that were not possible with traditional methods and resources (Sweden). They may even generate a complete reform (CERI).

Reflection on teaching methods leads to the core of the practical problem. Ever since their inception, the purpose of schools has been to impart knowledge through information. The fact that the sheer quantity of information now available no longer enables individuals to amass encyclopaedic knowledge is of growing significance. Rather than committing information to memory, it is often more important to be able to find it whenever it is required. Data banks may consequently be expected to play an increasing part both in training and in occupational life. However, locating information whenever necessary is not enough: it still needs to be put to proper use. It is here that the importance of being able to apply the higher cognitive processes, at least in order to construct solutions and take enlightened decisions, becomes evident. The French report, in particular, draws attention to this, emphasizing that new instruments, such as computers and interactive video disk players, enable teachers to stress the active nature of reasoning and learning.

Here, too, there is unanimity: prescriptive, one-way teaching which transmits knowledge, skills and ready-made rules of conduct to be swallowed whole or applied unthinkingly must give way to active learning where the learner, in accordance with Piaget's theories, builds up his or her own knowledge by functionally interacting with the environment, whether near or far. The Spanish report, among others, gives considerable weight to this aspect.

Because of their almost inevitably multi-disciplinary nature, educational projects which open a window on to the outside world enable account to be taken of manifold sources of information to which pupils are exposed: study of the press, televised messages, etc. (France). The multi-media approach sharpens interest (Portugal); the degree of concentration displayed by pupils working, for instance, on the creation and operation of a database has come as a surprise to many observers. Wherever students have such freedom of access to media-transmitted information and data, their intellectual autonomy grows visibly. Furthermore, the sheer diversification of teaching material (texts, audio material, video, computer programs) is breaking down the unidirectional character of traditional teaching by encouraging the development of a variety of types of communication between teachers and pupils (Portugal). NICT is also amplifying the long-standing active methods of teaching and giving them a new lease of life.

Sweden deplores the fact that all too often computers in education are, as it were, forced into traditional school work, as a result of which not only do teachers fall behind in their efforts to cover the curriculum but also teaching methods are often imposed from outside. To derive full benefit from the computer as a teaching aid, a teacher must be given opportunities to replace traditional methods with others that are more suited to contemporary situations.

In its discussion of the effects of NICT on school life, the French report cites the example of the transformation of the humble school magazine into a professional-standard publication, with a large circulation among all involved in the educational process as well as local companies. There is also mention of press briefs being compiled in connection with major events, open days and so on, as well as of pupils themselves producing brochures or videos about their schools. Audio information is broadcast either for internal consumption or externally, to the local community.

New methods of instruction are emerging. Sweden, for instance, is currently experimenting with different forms of computer-assisted music teaching. A further possibility is the individualization or semi-individualization of teaching. The sheer multiplicity and flexibility of the new information and communication media, together with the enormous storage capacity of computers, means that increasing personalization of teaching and learning processes may now be envisaged.

In short, the information society offers opportunities for new thinking and experimentation in the field of educational methodology. NICT allows changes to be made in curriculum content, classroom organization, teacher–pupil relationships and evaluation techniques (Spain).

EFFECTS ON THE RECRUITMENT AND TRAINING OF TEACHING STAFF

Recruitment

The national reports provide no information on any communication knowledge and skills required for the purposes of initial teacher training. France mentions an optional test in computerized information processing, for all state employees as well as an assessment of proficiency in NICT-assisted self-expression and communication in certain competitive examinations for teaching staff.

Initial teacher training

NICT offers vast scope for reforming teaching methods but cannot by itself bring them up to date. Unless competent and motivated teachers take on the task, no reform will occur.

According to the Austrian report, all teachers should be able to use computers for teaching purposes with the same ease as other teaching aids or audio-visual techniques. However, as Sweden points out, software is of no value in itself – everything depends on the reasons why it is to be used. Obviously, it is far easier to provide sound initial training for a relatively small number of trainee teachers than to retrain the millions of teachers already in post throughout Europe (Portugal). For the latter, not only do knowledge and skills have to be improved but – and here lies the most difficult aspect – time-honoured attitudes have to be changed.

Almost everywhere – although, of course in differing ways and degrees – information technology has already become part of initial teacher training. In Ireland, for example, trainee teachers can take an option course on the use of NICT in education, and all colleges of education are equipped with computers to demonstrate their value in primary education. In Belgium, future primary and lower-secondary teachers attend a compulsory information technology course which focuses on programming logic, the use of software packages and the educational applications of computers. It may be supposed, however, that training will suffer for a long time yet from the effects of poor quality in educational software. Indeed, the importance of observing proper practices in the use of NICT in actual teaching and learning situations, whether for initial or for in-service training, cannot be overrated (Spain). Unfortunately, the declining birthrate is resulting in fewer new graduates with a practical knowledge of NICT being recruited. Teacher training is no doubt also affected by the fact that the trainers themselves do not possess sufficient knowledge or experience of the effects of the use of computers on learning processes (OECD/CERI).

Matters are less clear-cut in the case of audio-visual techniques and mass media. It appears that in the great majority of countries an introduction to these fields is provided during initial and/or in-service training (sabbatical periods, short courses, etc.). In French-speaking Belgium, in-service training courses are run in the management of media libraries or audio-visual production centres as well as in the operation of closed-circuit television.

The report from the Federal Republic of Germany mentions the absence of information technology courses which could be described as comprehensive and applicable to all categories of teachers. In Norway, by contrast, media education is widespread: each institution is free to adopt a particular programme, provided that it conforms with the general guidelines laid down by the Ministry of Education. These programmes are also available as part of in-service training.

The French report states that communication and information are treated as important elements in the teaching of all subject areas. Training in audio-visual techniques occupies a prominent place, and this seems to be more or less the case in virtually all the other countries. Austria provides an example of the systematic implementation of a long-term plan. From 1972 onwards NICT, especially computer techniques, was introduced into teacher training – first for mathematics, then for chemistry and descriptive geometry. Now, all areas of general and technical education are gradually being covered.

In-service teacher training

Such training exists everywhere, but the reports give no clear idea of the emphasis placed on information and communication education, apart from computer science (which clearly has priority). Nevertheless, France has for some years made a major effort to inform and train teachers (Centre de Liaison de l'Enseignement et des Moyens d'Information, CLEMI). Significant steps have also been taken in Portugal, Spain (Mercury Programme) and the Netherlands, among others. France reports that more than one-quarter of all resources available for the in-service training of secondary teachers is allocated to NICT.

Luxembourg runs modular training programmes (4, 8 or 16 hours) for all its teachers, which may be attended partly during and partly outside working hours. The aim is to impart a general knowledge of information technology and encourage the carrying out of educational projects where it is harnessed to the needs of all subject areas.

With the exception of some special cases such as Denmark, where for decades there has been a comprehensive system of in-service training truly accessible to all the country's teachers, it is rare for in-service training schemes to exceed, in either quality or quantity, the critical threshold below which there are no really perceptible effects on the education system as a whole.

In Flemish Belgium, the conclusion has been reached that distance education is the only means of providing retraining on a large scale. Television programmes designed for this purpose began in January 1989. One of the main reasons for this is that many teachers are at a complete loss in the face of the flood of hardware arriving on the market and the welter of information and other material offered to them. Strict quality checks are to be carried out, and teachers will be informed of their results. Multimedia self-instruction packages could also play a significant part. Yugoslavia appears to be moving in this direction by preparing modules covering the different aspects of education.

In a small country like San Marino, the majority of teachers can be trained fairly quickly if determined action is taken. Thus in connection with the major project begun in 1988 to introduce information technology at lower secondary schools (11–14), a computer literacy course designed for all teachers of all subjects was attended by two-thirds of them (82 out of 124).

Obviously, conditions are very different in countries where tens of thousands of teachers have to be trained. In order to reach the vast mass of teachers, Portugal is providing fairly advanced training for a relatively small number of teachers throughout the country, who will have a 'cascade' effect on their colleagues. Spain is relying on its provincial teachers' centres and its experimental centres, within which teaching teams are being set up with a coordinator. Norway has been running a two-year intensive course on the theory and practice of media education for the retraining of teacher trainers.

The Austrian report gives a clear picture of the methodology of in-service training. It is based on the principle of using teachers' own experiences as the starting point. Teachers undergoing in-service training draw up and carry out projects. Discussion of any difficulties encountered is treated as a source of learning. The primary concern is to remain at all times in touch with classroom realities and not to attempt to change everything at the very outset. The Swedish government recommends that experimental projects should preferably be conducted by universities which run in-service training courses for teachers, so that the latter may be directly informed and the new techniques brought more quickly into schools. So as to provide an incentive for in-service training, in the Netherlands computers are supplied only to those primary schools whose staff have attended training courses.

A novel scheme is to be found in French-speaking Belgium: a network known as 'Computers for Education', set up by university educational research centres, is permanently available to teachers, parents and other interested parties in order to keep them abreast of questions regarding information technology in relation to education. Demonstrations are given on request and seminars held from time to time. Moreover, a Club

Athena establishes contacts between leading NICT companies and education officers.

In Ireland, the National Institute of Higher Education plays a similar role, acting as a national resource centre for an exchange of information on NICT. The French Ministry of Education's telematics information service, EDUTEL, is on an even grander scale. Set up in March 1987, it had already received more than a million calls one year later. Another example is the Computer-Assisted Learning Centre at the Education Department of the University of Geneva.

Finally, the network of interconnected computers that Iceland is installing among all its schools to enable all teachers to communicate with colleagues far and wide for the purpose of exchanging ideas, working together and keeping up with new developments may also be considered a powerful factor for educational progress.

From the above as well as from odd references in other national reports, it transpires – particularly in the field of information technology, but no doubt elsewhere too – that most in-service training activities consist of short courses focused far more on the technology itself than on its implications for teaching methods. Summer schools run by the Commission of the European Communities are attempting to reconcile these two concerns, but they last for only 10 days at a time. As CERI points out, reforming teachers' theory and practice is a slow and difficult process and the most that such short courses can do is to get the process under way. In any event, no really serious assessment has yet been made of the number and duration of courses to be organized in a given situation. Moreover, while current research has demonstrated the crucial importance of 'opportunities to learn' (to learn to play the piano, both the instrument itself and time to practise are required), it is noticeable that very few teachers are well-off from this point of view. In some countries, nevertheless, experience has shown that just two or three computers available outside the information technology room are sufficient to stimulate a significant increase in the use of computers in the various subject areas.

2.6 NICT AT THE SERVICE OF TEACHING AND LEARNING

AS AN AID TO SUBJECT STUDIES

This point was raised when teaching methods were being discussed. It is generally acknowledged that all disciplines are concerned. The experimental sciences benefit enormously from computer simulations and the eradication of long and complex calculations; spatial images are of value to geography, geology and biology, etc. Television is of great help in the human sciences, in foreign-language studies (original-version films) and in other subjects which benefit readily from its vivid illustrations.

The National Curriculum English Working Group (UK) has recently stressed the importance of media education in developing major aspects of learning the mother tongue. There is also interesting information in the United Kingdom report on the role the computer can play in the learning of mathematics. The support which NICT can now offer to the learning of basic skills – reading, writing, arithmetic and 'discovery' subjects – is increasingly recognized. The CERI report describes the current scope for enhancing these learning processes as historic (see OECD, 1987). A discordant note is, however, sounded by the Swedish report, which mentions the existence of widely divergent views in Sweden concerning the use of computers for teaching subjects, especially in primary schools. Some seem to fear that early use of computers may be prejudicial to children's development without offering any significant compensatory contribution.

NICT can be of considerable assistance to pupils in overcoming learning difficulties by permitting an individualized and interactive approach (France, Sweden). This point is of special importance at a time when most countries are trying to combat widespread *academic under-achievement* and, more generally, feel the need to boost educational productivity. So far, however, it would appear that, despite all its potential, NICT has led to little significant improvement in the situation but rather to have benefited the brighter type of pupil. (France)

Open universities

Wherever open universities (which owe their very existence to recent developments in mass information media) have been fully organized, as in Great Britain, the Netherlands or Denmark, they have proved their worth. While it is true that the initial aim of making higher education available to all has had to be trimmed back because of the process of natural selectivity which has occurred among potential students – those already possessing a sound educational basis, such as teachers, are the ones that derive the most benefit from these new structures – the long-term effects may yet prove greater than at present seems likely, since open universities offer advantages which will increasingly be in demand as listed in the Netherlands report:

the only admission requirement is adulthood;

students can construct their own courses;

they can study wherever and whenever they wish;

they can progress at their own pace.

Open universities are an invaluable testing ground for adult education methods as well as for the educational applications of information technology.

From an organizational point of view, Finland is unique in not having set up any new institutional framework for its open university. Each higher education institute makes its own open university arrangements, generally in cooperation with civic or workers' institutes. At first, conventional courses were offered, but now distance learning is developing (radio, television, tele-conferences, video conferences, etc.). Optimum results are being achieved with a blend of the two types of teaching. An exploratory project intended for secondary education is currently underway in the Netherlands. Several countries are planning to establish open universities. Portugal, in particular, has recently completed preparatory work on its Universidade Aberta, which in 1992 will be able to cater for some 40 000 students.

Pupils must be initiated in *independent learning* at a very early stage, if only because they will be required to go on learning throughout their lives. This accounts for the creation, particularly in school documentation centres, of autonomous work stations where pupils may consult imagebases or databases, use computer-guided video disks, access Minitel-type computerized information networks and so on. In countries like Belgium where dense tele-diffusion networks cover the entire national territory, opportunities for home study will expand rapidly once interactivity becomes possible.

Distance learning

The beginnings of distance education go back to the nineteenth century, but NICT is giving it new impetus. For example, as early as 1970, Portugal launched a vast programme based on television.

Because of its outstanding experience in the matter, Denmark occupies an exemplary place in distance learning. It distinguishes between three models historically linked with technological progress:

1. Correspondence learning, which experienced a boom in the late nineteenth century with the advent of new printing techniques and the railways.
2. Multi-media distance learning, which has been developing since the 1960s with the combined use of printed material, radio, cassettes and, to some degree, computers. Telephone counselling is sometimes provided and face-to-face tutorials are arranged.

   A feature of models 1 and 2 is the practically one-way direction of information: it is sent to the learner, whose interaction with his instructors is minimal. The distance marker either approves or disapproves, the student attempting to give whatever answers he thinks will please the tutor. The result has been a social bias – those who are already well educated benefit most from the opportunities offered.

3. Communication is the key-word of the third-generation model. Thanks to interactivity, pupils can at last use their own language. Tele-conferences are destined to play a major role here: the Open University of Jutland is currently carrying out a series of searching experiments with the relevant technological aspects.

Further noteworthy distance-learning schemes are Austria's 'radio college', broadcasting a wide variety of programmes which may be borrowed or bought by the public, and France's extensive CNED (National Centre for Distance Learning – previously the National Centre for Correspondence Learning), which makes increasing use of the new communication techniques and caters for all students, levels and subject areas; 240 000 students are currently registered, including 160 000 adults. In 1977 Norway created a state-run distance learning body (State Institute of Distance Education): television, video recordings and conventional textbooks were from the outset selected as means of transmitting information. Finland has a more selective approach, giving priority to general or vocational education for adults.

Finally the growing feasibility of distance learning is clearly of special interest to certain thinly populated countries or regions (Iceland, Sweden). Sweden, for example, uses videotext, radio and television as teaching aids for pupils living in remote country areas. Economics programmes for companies and information technology courses for adults are distributed in the same way.

The following conclusion reached by UNESCO seems appropriate: 'Application of NICT to distance education is growing with the development of network facilities, improved accessing to active information banks, home learning stations, videotext and electronic mail, digital transmission, diversification of interactive tools allowing home tuition and individualized learning assistance.' In May 1988, the Commission of the European Communities emphasized the need to exploit the potential of distance learning for education and in-service training.

EDUCATION OF THE DISABLED

Virtually all disabled people will soon have access to substantial technological support. Just as, thanks to advances in robotics, sophisticated prosthetic appliances are being developed for those suffering from motor handicaps, so information technology is providing increasingly valuable help for those with sensory handicaps, particularly by means of computers conveying speech (synthetic or natural) and images (digitalized or otherwise). The United Kingdom mentions in particular the use of information technology for helping children with severe communication problems generally arising from cerebral palsy or head injury.

Many countries refer to the education of the disabled. Norway, which has a National Institute of Special Education, runs a half-year course for trainee teachers in NICT-based education for the disabled, and comparable in-service courses are also available. A number of advanced schemes exist in France, the Netherlands, the Federal Republic of Germany, Switzerland and elsewhere. In Sweden, special funds are set aside for the purchase of hardware and software for educational establishments. It is hoped in particular that the variety of aids provided by computers will enable even the seriously disabled to be better integrated into the regular education system.

The role computers play in the education of the disabled is primarily of a technical nature. As France points out, the problems and potentialities of computer-assisted learning are practically the same for the disabled as for others.

2.7 COPYRIGHT

The copyright problem is becoming increasingly acute. Photo-copiers, tape recorders and video recorders are to be found in many schools and homes. The ease with which sometimes highly expensive software packages can be pirated is well known.

It emerges from the Austrian report, which pays particular attention to this question, that except where production, copying and distribution are covered by proper contracts, the situation is far from clear. Whenever legal proceedings are instituted, the courts tend to side with the authors. Two important legal concepts are examined: 'free use of productions for one's own use' and 'public character'.

An event is deemed to be public if it is open to all. It is not public if it is restricted to participants who are not directly related to each other but have real personal ties with each other or who have a personal relationship with the organizer of the event. These conditions seem to apply, for example, to a pupil who records a TV programme with his private video recorder and then shows his recording to his class for purely educational purposes. Problems may arise when such recordings are shown, whether simultaneously or not, to several classes or when a teacher records a television programme for several classes. A similar distinction applies to photocopies, although here the legal situation appears even vaguer. The Austrian Ministry of Education supplies schools with regular information on copyright problems and the relevant statutory provisions.

In Switzerland, new statutory arrangements envisage reduced rates for schools, but without giving schools any kind of privileged position with regard to the actual principle of copyright. The Nordic Countries' Council of Ministers is currently concluding a series of copyright agreements. The European workshop held by UNESCO in 1986 on mass media and education recommended that copyright be abolished in respect of the use for educational purposes of all publicly issued material.

On the level of general principle, the European Audiovisual Charter – the European Charter for the defence and future of audio-visual creation adopted in Delphi in September 1988 by participants from 20 countries – stipulates (Article 4) that the author has 'an exclusive incorporeal proprietary right which shall be valid *era omnes*'.

SELECTIVE BIBLIOGRAPHY

Amidei, G.B. (1984). Journalism and pedagogy. In *Media education*. Paris: UNESCO.

Bevort, E. (1986). *Report of the 33rd Council of Europe Teachers' Seminar on*

'*Mass media education in primary schools*' (Donaueschingen, 6–10 October 1986). Strasbourg: Council of Europe, CDCC; DECS/EGT (86) 73.

Bloom, B.S. (1986). Le problème des deux sigmas: trouver des méthodes d'enseignement collectif aussi efficaces qu'un précepteur. In *L'art et la science de l'enseignement*, Crahay, M. and La Fontaine, D. (eds). Brussels: Labor.

Commission of the European Communities (1988a). *Education in the European Communities. Prospects 1988–1992*. Brussels: CEC.

Commission of the European Communities (1988b). *Activities of the Commission of the European Communities in the field of education, training and youth policy during 1987*. Brussels: CEC.

Council of Europe, CDCC (1988). *The new information technologies and education. Report on the activities of the Council of Europe with regard to NICT and education 1982–1988*. Strasbourg: Council of Europe, CDCC; DECS/Rech (88) 3.

Corset, P. (1982). *Report of the Symposium on 'The secondary school and the mass media'*. Grenoble, France, 29 June to 3 July 1981. Strasbourg.

Gambiez, C. (1981). '*The use of the media at school to prepare youngsters for life*', prepared within the framework of the CDCC's Project no. 1, '*Preparation for life*'. Strasbourg.

Gerbex, R. (1985). *Report of the Colloquy on 'The Press in School'*, organized by the Council of Europe and the Association régions, presse, enseignement, jeunesse (ARPEJ), Strasbourg, 20–22 March 1985. DECS/EGT (86) 7.

McBride, S. (1986). *Many voices, one world*. Paris: UNESCO.

Masterman, L. (1984). *Report of European Teachers' Seminar on 'Mass media education'*, Kristiansand, Norway, 8–14 August 1984. DECS/EGT (83) 82.

Masterman, L. (1986). *Report on the 'Impact of Mass Communication Media on Curriculum Development and Educational Methods'*. Paris: UNESCO.

Masterman, L. (1988). *The development of media education in Europe in the 1980s, particularly in the field of TV and electronic media*. Strasbourg: CDCC.

Melmed, E. (1983). *Educational productivity, the teacher and technology* (mimeograph). Washington, DC: US Dept of Education.

OECD (1987). *Information technologies and basic learning: reading, writing, science and mathematics.* Paris: OECD.

OECD/CERI (1988). *The use of microcomputers in education. Implications for teachers* (note by the Secretariat). Paris: OECD/CERI.

Pigasse, J.P. (1981). La révolution de la communication. *Communication et Langage,* **50**, 17.

Schaeffer, P. (1984). Mass media and the school: Descartes or McLuhan. In *Media education.* Paris: UNESCO.

UNESCO (1977). *The study of the media in education.* Paris: UNESCO.

UNESCO (1982). *International Symposium on 'Education of the public in the use of mass media' (Grünwald),* Final Report. Paris: UNESCO.

UNESCO (1984). *Media education.* Paris: UNESCO.

UNESCO (1987). *Report and papers on mass communication,* no. 80. Paris: UNESCO.

UNESCO (1988). *Informatics in education,* ED-88/MINEDEUROPE. Reference document 5. Paris: UNESCO.

CHAPTER 3

The Information Society – a Challenge for Education Policies? Policy Options and Implementation Strategies

Michael Eraut

3.1 SUMMARY

The assessment of the educational potential of various applications of new information and communication technologies (NICT) is a difficult process. There is much experiment and little evaluation, and the situation is changing quite fast. Hence the important debate about priorities lacks reliable evidence on effectiveness. That debate, however, also concerns the relative merits of different educational goals. The argument is partly ideological and partly about predicting the nature of our society in 10–20 years' time.

Many of the problems of introducing NICT-related change into education can be predicted from what is already known about innovation in education. But such knowledge is not being fully used in spite of early indications that it is still valid and relevant. What emerges from current evaluative research is the need for planned change towards a future that is yet uncertain, while the relevant evidence is only slowly being gathered. In such circumstances, priority should be given to developing a NICT infrastructure within the educational system which can respond flexibly and with increasing capability and capacity to new opportunities and policy changes. The most important part of this infrastructure is people, especially courseware designers and teachers. It is their training and continuing development which should be given the greatest attention.

The educational aims advocated in connection with NICT can be conveniently grouped into the following seven categories:

1. The more effective achievement of existing goals by using new methods such as video presentation or computer-assisted learning.
2. Enabling new goals to be taught within the current curriculum framework of subjects. For example, the vicarious experience brought into the classroom by television, the information-processing potential of computerized databases and the modelling capacity of new interactive software have significantly changed what can be taught in subjects like science and geography.
3. Learning about society and its technology. The onset of the information society must have a major effect on what is taught in the social science and science/technology areas of the curriculum. One major issue is the extent to which this should have a future orientation.
4. Learning to use new information and communication technologies as part of a general programme for developing information-handling and communication skills. This can be taught either as a separate subject, or as part of a cross-curricular approach like study skills. The most ambitious claims in this area relate to the use of computers in developing metacognitive or thinking skills.
5. Learning knowledge and skills appropriate for some specialist occupation. This would be a form of prevocational or vocational education. Computer science, technical graphics and office skills are common examples.
6. Learning to criticize the programmes and products of NICT. The purpose is to develop a more critical approach

from a variety of perspectives. Media studies has tended to follow the tradition of art or literary criticism, while consumer education has focused more on technological or economic aspects. The appraisal of computer software could profitably draw on both traditions.

7. Creative use of NICT for purposes defined by the students themselves. The assumption is that students should not be only at the receiving end of other people's communications. They should learn to produce communications of their own, e.g. class newspapers, videos, computer programs, partly to improve their understanding of the various media and genres but also to develop their enterprise and initiative; and to counteract any monopolistic tendencies in public communications facilities.

It should be noted that these seven categories of aim penetrate into almost every aspect of the curriculum, and include all those aims sometimes advocated under headings like 'media education' and 'computer literacy'. Thus sooner or later the challenge of NICT will have to be treated as a whole curriculum problem. The addition of one or two new subjects into the curriculum is only one approach and, even if it is preferred, will provide only a partial solution. What is eventually needed is a reappraisal of the shape and scope of the whole curriculum and the balance and emphasis within each part of it.

In the primary phase, aims in categories 1, 4 and 6 are particularly important, but their integration into the curriculum will need further planning and development. Both the quantity and the quality of teacher training are major limitations on the pace and direction of change.

At secondary level, too, strategic curriculum decisions are needed. Three alternative strategies have been advocated:

1. Incorporation into the traditional curriculum framework through use of NICT in the teaching of the current curriculum subjects.

2. Insertion into the curriculum for all students of a new subject or subjects. 'Computer literacy' or 'media education' are commonly used names for NICT-oriented subjects but

many other possibilities exist.

3. Addition of optional courses at the middle or upper secondary level. These could be very varied, with titles ranging from 'computer studies' or 'computer science' to 'video production' or 'journalism'.

In the long term, all three routes may be followed. In the short term, financial considerations alone might suggest a progression from route 3 to route 2 to route 1. But this strategy can also cause difficulty, because to start with route 3 alone would turn NICT into a specialist subject with its own distinct membership and culture. Once teachers, trainers and managers had become accustomed to this, it would be difficult to change direction. Deciding between the relative merits of routes 1 and 2 is also difficult, especially for information-handling skills. Finally, the use of school facilities and expertise to improve access for adult and handicapped students is recommended.

Introducing computers into the classroom causes many problems. These can be ameliorated by good management, teacher support and in-service education. So far, however, the needs of teachers engaging in this radical change in educational practice are consistently underestimated. Apart from getting insufficient access to equipment, they find the available software patchy and not well geared to their curriculum. Classroom organization and management pose many problems for which they are unprepared; and they receive little guidance on pedagogic strategies, in spite of growing research evidence of their importance.

At school level the developing NICT culture among teachers and pupils conveys hidden messages about access, gender, the character of NICT enthusiasts, the parallel curriculum of the mass media and the role of NICT in society. School managers need to monitor this hidden curriculum alongside their introduction of INSET into the official curriculum. Each school also needs an ambitious staff development plan, using both external and internal sources of expertise, and to make sure that staff development is properly tuned to the needs of teachers and pupils. Another priority may be the introduction of NICT into school administration. The hardware and software resources have to be managed and expanded according to a financial plan which matches the school's educational priorities.

National policies tend to be unbalanced with the provision of software and training lagging behind the hardware. There is also a clash between equity and effectiveness, because a 'critical mass' is often a necessary consideration when investing in NICT. Causes of the 'software famine' are discussed, together with some approaches to relieving the problem. Software development teams are needed to build the necessary expertise, and there is much scope for international cooperation in this area. However, such teams should be broadened into curriculum development teams which can prepare modules comprising both NICT-based and print-based learning materials and tested pedagogic strategies. Otherwise the software will not be well used or properly integrated into the curriculum.

Finally, teacher training needs are discussed. Provision for classroom teachers has been inadequate hitherto, both in quantity and in quality. It needs to give more attention to the implementation problems encountered by teachers, and to include a school-based component. For this purpose, each school needs a NICT coordinator/staff developer who is trained not only in the use of NICT but in staff development approaches and techniques. Other training priorities are headteachers, teacher trainers, local support personnel and software designers.

3.2 INTRODUCTION

In Chapter 1 Prof. Balle discusses how the development of new information and communication technology (NICT) is shaping our future society, and how the decisions of the next decade will in turn affect how NICT is developed and used. The challenge is two-fold: (1) how can education best prepare for the future information society; and (2) how can educational thinking contribute to the policy-making process and influence those future developments?

Two important features of the future information society that are difficult to predict are the control of communication channels and the nature of employment. What, for example, will be the eventual balance between the monopolistic, internationalizing trend in the ownership of mass media and the new opportunities opening up for local or community channels of communication. Similarly, it is still being debated whether the increasing computerization of work will lead to more skilled jobs or less. Both issues could be affected by the skills and attitudes of the next generation of youngsters and by the capacity of the adult education system to enhance the capabilities of those already in employment.

More predictable, perhaps, is the continuing influence of the 'parallel curriculum' offered by the mass media. This will continue to occupy a large proportion of young people's time and attention, and to provide a marked contrast with the formal curriculum offered by educational establishments. Less predictable is whether computers will also become more prominent in the parallel curriculum than in public education. The evolution of video games and a 'hacking' sub-culture suggests that this is not such an unlikely development; some children already spend many more hours on home computers than on school computers. Indeed, the very unevenness of this access is already causing concern about gender equity and social equality. While the parallel curriculum need not prevent the evolution of the formal curriculum to a shape and style that is seen both to be more stimulating and more relevant and to retain those traditional goals that are still highly valued, there must be considerable doubt as to whether this will actually happen.

Within education, there is still considerable debate about the most appropriate uses of NICT, and especially about which applications should be accorded priority. The debate encompasses two dimensions: goals and effectiveness. Arguments about goals are concerned partly with forecasting what our future society will be like – a process in which people tend to oscillate from scaremongering to complacency or even wishful thinking – and partly with different perspectives on the relationship between education and society, in particular the balance between conserving the past, preparing for the present and constructing the future. These arguments about goals are complex and value-laden, but so also, contrary to popular opinion, are arguments about effectiveness. For although there has been much experiment, there has been little replication and little independent evaluation. Moreover, there is no more agreement about criteria than there is about goals.

The more predictable aspects of using NICT in education derive from what is already known about change. Introducing change into education is a complex business, especially when it affects the nature of classroom life. It requires coordination and continuity over a long period of time, combined with the flexibility to modify programmes and strategies in the light of experience. It requires good management at all levels and a substantial investment in both programme development and teacher training. Evaluative research on the use of NICT during the 1980s has already confirmed that these lessons are often ignored, and that NICT-based innovations are far from being immune to the fate of many unsuccessful predecessors.

What emerges from this brief analysis is the need for planned change towards a future that is yet uncertain. Reviews of policy options and implementation strategies will need to become a regular feature of ministerial life, as this report has a half-life of only five years (i.e. half of it will be out of date by 1994). It is argued, therefore, that some priority will also need to be given to developing a NICT infrastructure within the educational system, which can respond flexibly and with increasing capability and capacity to new opportunities and policy changes as and when they arise. The most important parts of this infrastructure are the courseware designers and the teachers. It is their training and continuing development which should be given the greatest attention.

This report begins with a review of the educational reasons for using NICT and the thinking and experiences which lie behind them. Thus Section 3.3 identifies several types of educational aim that arise when considering the future uses of NICT. Some are traditional aims, built into current practice, the pursuit of which may be aided by the involvement of NICT. Some are new aims which are made possible, perhaps even urgent, by the advent of NICT. The purpose is to clarify the nature of the curriculum debate and to indicate the issues that need to be considered when formulating curriculum policy. Section 3.4 explains the particular form that this curriculum debate is likely to take in primary and secondary education, with a brief additional reference to access by adults. Section 3.5 focuses on implementation, first by reviewing the problems encountered when introducing computers into classrooms, then by considering school-level policy and management issues. Finally, Section 3.6 examines national policies for introducing computers into education, giving special attention to software development and teacher training.

3.3 EDUCATIONAL REASONS FOR USING NEW INFORMATION AND COMMUNICATION TECHNOLOGIES

This section discusses the range of educational aims that can be promoted through the use of NICT. As the list below indicates, some are existing aims pursued by the current curriculum, some require an extension or transformation of existing aims, and some suggest entirely novel curricular goals. All the aims have strong advocates, and most are the subject of pilot projects or developmental research in several European countries. The challenge to education is how to decide priorities between these and other aims and how to accommodate these new opportunities within a curriculum that is already perceived as too crowded.

The educational aims advocated in connection with NICT can be conveniently grouped into the following seven categories:

1. The more effective achievement of existing goals by using new methods such as video presentation of computer-assisted learning.
2. Enabling new goals to be taught within the current curriculum framework of subjects. For example, the vicarious experience brought into the classroom by television, the information-processing potential of computerized databases and the modelling capacity of new interactive software have significantly changed what can be taught in subjects like science and geography.
3. Learning about society and its technology. The onset of the

information society must have a major effect on what is taught in the social science and science/technology areas of the curriculum. One major issue is the extent to which this should have a future orientation.

4. Learning to use new information and communication technologies as part of a general programme for developing information-handing and communication skills. This can be taught either as a separate subject, or as part of a cross-curricular approach like study skills. The most ambitious claims in this area relate to the use of computers in developing metacognitive or thinking skills.

5. Learning knowledge and skills appropriate for some specialist occupation. This would be a form of prevocational or vocational education. Computer science, technical graphics and office skills are common examples.

6. Learning to criticize the programmes and products of NICT. The purpose is to develop a more critical approach from a variety of perspectives. Media studies has tended to follow the tradition of art or literary criticism, while consumer education has focused more on technological or economic aspects. The appraisal of computer software could profitably draw on both traditions.

7. Creative use of NICT for purposes defined by the students themselves. The assumption is that students should not be only at the receiving end of other people's communications. They should learn to produce communications of their own, e.g. class newspapers, videos, computer programs, partly to improve their understanding of the various media and genres but also to develop their enterprise and initiative; and to counteract any monopolistic tendencies in public communications facilities.

It should be noted that these seven categories of aim penetrate into almost every aspect of the curriculum, and include all those aims sometimes advocated under headings like 'media education' and 'computer literacy'. Thus sooner or later the challenge of NICT will have to be treated as a whole curriculum problem. The addition of one or two new subjects into the curriculum is only one approach and, even if it is preferred, will provide only a partial solution. What is eventually needed is a reappraisal of the shape and scope of the whole curriculum and the balance and emphasis within each part of it (DES, 1989).

This section, therefore, will attempt to characterize and examine each of the seven groups of aims listed above, to assess relevant findings from pilot projects and research, to highlight significant issues and to indicate those factors which curriculum policy-makers will need to consider. The situation is complex because the decision-making process involves:

deciding what priority should be given to each curriculum goal;

choosing between different curriculum approaches to achieve the selected goals;

assessing how much can be achieved by a particular approach in any given context.

These are interdependent rather than sequential judgements and the available evidence is limited.

Before I discuss these matters in greater detail, two major problems should be noted. First, curricular goals are rarely tackled one at a time, nor would it be economical if they were. So in pursuing one goal, a teacher is likely to take advantage of the opportunity to contribute to others. In particular, teachers will claim to be developing a range of general knowledge and skills while focusing on much more specific areas of content. Thus students may learn about computers or acquire general information-handling skills while primarily focusing on the study of a particular topic in a particular subject. There is little evidence, however, to indicate the extent to which such general knowledge and skills have been acquired in this way (see below). Some would argue, for example, that much of this learning is a natural part of a pupil's intellectual development and relatively independent of formal teaching.

The second major problem is closely related. Most assessment techniques were developed to measure achievement in the traditional goals of education: basic skills, comprehension and the simple application of concepts and algorithms in highly predictable ways. Hence, although the Assessment of Performance Unit in the UK and the International Association for the Evaluation of Educational Achievement (IEA) have expanded the testing repertoire in language, mathematics and science, there are still many educational goals for which valid methods of assessment have yet to be developed. Assessment is also a highly politicized aspect of education, with scores on public examinations and tests of basic skills being treated as major public indicators of standards. This makes it difficult to change curriculum priorities, as Alan Bennett noted in his play *Forty Years On*:

> 'But don't you think, Headmaster, that your standards are out of date?'
> 'Of course they are! They wouldn't be standards otherwise!'

Thus, partly because of technical limitations, partly because of limited time, partly because of political pressures, and partly because of the uncertainty surrounding the attribution of cause and effect in the development of general skills, evaluations of pilot projects have tended to focus on measuring achievement of traditional goals alone.

THE MORE EFFECTIVE ACHIEVEMENT OF EXISTING GOALS

The longest-running tradition in evaluation research is the comparative study, in which one method of teaching is 'tested' against another by comparing gains in student achievement over a period of time. For 30 years this approach has shown that in a large proportion of such experiments there are no significant differences between one method and another. Most evaluators have become disenchanted with this approach for a variety of reasons, including the following:

- Where either or both 'treatments' involve teachers, the variation between teachers exceeds that between methods. Indeed even when teachers are absent, within–class variations can be considerable.

- The quality of the message is at least as important as its mode of delivery. Many comparisons are made with programmes that educators consider to be of low or medium quality.
- The idea of using a single method alone for a long period of time is pedagogically naive. One should be looking for the best mix.
- Even when one method is shown to be 'superior' for one topic, no educator would seriously consider using it all the time.
- The cost factor is often conveniently omitted.

Media research proceeded along similar non-productive lines until researchers finally concluded that media selection was more appropriately considered at the level of the individual learning activity (Heidt, 1985; Levie, 1985). Only then can the most appropriate combination of attributes be selected for the particular kind of information being communicated and the particular kind of learning that is expected to occur. Other studies have shown that the main factors affecting the classroom use of audio-visual media are:

flexibility of use and ease of operation under normal classroom conditions;

availability of good audio-visual materials;

the pedagogic knowledge and media experience of the teacher;

cost.

Flexibility has significantly improved with the arrival of video-cassettes, and will be further enhanced by video disks. The introduction of video disks will finally solve the main technical problems, but may be considerably delayed by economic problems. The availability of suitable software, for example, will depend on the development of a specifically educational market. In the long term, the teacher factor may prove to be the most significant; that will be further discussed in Section 3.6.

With computers a rather different picture has emerged. Kulik and Kulik's (1987) meta-analysis of 200 comparative studies in the USA showed an average effect size of 0.31 standard deviations, i.e. examination scores were raised by about 6 per cent. Nearly all these studies involved courses or sections of courses, situated in computer laboratories with one work station for each student, and using drill and practice or a didactic tutoring mode of instruction. What is the objection to everyone installing computer laboratories for this purpose? The arguments centre round cost, pedagogy and uncertain effects.

The cost-effectiveness of computer-assisted instruction is still subject to considerable debate. Levin (1986), for example, has argued that peer group tutoring offers better value for money at primary level, and that in mathematics, a substantial reduction in class size would also yield better results. He also showed that in the school context the hardware accounted for only 11 per cent of the total expenditure. So although hardware costs may fall, the total cost of laboratory-based CAI will not decline much further.

It is often stated that it is the interactiveness of computers that is responsible for their superior performance in these comparative studies. Yet the main pedagogic criticism is that typical CAI is not interactive enough. Critics, often from within the computing fraternity, argue that CAI comes close to coaching students for tests which inadequately sample the subject domain, drilling them only in the more easily replicated surface features of a subject. To refute this accusation would require a detailed review of the software and the assessment instruments, neither of which is adequately described in the public research.

Against this background of pedagogic debate, there is very little evidence from process studies to suggest the reason for the apparent success of CAI. Even the Kuliks argue that more research is needed on this issue. Until we understand rather more about how and what students learn from CAI, few institutions are likely to invest in it on any significant scale.

The advent of microcomputers was responsible for the rapid diversification of computer-based learning away from the laboratory model, although that model still remains dominant in a large number of places, especially for courses in computer science or computer literacy (see below). During the 1980s computers have been increasingly tried out in normal or slightly modified classroom settings, where evaluation has been much more difficult. Comparative experiments are of little use when the computer is rarely given responsibility for the teaching of a whole topic, and interactions between student and computer are typically quite short. Moreover, the variations between contexts and patterns of computer use in classrooms have been far too great to characterize any one pattern as being 'the experimental treatment'. Research into this multitude of classroom-based experiments has been limited. It has necessarily focused on independent observations of process and product, and has rarely sought to intervene with special tests or examinations.

Nevertheless, researchers and other observers of the newly developing classroom-based computer scene are agreed on a number of points.

1. Only a few teachers have managed to integrate use of the computer into their normal programmes of classroom work.
2. Some teachers are engaged with their pupils on a voyage of discovery about computers.
3. There is much bad practice with students wasting time or engaged in relatively meaningless activities.
4. Much more teacher preparation is needed for effective classroom use of computers.
5. For a variety of reasons, there is still a desperate shortage of good software.
6. The potential of computers for aiding learning is still largely unexplored.
7. What is known is still relatively unexploited.
8. Large numbers of positive experiences continue to motivate teachers and students alike.

More detailed accounts of this classroom evidence will be given in Section 3.5. Here it can be noted that although greater time and effort needs to be given to implementation, there is still much to encourage the further development of computers as aids to achieving many current curricular goals.

The other major change in computer-assisted learning has been a move away from the tutorial mode of computer–

learner interaction towards more learner-centred approaches. In the *tutorial mode* the designer retains the initiative throughout, and the user responds as asked: user choice is confined to selecting an option on a menu, constructing an answer to a question or calling for repetition or help. The least sophisticated forms involve drill and practice exercises with facts, spellings or arithmetic – sometimes presented in interesting diagrammatic formats or as games. The most sophisticated involve what is commonly referred to as ICAI (intelligent computer-aided instruction) or just as 'intelligent tutoring'. In theory, it is said to build a tutoring system around knowledge of the subject, knowledge of the student and knowledge of how to help the student learn (Sleeman and Brown, 1982). But major problems immediately arise. How is knowledge of the subject to be represented? How is knowledge of the student to be obtained and used? How is knowledge of how to help the student learn to be raised above the current level of ad hocery? Some commentators (e.g. Self, 1987) believe these aims are unachievable. While the ordinary tutoring mode can make a useful contribution, especially to distance learning, we should not be deluded into thinking that enormous improvements in design technique are 'just around the corner'.

More learner-centred approaches start from two premises: that learning goals are defined by the users rather than the software; and the role of the computer is to assist users to achieve these goals. In the *inquiry mode* (see Table 1) the assistance may take the form of a calculating facility or providing information from various databases; or the student may be allowed to interact with a simulation or consult an expert system. The computer retains the role of knowledge provider, but the users decide what knowledge they want and how they will use it. In the *constructive mode*, however, even the knowledge provider role is abandoned. Both the goals and the relevant information come from the users. The role of the computer is to enable them to record, manipulate, organize, retrieve, present and communicate that knowledge. The simplest examples are the use of a word processor for writing, a graphics package for presentation, or a database for organizing evidence from surveys. More subtle software includes electronic notepads, writing aids, design aids and programmes for

Table 1 Student use of computers: a typology of modes and applications

Type of information	Mode of use		
	Tutorial mode (system knowledge, system goals)	Inquiry mode (system knowledge, student goals)	Constructive mode (student knowledge, student goals)
Facts	Drill and	Databases	Databases
Pictures	practice	(other data)	(own data)
Drawings			
Algorithms		Calculation	*Programming*
Diagrams			Electronic notepad
Outlines			Graphics package
Displays			
Tables			
Questions			Design aid
Answers	*Tutoring*		*Word processing*
Prose		*Information retrieval*	*Writing aid*
Models	Intelligent tutoring	Simulations	Modelling
Organized conceptual knowledge			*Desktop publishing*
Expertise		Expert systems	
Control of peripherals			

The italicized terms are broader in scope than the others, and cannot be located in a single position in their columns.

179

desktop publishing. Then at the most sophisticated level students may engage in constructing their own programs for computer-controlled devices or their own models of complex phenomena and their interrelationships.

While some of the work in the inquiry mode and the constructive mode falls within existing curricular goals, their exploration is increasingly causing teachers and researchers to realize that important new goals are now becoming attainable (see the next section). Indeed the proper balance between existing goals and new goals is becoming a matter for considerable debate. Recent discussions can be found in Cerych and Jallade (1986), Gwyn (1986), OECD/CERI (1986) and especially OECD/CERI (1987a).

NEW GOALS WITHIN CURRENT CURRICULUM SUBJECTS

This section reviews some of the new learning experiences now becoming available for inclusion in the curriculum as a result of NICT. While some are clearly directed at new curricular goals, others come closer to supporting existing goals but are still regarded as making a novel contribution to their subject. Indeed, deciding whether or not a particular application falls within old or new territory depends not only on the country but also on the criteria being used. The curriculum may be formally defined in terms of aims and content, informally defined in terms of expectations and tradition, and operationally defined in terms of textbooks and examinations. These new experiences often place a strong emphasis on inquiry skills and conceptual development.

The most easily appreciated advantage of NICT is the access it can bring to new kinds of information. The key developments here are in electronic communications and video disk technology. Electronic communications have already arrived. It is possible for schools to get up-to-date information from a wide range of external data sources, allowing the continuing analysis of such phenomena as economic trends, current affairs and weather patterns to bring a sense of immediacy akin to that so prevalent in the 'parallel curriculum' of the mass media. Electronic mail partnerships can also be used to develop students' communication skills and to enhance their understanding of peers in other countries, a boost to international understanding that has yet to be fully developed or evaluated.

Video disk technology, as suggested earlier, ought to help make the use of audio-visual materials far more flexible. It allows smooth and flexible transitions from still pictures to moving picture sequences, the facility to freeze or repeat, fast search and retrieval and the opportunity to follow up unforeseen needs for information. When more software becomes available, teachers will be able to use a much wider range of visual evidence, and to use it much more flexibly. One major limitation will be the teachers' skill and imagination. Another will be the quality and appropriateness of the disks. One can foresee the interconnected use of maps, photographs and diagrams in geography; the reference in history to archaeological evidence, portraits and manuscripts; the viewing of dangerous or difficult experiments in science; comparisons of dramatic performances in literature; and an enormous range of audio-visual experiences to support the teaching of foreign languages. Most of these things can be done with today's technology, but the time and effort involved is too great for most teachers. When those difficulties are lessened, wider and more integrated use of audio-visual material will follow, with consequent demands on resources.

The other major advantage of NICT lies in the tools it puts at the command of the learner for writing, calculating, information-processing and problem-solving. While writing forms a central part of the traditional curriculum there is evidence that changes in attitude and approach are being achieved by the introduction of word processors. Writing is being professionalized for children, not only in the quality of the final presentation but also in the way the task is being approached. The multiple drafting process is welcomed as it becomes less troublesome, and the criteria by which writing is judged are becoming more explicit, more widely shared and more meaningful (Broderick and Trushell, 1985; Marcus, 1984; Miller, 1986; Pearson and Wilkinson, 1986).

Mathematics can also be transformed by using the computer as a tool, not only because of its calculating facility but also because of the range of methods of data representation. This opens up the possibility of making greater use of numerical data right across the curriculum, for numerophobes and numerophiles alike. Mathematicians have suggested that the use of computers should enable greater attention to be given to iterative numerical techniques, statistics and probability, procedures and algorithms (including programming), geometrical topics facilitated by having a computer graphics facility, and matrices and vectors (which are used both for storing data in computers and for getting computers to draw pictures and representations of three-dimensional objects) (Ball *et al.*, 1986). More radical still is the approach of Papert and his followers, who advocate a programming/problem-solving approach to learning. Most of their work has been in the field of mathematics, where they have pursued an entirely different kind of mathematics curriculum (Feurzeig, 1986). Independent evaluations have been very varied, however, suggesting that more attention needs to be given to the context, purpose and pattern of use (Ennals, 1986; Govier, 1988; Hoyles and Sutherland, 1989; Hughes *et al.*, 1985).

The information-processing facility of computers is also used in databases which may be used in either the inquiry or the constructive mode, according to the purpose. In primary schools they are used to develop classification and inquiring skills in a variety of content areas; in secondary schools they are used in history and geography. Combining the database facility with the numerical data-processing facilities allows many aspects of the social science curriculum to take on quite a different character, with greater attention to data analysis and inquiry methods than would be possible in a computerless curriculum. Simulations are equally popular in these subjects, with the additional computer facilities allowing a more sophisticated and more numerical approach than would otherwise be possible (Kent, 1986; Wild, 1988). Again, many would argue that this kind of work gives learners a different view of the discipline and a deeper understanding of certain key features of its subject matter. In the natural sciences, for example, students can engage in simulated experiments in which they manipulate the variables, using the computer to perform any necessary calculations. Some of these experiments might be impossible to carry out in real life, as for example with a simulated ecological system; while others might be extremely lengthy to perform once, let alone ten times under a range of different conditions.

Similar arguments are presented by proponents of the use of the computer to support problem-solving or thinking behaviour (Pea, 1985). Appropriately directed programming often has this aim (Papert, 1980; Gwyn, 1986; OECD/CERI, 1987a). Papert's concept of designing a 'microworld environment' in which children can solve problems by developing appropriate programs, is one approach (Lewis, 1988). Another is provided by programs designed as tools to assist pupils to develop mental models of a knowledge domain (Bliss and Ogborn, 1988). Introducing work of this kind into the curriculum would give much greater attention to students developing their own theories and testing them out, in accordance with the increasing emphasis by some cognitive psychologists on the importance for learning of children's own informal theories.

Finally, there is a range of peripheral devices which computers can be used to control, ranging from lathes, through looms and robots, to electronic keyboards (SED, 1987).

To conclude this section, it should be noted once more that the question of whether a goal is new or not will often be difficult to answer, because some curricular goals have rather ambiguous status. For example, curriculum documents may contain references to problem-solving or inquiry skills, which are pursued by only a small minority of teachers. Yet these goals are precisely those given the greatest emphasis by advocates of using computers in the inquiry or constructive modes. The most promising development is that the use of database and modelling software and programming environments like Logo is making inquiry and problem-solving processes more explicit, and hence more easily incorporated into the curriculum experienced by pupils, rather than only the paper curriculum of educators' aspirations.

LEARNING ABOUT SOCIETY AND ITS TECHNOLOGY

One of the principal aims of education is to prepare future generations to take over from those currently making our society work. The complexity of even today's society, the increasingly rapid pace of change and the already foreseeable challenges that lie ahead in such fields as energy, environment, development and international relations make this a daunting task. But as Broudy (1986) has asserted, 'the central civic activity of the citizen is to participate in decisions concerning the public good'. We now have the capacity to educate future generations better than their forebears. But will we use it to prepare them sufficiently for the tasks that lie ahead? And will they emerge from schooling with a sufficiently positive attitude towards education to want to participate in periodic continuing education thereafter? The context of this paper makes it particularly apposite to ask:

- What will school leavers in the 1990s know about the society we live in, particularly about the role of information within it?
- What will they know of the mathematical, scientific, economic and technological knowledge that underpins the way information is organized, stored, distributed and achieved?
- What will they know about the interactive relationship between information technology, information control and society?

Although some lonely voices were heard long ago, it was not until the late 1970s and early 1980s that the onset of a future post-industrial information-dominated society began to be widely discussed. As a result few of our teachers or curriculum policy-makers are able to participate in a properly informed debate about its role in the curriculum. Hence there is a propensity to deal with the issue by creating new specialisms rather than reforming the current curriculum in such areas as the social sciences and citizenship education. To deal with the information society only in courses in 'computer literacy' or 'media education' is to separate it from mainstream discussions about the nature and future of our society. The Carnegie Commission on Education (Boyer, 1983) commented on the problem as follows:

> The great urgency is not 'computer literacy' but 'technology literacy', the need for students to see how society is being reshaped by our inventions, just as tools of earlier eras changed the course of history. The challenge is not learning *how* to use the latest piece of hardware but asking *when* and *why* it should be used.

This problem has already been encountered in science education, where such matters as the impact of science and society and science policy have traditionally been treated as 'extras', while the scientific and technology dimension has been so lacking from most history books as to give an entirely false impression of the nature of historical change.

This argument leads me to three conclusions. The first is that the role of communications and technology needs to be properly integrated into the study of the past, the present and the future. The second is that the rapidity of change is such that more attention needs to be given to the study of the present and the future than has been customary in most nations hitherto. Third, and possibly more contentiously, I would argue that much study will not lead to sufficient understanding of the issues if it cannot be based on a good grounding of economic awareness and understanding.

The conclusions present a considerable challenge to curriculum developers. How are they to make accessible to pupils the central concepts and issues discussed in important documents like the MacBride Report to UNESCO, *Many Voices, One World: Communication and Society Today and Tomorrow* (1979), or the Friedrichs and Schaff Report to the Club of Rome, *Microelectronics and Society, For Better or For Worse* (1982)? And if this material is to be discussed in the upper secondary school, what foundations will need to be laid for it in the lower secondary curriculum? However, comprehension may not be the only problem. A careful course has to be steered between a technological determinism, which treats change as inevitable and beyond social and political influence, and a wilful neglect of trends and phenomena which will have major effects on our society (Taylor and Johnsen, 1986). More difficult still is the pedagogic skill required of teachers in areas where there are political pressure groups and value differences can be highly politicized. But this is equally true of other areas of the curriculum, where properly professional approaches to handling value issues in the classroom have been developed. It would also be a mistake to overestimate the likelihood of teachers having any effect at all on the values of upper secondary students. Opportunities to clarify values and discuss important issues are welcomed, but the imposition of a teacher viewpoint is always rejected.

Finally, I wish to draw attention to the problem of how much understanding of computers should be included in the technology component of the curriculum. The pedagogic challenge is that of linking pupils' concrete experiences of computer use to generic knowledge about such matters as programs, computer architecture and even expert systems, which will provide them with some background to follow the changing technology and better understand the impact of computers in daily life (Neuwirth, 1986). The widely quoted syllabus prepared by the Association for Teacher Education in Europe (van Weert, 1984) suggests that pupils should study the societal impact of NICT, the applications which are making the impact, principles of programming and principles of software and machine architecture. This was conceived as part of a proposed 'computer literacy' course. Recently, however, more integrated approaches have also been considered, and the new national curriculum in England and Wales is concerned to build these particular aspects of NICT into a foundation design and technology component for all pupils from 5 to 16. This will enable NICT to be integrated with other technologies in a general problem-solving approach to design and technology which involves designing, making and evaluating artefacts and systems (DES, 1988).

GENERAL INFORMATION-HANDLING AND COMMUNICATION SKILLS

For some time, advocates of student-centred learning have argued that students need to develop information skills. This phrase can include aspects of what are sometimes called 'library skills', 'study skills' or even 'reading development' (Marland, 1981). An extension to include the interpretation and use of a whole range of graphical modes of representation would also seem appropriate. It can then be argued that the use of computers can play a significant part in facilitating the development and use of these skills, although it also adds to the 'syllabus' the additional skills required to use the computer itself in a range of applications. Carter and Monaco (1987), who studied computer usage in ten schools from an information skills perspective, report that 'the introduction of IT into schools does *not* appear to require pupils to acquire information skills which differ significantly from those required to utilize all media'. Moreover, the use of IT was the least of the pupils' problems. Far more important were lack of understanding of what they were doing and the inability to visualize the information in a different way. More appropriate use of IT could help tackle some of these problems. This suggests that IT applications can be profitably learned and practised as part of the development of information skills.

The applications studied by Carter and Monaco, mainly databases, word processing and teletext, are often taught as part of a general 'introduction to computing' course. They would argue that this is likely to divert attention from information skills *per se* on to computer operating skills alone; but this would depend on the kind of activities pursued. Theoretically, it should be possible to develop information skills within any curriculum area. Other applications commonly included in such courses are spreadsheets and simple calculations and graphics. Here the additional facilities provided by the computer could profitably be used to extract meaning from print-based media such as books and newspapers, and hence to develop a much more critical approach to graphically displayed information and statistics. Sometimes programming is also included in such courses, but it does not really belong in this category of aims.

Other media which might usefully be included in a course on information and communication skills are photography and sound recording. They are particularly well suited to work with young children and vividly illustrate how information is always selective and sometimes deliberately misleading. Sound can be used to develop listening and speaking skills, and photographs to stimulate or illustrate written communication. The use of more complex media is discussed below.

Finally, this is probably an appropriate place to examine the claims of Papert and others that programming enhances general cognitive skills. On the whole these claims have not been substantiated. In those few cases where positive evidence was obtained, there was considerable intervention to provoke reflection and metacognitive analysis while children were at work. Salomon and Perkins (1987) conclude from a penetrating review of the issue that computer programming is no more effective in achieving this aim than other specially designed procedures for developing problem-solving skills. As with information skills, the thinking is the key and that takes place in the mind of the thinker, whether or not the stimulus is a computer program.

PREVOCATIONAL OR VOCATIONAL EDUCATION

The strategic argument about the relative merits of a 'computer literacy' course for all, incorporating many of the goals outlined above, and a 'computer studies' course for a few will be taken up in Section 3.4. Meanwhile it is useful to consider 'computer studies' as a prevocational or vocational course, recognizing that such courses may be offered in the later stages of compulsory education, in post-compulsory upper secondary education or in technical/vocational colleges.

Jallade's (1984) review of NICT and technical education defines four groups of NICT users:

1. Specialists at three levels: (a) high-level specialists who receive university training in NICT and become designers of systems, designers of applications and specialist teachers of NICT; (b) middle-level specialists who receive 'short cycle' higher education plus in-company training; (c) maintenance and service personnel, who obtain technical/vocational qualifications and also receive in-company training.
2. Professional 'appliers' who combine professional qualifications with an additional qualification in NICT.

188

3. NICT users 'on-the-job' whose jobs now require fairly routine use of NICT: this is being built into a large number of technical/vocational qualifications, and is also a major concern of in-company training.
4. NICT users 'off-the-job', for whom NICT training is about uses of NICT in the home and community.

Evidence suggests that the recruitment of high-level specialists does not depend on the presence of 'computer studies' in the school sector, but rather on strong and appropriate science education at the upper secondary level. Maintenance and service personnel receive their vocational training either in upper level secondary education or in technical colleges, but there are signs that much of this work will soon be at 'higher technician level'. In either case the requirement from compulsory schooling is not an early specialism in computer studies but a good general education in mathematics, science and technology. Some prior experience in working with computers would seem to be an important element in career choice but that should be offered within the core curriculum, with an emphasis on the general development of thinking and problem-solving skills.

This same theme is echoed by a recent OECD/CERI (1988) report on human resources in one major group of IT users, the banks and insurance companies. This reported that the new skill requirements of middle-tier workers seem to place a premium on 'liberal arts' education at the secondary and even early post high school level, and quoted a bank official as follows: 'The bank can train anyone in becoming proficient in the use of specific techniques and procedures; the bank cannot train individual workers in thinking for themselves, in being at ease with broad and complex environments.' Bertrand and Noyelle continue with the following comment: 'Most firms regard such training (in the use of new technologies) as quite trivial when compared with other training needs. In the long run, also, it is widely assumed that the new generation of workers will graduate from high school and college proficient in the use of the new tool.'

From this analysis it appears that the main challenge for vocational education will be not the creation or continuation of separate computer studies programmes, but the transformation of existing vocational programmes to take the developing role of NICT more fully into account. As with modern languages, competence in NICT is likely to become an additional requirement of many existing occupations, though, at some stage in the future, vocational courses may be able to assume that their students arrive with some computer-related skills already acquired. Another point stressed in a useful review by Hunter (1986) is the need, when considering computer applications, for an increased focus on the cognitive aspects of tasks, such as analysis, decision-making, troubleshooting and problem-solving. This is particularly urgent in business education/commerce courses.

The arguments above should not be applied to optional courses which allow students to develop their interests and talents. These allow the use of NICT for personal and community purposes to be explored in a context free of purely vocational considerations. Such opportunities should apply across the full range of NICT and not be focused primarily on computers. Video production, for example, could be equally valuable; this is more fully discussed below.

NICT CRITICISM

While the general study of the role of NICT in our society was discussed above, one aspect, the criticism of particular programmes and products, needs separate consideration. Claims and assumptions about the quality of programmes need to be properly substantiated, and this is a prime goal for media education, in whatever curricular form it appears. Historically, an aesthetic approach has tended to dominate, but from a wide range of viewpoints. Many teachers have traditionally treated the mass media as an undesirable influence against which children have to be protected. Others have challenged this 'high culture' perspective by treating programmes as forms of popular art and helping children to discriminate between good and bad examples of each genre. Given the range of mediated messages this poses enormous problems of priorities. A recent UNESCO conference (Masterman, 1986) suggested that this be resolved by reference to the primary aim of developing critical autonomy in pupils. The acid test of any media education programme is for students to have the confidence, experience, skills and maturity 'to apply critical judgements to media texts which they have not yet seen' and to be 'critical in their own use and understanding of the media when the teacher is not there'.

To achieve this purpose, media education has to move beyond the exchange of opinions to a deeper understanding of how media structure and represent information (UNESCO, 1984). Mediated messages are not neutral, transparent windows on the world but constructed by particular people with particular goals and assumptions for transmission to particular audiences. Moreover, these audiences are not passive but actively make their own meanings and interpretations of what they receive. Such an approach combines the concerns of the literacy critic with the construction and personal impact of texts and the social scientist's concerns with public meanings, the control of communications and ideology. Both humanists and social scientists are agreed on the need to understand how mediated messages are constructed in order properly to appreciate and criticize them – though their subsequent judgements may be made according to rather different sets of criteria. Some of this understanding can be developed by including discussions of media images in a range of traditional subjects. History and geography are particularly important in this regard because so much knowledge in this area is acquired outside school. But more detailed study will depend on the teachers themselves being adequately trained in media education (Masterman, 1988).

Another theme that falls within this section is that of consumer education, where aesthetics, economics and technology may be brought together to assess the relative merits of various consumer products. Again it could be argued that some background knowledge of industry would be helpful, as suggested above. This is also an area where the information skills described above should be used to find useful paths through the maze of consumer guides. In this context, we are primarily concerned with NICT-related products, such as players, receivers and recorders of audio and audio-visual messages – many of which are bought by students of school age.

However, attention should also be given to computer software. Although such consumer education involves quite different areas of knowledge and expertise, it could still be based on the same primary aim as that adopted by media education, namely the development of critical autonomy.

CREATIVE USE OF NICT FOR STUDENT-DEFINED PURPOSES

Several reasons have been advanced for giving students facilities and space within the curriculum to construct images, programs or products for their own purposes. One reason follows from our discussion about critical autonomy. The argument is that first-hand experience of constructing a photograph, a video, a newspaper or a computer program is central to understanding the central concepts of structuring and representation of communication. Another argument is more instrumental, suggesting that having to construct a communication develops a deeper understanding of the content of that communication, partly by developing motivation and enthusiasm for the task and partly from the learning that comes from engaging in groupwork, when ideas that might be passively accepted from a teacher or a textbook can become the centre of prolonged and searching discussion. A third argument sees such creative work with NICT as a natural extension of expression in written text, in art, in music or in technological design.

For me the most powerful argument of all comes from an analysis of the role of NICT in society. Control of communication is not only a matter of political and economic power, it is also a matter of confidence, determination and perception. NICT can be used for personal purposes and to empower local communities, provided people develop the skills and motivation to make NICT serve their own interests as much as other people's. Moles (1984) discusses the role of the self-media in communicating from oneself to oneself over a period of time. In addition to diaries and snapshots, we now have home videos and electronic notebooks. At community level the arrival of cheaper sound and video equipment of near broadcast quality, of increased channels for electronic communication and of desktop publishing has transformed the potential for quality communication. Apart from the enormous enthusiasm such work engenders in students and the concomitant development of their communication skills, this aim must surely be justified as central to the emancipatory role of education. Those very aspects of education that some people fear will be eroded by NICT could become the areas where it has some of its most positive impact.

3.4 INCORPORATING NICT-RELATED AIMS INTO THE CURRICULUM

This section takes the seven types of aim described in Section 3.3 and assesses their significance for curriculum policy in primary and secondary schools. The presentation is intended to clarify policy options and critical issues for policy-making, through discussion not only of priorities but also of the curriculum formats in which the various aims may be pursued. A final section then looks at access to school-level provision by adults and by children with special needs.

THE PRIMARY PHASE

Many European nations have deliberately not introduced computers into primary schools but other new technologies, notably television, usually play a significant role. One distinctive feature of primary education in some countries is the greater flexibility of organization of both the classroom and the curriculum. This makes it possible for a good primary teacher to use a television programme as a stimulus for a series of activities with a whole-class thematic focus and to use a microcomputer with two or three children working on their own. Most would like to have at least three such computers but do not necessarily need many more. This adaptability has led many observers of the British scene to comment that computers have been better used in primary than in secondary schools. However, primary teachers have not found it easy to integrate computers into the curriculum, and typical practice lags well behind that reported by the enthusiasts (see Section 3.5).

The best use of NICT in primary education has possibly been in language development, perhaps because teachers feel most confident in this part of the curriculum and have been quickest to see the potential. Audio-visual media have been used to capture children's imagination and hence to stimulate language production in speech and in writing – a use that is highly dependent on the skill of the teacher. Adventure games on computers have now begun to be used in a similar kind of way, while sound is used both to stimulate and to record children's own stories. The impact of word processing appears to be of quite a different kind. Although the exploration of its potential is still in its infancy, already there are signs that it could have a dramatic effect on children learning to write. Not only is the improved appearance of the product motivating, but the ease of redrafting and discussion of drafts brings within most children's reach the kind of attention to language structure and audience that linguists have always considered desirable but difficult to achieve in practice. It has the power to transform writing from a physical chore to an exciting meta-cognitive activity (Dunstan, 1988).

Applications in mathematics may eventually prove equally exciting but await improved access, more and better software, and increased teacher understanding before their potential is realized. The prevalence of thematic or topic work in the primary curriculum creates information handling demands which computers are well suited to meet. It also offers opportunities for introducing information in a variety of media forms. This kind of use is less demanding of regular access to equipment and therefore more readily introduced. What frequently happens, though, is that topic work is claimed to be developing language and information skills when it is presenting little real challenge to the children. Making the process more visible may alert teachers to the realization that such things have to be taught.

Finally, one should stress the real potential for introducing media criticism and production into primary education. Children are already receivers of mass communications and enjoy critical discussion and especially developing mediated messages of their own, such as newspapers, radio programmes or photoplays. Such work is often easier to organize at primary level because timetables are less rigid and motivating cross-curricular themes are considered to be a bonus (British Film Institute, 1989).

THE SECONDARY PHASE

There are three routes by which NICT can be incorporated into the secondary curriculum:

1. Incorporation into the traditional curriculum framework through use of NICT in the teaching of the current curriculum subjects.
2. Insertion into the curriculum for all students of a new subject or subjects. 'Computer literacy' and 'media education' are commonly used names for NICT-oriented subjects, but many other possibilities exist.
3. Addition of optional courses at the middle or upper secondary level. These could be very varied, with titles ranging from 'computer studies' or 'computer science' to 'video production' or 'journalism'.

In the long term these three routes are not competitors, because one can envisage all three being followed at once; it is certainly difficult to imagine the first route not being part of any future strategy. However, in the short term, the extreme shortage of what is still very costly equipment (in the context of public education budgets) and of teachers trained to maximize the potential of NICT, the three routes appear as alternatives. This is particularly true for computers, which have arrived on the educational scene rather more suddenly than television, and with stronger community expectations for immediate responses from schools.

Route 1 is increasingly favoured by educators, as it makes the technology the servant rather than the master of the curriculum. This argument welcomes routes 2 and 3 alongside route 1, but opposes the segregation of NICT implied in pursuing routes 2 and 3 alone. However, route 1 is also the most ambitious and expensive approach. It requires as much hardware as route 2 and considerably more software; above all, it requires that all teachers become confident users of NICT. Routes 2 and 3 require only that specialist teachers are trained. From a purely financial viewpoint there is an obvious progression from route 3 to route 2 to route 1 as each transition involves a step-up in funding. But there are strong arguments against regarding such a progression as easy.

Treating NICT as a specialist area of knowledge will establish it as a separate subject, both distinctively technical and threatening to other subjects' resources and 'territory'. This will create a psychological barrier for many would-be NICT users, and make it more difficult for teachers of other subjects to take up NICT later when route 1 is finally pursued. Even the transition from route 3 to route 2 is fraught with difficulty, because research in curriculum history has shown that subject communities play a very powerful role in determining how knowledge is conceptualized and which educational goals have been given priority (Goodson, 1983). If one defines a new subject in terms of specialist expertise, then one is giving the pioneers of that subject, on whom one will have to rely for its future development, a particular kind of occupational identity. To switch at some later stage from route 3 to route 2 is likely to make the kind of course offered in route 2 similar in emphasis to the original specialist provision. This is because to start with a specialist option is to develop a subject community whose attitudes and predilections are oriented towards specialist goals.

Another danger in pursuing route 3 on its own is that different groups of students will take advantage of it to different degrees. Girls, in particular, are less likely to choose specialist options perceived as technological. Hence, although British curriculum policy has now endorsed route 1, the effect of the increase in computer studies courses at school level over the past ten years has been to lower the proportion of women taking computer science degrees (Large and Bradbury, 1989).

These comments are not meant to imply that route 3 would not be the most appropriate choice in some national contexts. That would depend on the existing location of prevocational and vocational courses. Where vocational training is primarily located outside the upper secondary school, it would seem anomalous to have such options within the school sector, although, as discussed in Section 3.3, it is still possible to have NICT-related options that do not have a primarily vocational orientation. Within the vocational course sector, there is also the danger highlighted by Hunter (1986) that provision will be dominated by preparation for specialist NICT jobs at the expense of the growing NICT-related requirement of a large number of traditional occupations.

The introduction of new NICT-related subjects into the common curriculum offered to all children (route 2) also requires careful consideration. Let us begin by considering the long-term situation. If NICT becomes sufficiently available for use by all secondary school teachers to support teaching and learning in every area of the curriculum, will these new NICT-related subjects still be needed? For the sake of this argument, I shall assume that the role of NICT in society and some understanding of its technology will have been fully incorporated by then into the core curriculum in the social sciences and technology. The debate then hinges around the most appropriate way to pursue the aims of information-handling skills, criticism of mediated communications and programme/software production.

Let us begin with information-handling skills. Since this has been taught in some schools since the pre-computer era, there is relevant experience to build on. Evidence from UK schools suggests a genuine dilemma over whether it is better to have a separate subject or a cross-curricular approach. One argument is the impossibility of teaching skills without content – and if there is to be content why should it not be content taken from the normal curriculum? If the content is not seen as important by the children, then the whole process can become self-defeating. A second argument is that of transfer. Will the information-handling skills acquired on a separate course be reinforced and further developed in the rest of the curriculum? The third is the converse of the second: if information skills are to be taught through a cross-curricular approach will there be sufficient coherence and progression? Indeed, will some aims ever get implemented? There is good evidence that very few schools have successfully translated cross-curricular rhetoric into actual practice. These arguments focus around two main issues:

1. Within any particular information-handling task, how much of the initial know-how can be ascribed to generalized information-handling skills and how much to content-specific knowledge and methodology?
2. Will teachers in general become sufficiently learner-centred to see developing pupils' approaches to learning and inquiry as a major part of their task?

The first is an essentially curricular issue, the second a challenge for teacher training. I would be surprised if any nation was able to reach a consensus on either!

One rather complicated strategy that straddles these two alternatives would be to devise an information skills curriculum to be taught by teachers from several subjects on a modular basis, each teacher using his or her own subject content in the allotted module but also being responsible for liaison between his or her own subject and the information skills team. A strategy similar to this is used in Sweden (Makrakis, 1988). Certainly, there is a good argument for locating at least the initial teaching of information skills with one person, in order to avoid duplication. In some countries, that may have been already achieved in the primary school.

While some aspects of the criticism of mediated communications clearly ought to be incorporated into the teaching of the subjects concerned (UNESCO, 1986), a substantial part of this work falls within the area of communications. As such it can be treated as a separate subject, as part of the social studies curriculum or as part of the first language curriculum. In Britain decisions of this kind have usually been made at school level, taking into account the interests and talents of the teachers available. This strategy probably works better when this is an optional rather than compulsory element in the curriculum. In the latter case, staffing can be a problem. Unless all first language or social studies teachers become media educators (not a bad long-term strategy, but difficult in the medium term) there will be teachers reluctant to take on this responsibility in some schools to counterbalance the enthusiasts in others. But if media education becomes a special subject, will one not be creating a cultural bifurcation between print and not-print that will seem increasingly anachronistic?

The program/software production aims would logically fit alongside the criticism of other people's products. However, other strategies are equally worth considering. A case can be made, for example, for making production an optional course while criticism remains part of the compulsory curriculum. In some schools it presently appears not even as an option but as an extra-curricular activity. Another strategy arises when schools depart from their normal timetables for a few days in the year in order to pursue special activities intensively. This is particularly well suited to activities like video production, which cannot be easily fitted into the short period structure of a standard timetable. This is also an area of the curriculum where it might be possible to import help from experts and enthusiasts in the local community, rather than making it a teacher-led affair.

Route 1, the direct incorporation of NICT into the traditional curriculum frameworks, best achieves the subject-based aims discussed above, and we have just argued that it is the most appropriate route for discussing the role of NICT in society. It is also a possible, but not necessarily preferable, strategy for information handling, criticism and production. Being the most ambitious strategy, however, it requires the most complex planning and the greatest level of resourcing. I discuss this further in the later sections, but meanwhile it should be noted that progress would be greatly facilitated if there was at least one teacher in each subject who was prepared to take a leadership role in introducing NICT, and who was in turn able to receive support from a NICT specialist located either inside the school or in its immediate locality.

THE WIDENING OF ACCESS

Cerych and Jallade (1986) refer to the danger of developing a division in our society between those who are 'computer literate' and those who are not, the most likely divisive factors being age, class, gender, ethnicity and handicap. However, even if the schools succeed in delivering an appropriate level of competence to all their students, a large population of disadvantaged adults will remain. Not only do a very large proportion of adults need to acquire some NICT-related skills to adapt to the changing nature of employment, but NICT has an extremely important role to play in making educational opportunities available to adults. The acknowledged success of the open universities is probably only the beginning of a more general transformation of the means by which adults gain access to learning opportunities (Graebner, 1989).

The resources, facilities and expertise available in schools could play an important role in supporting this transition, because some adults find it easier to get to schools than other education centres, and joint use of resources and facilities is likely to be cheaper than separate provision for adults. Indeed it would be wasteful to make future plans for the use of NICT in schools which did not also take into account parallel plans for adult education.

One should also note the great potential of NICT for making the curriculum accessible to children and adults who have difficulties in receiving it because of distance, physical handicap or some other form of disability (Geoffrion, 1983; Hawkridge *et al.*, 1985; Morocco and Neuman, 1986; Weir, 1987).

3.5 IMPLEMENTATION PROBLEMS WHEN INTRODUCING COMPUTERS INTO SCHOOLS

COMPUTERS IN THE CLASSROOMS

This section first focuses on classroom issues that arise in connection with the introduction of computers into the teaching of traditional school subjects. The rather different context of courses in computer literacy or information technology is then discussed. Then the section concludes with a review of the innovation problems facing school management. Four main types of classroom problem are discussed: incorporation into the curriculum, classroom organization and management, the teacher's role during computer-aided learning, and the impact of the innovation process on teachers' attitudes towards using computers.

Incorporation into the curriculum

Teachers are acutely aware of the strong community expectation that schools will make increasing use of computers. They also find that as a result of a variety of decisions made by others they have inherited a motley collection of hardware and software. They may have been on a short computer awareness course, and may even have a colleague who is a bit of an expert. But they probably have had very little advice on what they are expected to do, apart from using the computer and having some good stories to tell about it.

If they are working to a tightly prescribed curriculum, teachers are likely to find that the software does not match it too closely – or that the software covers half a topic but also goes well beyond the objectives, so they have to decide whether to use it at the expense of skimping or omitting something else. Even if the curriculum is loosely structured, teachers still have the problem of how to develop a unit that combines computer-linked activities with other activities in a coherent and manageable way. Neither of these planning tasks is impossible, but they are time-consuming and demand considerable knowledge of the software and its effects on learning.

Large gaps are reported in many countries between the use being made of computers in the 'good practice situations' reported by the enthusiasts and the use observed in the majority of schools. This is true of British primary schools even though they have been reported as among the best adopters of computers. Govier (1988) summarizes research reporting that the insertion of a computer rarely affects either the curriculum or normal classroom practice: its use is assimilated to existing pedagogic assumptions. Many teachers still regard the computer as a distraction in the classroom and do not believe it has yet had positive effects on pupil learning (Hall and Rhodes, 1986). My conclusion is not that the accounts of the enthusiasts are wrong, though some might seem a little uncritical, but rather that good practice has not been very widely implemented.

Where there has been long-term well-supported use, and changes in practice are noteworthy, the problem of the relationship between the new practice and the regular curriculum is repeatedly raised. Olson and Eaton (1986) regard this as generally healthy, because it leads to teachers reappraising the curriculum. Hawkins and Sheingold (1986) are more ambivalent, pointing to the difficulty of using computers to introduce problem-solving skills that were not in the regular curriculum and could not easily be monitored or assessed. Teachers felt uncomfortable when they could not judge the success of their work and did not know what kind of standard to expect. This, together with much of the pedagogic evidence cited below, leads to the conclusion that it is not just more and better software development that is needed. It is curriculum development with computer-aided learning built in. Then new goals and assessment, computer-based and computer-free learning experiences, and pedagogic guidance for teachers can all be developed in an integrated manner. A tightly structured package might be inappropriate but more support is needed than that provided by isolated pieces of software.

Classroom organization and management

Much work with computers is carried out under considerable practical difficulty, because of circumstances beyond the teachers' control. First, there is the problem of access to equipment. The introduction of computers into schools is good public relations and apparently large sums of money are seen to be spent. But what is provided may amount to only 20 minutes access per pupil per week (Becker, 1984). While recent evidence from the USA (Congress, 1988) suggests that pupil users now have an average access time of 60 minutes a week, this is unlikely to be reached by many European schools (except in vocational courses). It also falls short of the 20 minutes a day regarded by many educators as a minimum for proper exploitation of computers' potential. To use computers profitably with such low access times requires close integration with non-computer-based activities and users who are already familiar with the software.

Second, there is the problem of location. If computers are moved around, then classrooms constantly have to be reorganized. But the alternative strategy of moving classes to a computer room raises other difficulties. For the computer work to be properly integrated with other activities, learning resources such as reference books and practical apparatus will need to be available. There may even be pressure on the teacher to organize the work to maximize computer usage rather than achievement of learning goals (Johnston, 1985).

Teachers feel threatened by the computer because it forces them to organize their classrooms differently, reduces their control and makes their normal approach to monitoring progress difficult to implement. Discipline is rarely an overt problem with children working at computers, because their motivation is high. However, this only reinforces the common practice whereby teachers leave pupils at computers more or less to look after themselves. Although this enables the teacher to give more attention to the rest of the class, it also serves to isolate computer-based activities from the 'official curriculum' and gives them an ambiguous status. Teachers gain the opportunity to practise an apparently more pupil-centred pedagogy within this isolated setting of a class within a class, and to acquire a modern image. But they also feel bereft of influence, unable to monitor what goes on and uncertain about their proper role (Olson, 1988).

This points to yet another management problem for teachers. Not only do they have to plan for computer-based activities to lead into and develop out of non-computer-based learning experiences (longitudinal planning), but they also have to plan for computer-based and non–computer-based activities to take place at the same time (lateral planning), though not necessarily as part of the same topic. Coordinating and sharing the work of the different groups may also be advisable from time to time, and this demands careful thought about when and how to return to a whole class focus. No wonder the Scottish Inspectors reported that 'the skills required by the teacher in using the computer are predominantly pedagogical rather than technical' (SED, 1987).

The teacher's role during computer-aided learning

Not only do many patterns of computer use require the teacher to plan an integrated series of activities but there is increasing evidence that educational benefits are diminished by the common practice of leaving children working with computers entirely alone. Olson and Eaton (1986) found that not being able to diagnose and respond to pupils' problems quickly was a major concern of teachers, only remediable by careful monitoring and close familiarity with the software. Carter and Monaco (1987) note that information-handling skills cannot be assumed but have to be taught to children using NICT. Robert (1984) reported that children using Logo tended to adopt 'a proper experimental approach' only when appropriately guided by adults. Children may also need teacher coaching on how to work collaboratively. Indeed most researchers seem to agree that the teacher has a crucial role to play during computer-aided learning if higher order thinking is to be developed.

Hawkins and Sheingold (1986) summarize the challenge to teachers as follows:

> Teachers may be managing pairs or groups of students rather than conducting the more typical whole-class or individual activity. To manage and support such work effectively requires observational skills different from those teachers normally apply and new intuitions about when and how to intervene in student-based activities, as well as raising questions about how to monitor the progress of individual students.

Impact on teachers

Heywood and Norman (1987) suggest two major causes of low or zero use of computers by teachers – competence and confidence – and they are closely related. However, teacher anxieties are not, as is often assumed, based primarily on the technology but on their own ability to use it for good educational purposes in their classrooms. This is often accompanied by real doubts about the extent to which their pupils will benefit. The heart of the problem lies in curriculum and pedagogy, for these will determine whether or not the innovation is beneficial for their particular class. So it is only when these practical concerns are addressed that their anxieties are likely to be assuaged.

In reading accounts of the introduction of computers, one is constantly reminded of research into other earlier educational innovations in curriculum or educational technology. Gross's (1971) account of curricular innovation in a primary school suggested that 'lack of clarity' was a major cause of failure. Teachers were prepared to support the rhetoric of what was being advocated but found themselves unclear about precisely what was meant to happen in practice. Often the introduction of computers into a school shows a similar lack of clear educational purpose, and the proponents of change fail to appreciate the magnitude and difficulty of the necessary change in pedagogy. The lack of integration with the regular curriculum is also reminiscent of the fate of many 1960s experiments in educational technology.

More recent research into curriculum implementation has suggested that the initial adoption of an innovation has to be followed by adaptation and refocusing if the innovation is eventually to become institutionalized as part of normal practice (Berman, 1981; Hall and Loucks, 1978). Similarly, Wright (1987) has noted that even regular users of computers in primary schools tend to reach a plateau after one or two years. She argues that this is because their practice is based on somewhat haphazard trial and error with little time for reflection. Further help is needed if they are to go beyond that point, 'to develop their understanding of microtechnology's capacity to transform certain aspects of the primary school curriculum'.

From this and other accounts it is possible to identify at least three different teacher responses to the introduction of computers into schools. At one extreme there are those who are extremely fearful of any technical innovation and any possible disruption to their established classroom practice. At the other extreme are the enthusiasts who adopt the use of computers unreflectively and are always pursuing the latest new development. In the middle are teachers who, having overcome their initial anxiety, become excited by the capacity of computers to motivate their pupils. They then reach a point where the novelty is less, and begin to consider the costs and benefits. Where and how should computers fit into the curriculum and the life of the school? These are the true educators and it is their contribution which must be further developed and expanded if NICT is to realize its potential.

TEACHING COMPUTER LITERACY AND INFORMATION TECHNOLOGY

Under this heading I refer only to courses taken by all pupils, not to specialist options. Introducing such courses is probably the easiest response to external expectations that schools should use computers, but external pressures do not often provide any clear objectives. Hence courses of this kind carry a variety of labels and vary enormously in length, from 10 to 200 hours. Sometimes, considerable thought has been given to the selection of the content at national or district level. Sometimes, teachers are put in the position of 'having to make it up as they go along'. Even when they are carefully planned, it is common for courses to attempt to cover far too many of the aims discussed in Section 3.3 – thus becoming superficial rather than challenging, and patchy rather than coherent.

In a few countries these courses are taught by teachers specially selected and trained for the purpose: these teachers are likely to have backgrounds in computer science, physics or mathematics, and to be predisposed towards a mainly technocratic approach. In other countries, teachers may be either enthusiastic volunteers or conscripts who have spare time on their timetables, according to local circumstances. The enthusiasts will actively seek training, the conscripts may not. All teachers of this new subject are likely to have problems in developing and sustaining an occupational identity, because they have no prior curriculum tradition or group of experienced teachers to follow. Their place in the school is uncertain, and even the future of their subject is unclear. As Section 3.4 indicated, computer literacy may be incorporated into the curriculum in a variety of ways, and separate courses may be only a step on the way to a more integrated form of provision. Those teachers who have painfully developed a new identity may find themselves having to change yet again (Petch, 1988).

Many of the problems discussed in this section also apply

206

to teachers of computer literacy or information technology. Since pupils will expect regular access to computers, shortages of equipment will pose greater difficulties than for teachers of other subjects. The curricular and pedagogic problems will still be significant, and the role of the teacher a matter for considerable concern. There is a natural temptation in such circumstances to keep pupils fully and enthusiastically occupied with a series of computer applications or programming tasks, without giving serious attention to what is being learned, to important information-handling skills and to wider discussions of relevant social and values issues.

SCHOOL LEVEL POLICY-MAKING AND MANAGEMENT

Research on educational innovation has confirmed that the role of the headteacher is crucial, even in a centralized system where he or she is given relatively little devolved authority (Fullan, 1982). This has been acknowledged in the innovation strategies adopted by some districts (Peper, 1986). However, in many schools the development of NICT has by-passed normal school management decision-making to a remarkable degree. Both in the USA and in the UK the policy and practice found today are almost a historical accident, resulting from the interests and preferences of school personnel and a variety of interactions with the district authorities and the local community. Few schools have had either the expertise or the decision-making time to develop, let alone implement, coherent whole school policies. The results, as Walker (1986) reports are:

slow, haphazard, and scattered acquisition of equipment (because there is no budget for this purpose);

use by a few enthusiastic teachers who become specialists (because there are no plans for staffing, in-service education or staff development);

use in isolated individual courses (because adoption throughout a department or curriculum component would require an institutional commitment);

improvisation, year-to-year adjustment (because strategic planning requires an institutional commitment);

highly variable quality (because individual users will not assert a right to pass judgement on the quality of what another may do, and the institution, having washed its hands of the matter, will be powerless).

The enterprise tends to be run by local 'experts', teachers who have acquired knowledge about computers, and are networked with other 'experts' outside the schools. They retain the tacit approval of headteachers, for whom the prospect of having to make independent judgements about school computing policy is often quite threatening. So policy may be determined by: (1) the curiosity and drive of a small band of enthusiasts whose developing peer culture leads them away from today's children towards tomorrow's utopia; and (2) the availability of free or subsidized hardware and software of many kinds (usually incompatible and variable in quality). The need to bring this situation under critical control is increasingly recognized (SED, 1987) and this is clearly a priority area for headteacher training.

Before proceeding to discuss more specific aspects of school policy, it is useful to reflect for a moment on the wider implications of the introduction of computers into schools. A school is a microcosm of society, which both reflects the norms and values of society and provides some of the new perspectives that will influence the future. There are grounds for thinking that this is particularly true for NICT. The experience of NICT in school during the 1990s will help to shape the role of NICT in our wider society during the twenty-first century. Every school contains elements of a NICT-related culture from which children absorb and acquire views about issues such as:

whether NICT is a technocratic or humanistic influence;

whether it enslaves or emancipates individuals;

whether it is more for men than women;

whether it constrains or enhances personal thinking;

what kind of people tend to be high NICT users;

how to relate to the parallel curriculum;

whether they will be able to influence decisions about the future or merely sit at the receiving end of a technological imperative.

These attitudes will be influenced by formal decisions about access to equipment, the content and ethos of NICT-related courses, and the selection of teachers to work in the area. But they will also be affected by the attitudes and behaviour of teachers during daily school life, and by the developing NICT-related peer group culture (Diem, 1986; Turkle, 1984). Not only does a school need to be aware of its subtle influence on its pupils, but it will also need to raise issues of this kind with the local community. It is important to keep educational issues on the agenda when people are responding to NICT in a mood of 'technological panic' (Jamieson and Tasker, 1988; Sloan, 1984).

This naturally leads us to those areas of school policy for computers which most directly affect the way NICT is perceived: the curriculum and staff development. The curriculum actually received by pupils will carry hidden messages about NICT as well as overt learning objectives, and the balance and emphasis will vary considerably from one teacher to another, and according to the resources available. From this can be seen the importance of good staff development if curriculum implementation is to proceed in the desired direction. To achieve this school managers have to make good use of external courses by selecting wisely, sending the most appropriate teachers, and organizing in-school follow-up. In addition, a great deal of in-school staff development will be needed, almost certainly an ongoing programme (Anderson, 1987). This problem is discussed in greater detail later.

The use of NICT for school administration will also be a management concern, and if it is organized in a manner that engenders a negative response from teachers, the view of humans as victims of the inexorable march of a hostile technology will prevail. The effectiveness of both administrative and curricular usage will depend on resource management. On the hardware side this means a coherent purchasing policy, reliable maintenance and the optimum deployment of equipment; on the software side, arrangements for searching out, evaluating and purchasing need to be combined with cataloguing, good access and storage. There is also the problem of converting spaces to improve usage and the perennial problem of security. These activities have to be delegated to appropriate teachers or technicians, who then need to be given clear policy briefs and properly managed, not just left alone.

Problems have often arisen when a single teacher with computer expertise, or sometimes only enthusiasm, has been given responsibility both for managing the computing facility and for staff development without regard for whether he or she has the skills needed for either job. In some schools, this problem has been resolved by creating two distinct roles: a system manager with responsibility for managing the computing facility and its hardware and software resources and a NICT coordinator to oversee staff development and take responsibility for the curricular implications of NICT. The former requires technical expertise and administrative skills, the latter pedagogic expertise and inter-personal skills. Whatever the arrangement, teachers will need training for these management tasks, and will benefit from the regular exchange of experience with their counterparts in other schools. It is particularly important for schools to have a long-term policy, so staff development can be planned ahead, key people given some incentive and direction, and special offers of equipment and/or advice can be accepted or rejected according to proper policy criteria (SED, 1987).

Further management issues arise when the school is also used as a resource for adults, or a centre for adult education. NICT facilities might be important for the adult programme, which would have to be carefully meshed with other aspects of the school's work. One can also envisage situations where parents have bought equipment for the school, which they then want to use in the evenings or during weekends.

3.6 NATIONAL POLICIES, SOFTWARE DEVELOPMENT AND TEACHER TRAINING

NATIONAL POLICIES

An extensive and helpful review of policies in OECD countries was published in 1986; more recent and detailed information for Council of Europe nations is provided in the National Reports for this conference. In order to avoid duplication, this section is confined to a few salient points. First, special attention is given in the two following sections to software development and teacher training. This is not because these are the only important aspects of a national policy, but because they are the least appreciated by policy-makers. Their attention is repeatedly drawn to hardware, partly because it is indispensable and visible, and partly because of concern for each nation's own information technology industry. Yet expenditure on hardware does not provide the desired positive effect on pupils, unless software development and teacher training are given an equivalent priority. The discussion of NICT implementation in Section 3.5 highlighted several issues relevant to developing a balanced policy.

1. A certain 'critical mass' of equipment is needed to support specific educational policies.
2. Software development needs to be closely integrated with curriculum development; and is lagging behind hardware provision.
3. Pedagogic issues are vital to the effective use of computers, yet neglected in training.

As the OECD report noted, hardware policies usually favour equity rather than efficiency, and this problem is compounded by the 'software famine' and inadequate teacher training.

All these points are highlighted by the few published evaluations of national policies. However, Makrakis's (1988) case studies of Sweden and Greece were for a doctoral thesis rather than part of a commissioned evaluation; HM Inspectors' report on the Microelectronics Education Programme in England and Wales

(DES, 1987) was much too late to be useful. Only Norway, to my knowledge, commissioned an independent evaluation (OECD/CERI, 1987b) to guide its policy-making process. Given the level of investment and the degree of uncertainty surrounding both innovation strategies and classroom implementation, this lack of policy evaluation seems extremely unwise. When an OECD report (1986) suggests that 'One way to look at the present situation is to see education as engaged in a vast exercise of trial and error', one has to ask how much and how effectively we are learning from such an expensive experience.

We should also note at this point that, although it is important for major policy issues to be widely debated in democratic societies, there is a danger that the public are particularly ill-informed about some of the issues raised at this conference. Three recommendations follow. First, more realistic estimates of cost need to be available in a form that makes the question of 'value for money' more easily discussed. System and training costs should be included, not just expenditure on hardware. Pupil access time should be used as a simple indicator of the level of implementation, not pupil/machine ratios. Second, the curriculum aims outlined in Section 3.3 need to be rationally discussed and prioritized, in a mood free from either salesmanship or technological panic. Third, much closer attention needs to be paid to the side-effects of various innovations and policies, on attitudes towards NICT, on career choice and on equality of opportunity.

SOFTWARE DEVELOPMENT

Several factors contribute to what most writers perceive as a 'software famine' (Smith, 1989):

the educational software market is small in comparison with either the commercial software market or the textbook market;

small linguistic groups are especially disadvantaged;

software is tied to hardware, which reduces the market still further, limits cross-national transfer and shortens its lifetime because the technology is changing so rapidly;

software is expensive to produce;

software development expertise is in short supply;

mechanisms for finding and evaluating software are inadequate;

software is available only as an isolated item, not as part of a coherent curriculum package;

good-quality software is still exceedingly scarce.

The size of the market may be increased: (1) by having more users, i.e. increasing access to equipment; (2) by standardization, which reduces the number of operating systems and user interfaces; and (3) by reducing the quantity in favour of quality. However, even in the large North American market software manufacturers tend to play it safe. Thus a recent policy review (Congress, 1988) reported 'substantial concern for the long-term quality and diversity' of commercial products, and recommended further underwriting of software research and development.

This is an area where European cooperation could make a significant difference, not only through standardization but also through organized co-production (the parallel development of similar software between two or more countries) and through joint activities (such as exchanges and workshops) for the further development of expertise. Some such arrangements already exist among the Nordic countries. These ideas were further developed at a recent conference organized by the Commission of the European Community (CEC, 1987), which also provided a useful review of national software policies.

Most reviewers of the software situation see an important continuing role for software development teams, where special expertise can be developed (Cerych and Jallade, 1986). Several such teams are described in Moonen and Plomp (1987), in which some contributors also discuss software evaluation. To produce the best results, such teams need an understanding management which can find a balance between productivity and quality, very close links with schools and an independent formative evaluation facility. Nevertheless, there is still a danger that they will produce

213

software, which is not accompanied by good pedagogic advice and is not sufficiently integrated into a larger curriculum package.

This highlights a problem that is central to any national policy for NICT, its relationship with other educational policies. Most of the problems identified in Section 3.5 concern management, curriculum and pedagogy, and none of them can be resolved within an exclusively NICT-based framework. Software development teams probably ought to be expanded into curriculum development teams for whom software is only part of their remit; such teams should also be closely involved in the development and evaluation of pedagogic strategies.

TEACHER TRAINING

Practically every issue raised in this report has implications for teacher training. At every level and in every country further training is needed both to extend training to people who have not yet received NICT-related training and to continue to improve the capabilities of those who have been trained. Section 3.3 has identified the curricular goals which teachers may have to deliver, and Section 3.4 the extent to which these are likely to be the responsibility of specialist teachers or teachers of traditional school subjects. Section 3.5 then demonstrated that, in addition to the more obvious needs for competence in using the appropriate NICT software, there are vital training needs relating to curriculum implementation, classroom management, pedagogic approaches and monitoring of student progress.

This sub-section is organized according to the tasks which a teacher may be expected to perform. First, the training of specialist teachers of computer studies is considered together with that of semi-specialists who teach computer literacy. The training of all other secondary school teachers and primary school teachers is then discussed. Next, training needs are suggested for school-based management roles, such as NICT coordinator, system manager and headteacher. Finally, I consider the needs of out-of-school personnel, such as advisers, administrators, NICT trainers and software developers.

The training of specialists and semi-specialists

Those countries introducing computer studies or computer literacy as a new curriculum subject face the problem of recruiting and training sufficient specialist teachers. These may come: (1) direct from the diminishing cohort of secondary school leavers; (2) from the highly demanded group of computer science graduates; or (3) by conversion training for teachers of other subjects. This section will only cover their needs as teachers. Further needs resulting from the expectation that these specialists will also assist other teachers, deliver in-school training, and generally spearhead the innovatory introduction of NICT will be dealt with below in the examination of the needs of NICT coordinators. The teaching role will itself present many problems. Those teachers with computing experience are likely to find school equipment somewhat inferior to that to which they have become accustomed. There will be considerable pressure to keep their knowledge constantly up to date. Above all they will be pioneering the teaching of a new subject, in which there is no established pedagogy and few teacher educators with any substantial teaching experience.

In order to teach computer studies, a computer scientist will need a combination of practical in-school experience with courses in education and on the teaching of the subject. In most countries this introduction of graduates into teaching takes several months. A conversion course, on the other hand, would have to cover a wide range of specialist knowledge, courses in subject pedagogy and practical experience in teaching computer studies. This would take at least a full year (OECD/CERI, 1986). Most countries have now developed and successfully delivered the computer science components of such a course, but hitherto the equally important pedagogic aspects have received much less attention. This is hardly surprising since a new subject pedagogy is still in the process of creation, so only limited expertise is available for incorporation into training. If it is given sufficient priority, this problem ought to diminish over time.

These pedagogic problems are greater still for teachers of

215

computer literacy in lower secondary or primary schools. Their training is less, their equipment is often worse, their students are less mature, not necessarily volunteers, and their curriculum is usually less well defined. I have used the term semi-specialist, because these teachers rarely receive specialist training. Yet they still have to forge a new subject identity, often on the basis of minimal experience and expertise. The knowledge base appropriate for this group of teachers will depend on the breadth of the information technology syllabus. While the model suggested by the Association for Teacher Education in Europe (van Weert, 1984) is broader than many current courses in computer literacy, it still leaves out some of the goals discussed in Section 3.3. In particular, it fails to put the use of computers into the wider context of information skills and communications or to consider algorithmic procedures as only one approach to thinking and problem-solving. The evidence of Section 3.5 suggests that the methodology or didactics course would need to be more substantial than the others if it was to include sufficient practical teaching experience. Olson and Eaton (1986), for example, suggest that such a course should include: (1) discussion of the competencies and understanding pupils should be expected to achieve, and how their development can be monitored; (2) exploration of a range of pedagogies, including whole-class teaching with a computer, groupwork and appropriate off-line learning activities; and (3) practical study, experiment and reflection on the teacher's role in various IT teaching contexts. It is difficult to imagine these goals being achieved by a course of less than 200 hours.

Specialist training in media education presents a rather different set of problems. First, the curriculum debate in many countries has left media education in a somewhat ambiguous position, and arguments for media education currently command less political support than those for computer literacy. Second, there is a substantial knowledge base required for teaching about the media and engaging in media criticism, even if this is not always recognized. Third, on a more positive note, the pedagogic skills required are fairly similar to those already possessed by many teachers of literature and social studies, and therefore present less of a problem. As a result, specialist training in media education is

216

more easily delivered by distance learning, except in the area of production skills which, like many computer-based skills, requires practice with feedback and coaching.

The training of teachers of other subjects

The magnitude of this task was aptly described in a report from OECD/CERI (1986):

> We face the need to train, as rapidly as possible, the entirety of the teaching profession to use the new technologies. Given the rapid evolution of the whole NIT area, it is scarcely any exaggeration to say that the whole profession would need, by some means or another, to be placed in semi-permanent retraining. There are many reasons why it is wildly impracticable to think in these terms; not least a lack of trained trainers, economic constraints, insufficiently clear agreement on the directions to be followed. The logistics of such an exercise, too, would be overwhelming. Yet this is, in fact, the fundamental task facing the various agencies of teacher in-service training and its seriousness should not be ignored.

Some countries have made a substantial start, most notably the Nordic countries, France and the United Kingdom. Denmark has just completed a five-year programme to train all its upper secondary teachers. Not only have 95 per cent of teachers at this level completed both a 20-hour local course and a 40-hour regional course (partly differentiated according to subject), but three teachers from each school have completed 200-hour courses. An evaluation of this programme would be extremely useful.

Typically, introductory courses have been much shorter than those in Denmark, and evidence is reported that their impact has been extremely variable (Vickers, 1987). Several reasons for this have been reported. First, training has not been closely coordinated with access to hardware and software in schools; so some teachers have received training and found themselves without any opportunity to implement what they had learned, while others were given access without any training opportunity.

217

Second, some teachers were given longer training courses in the expectation that they would later assist and train their colleagues, but then found themselves given no release time from teaching to carry out these additional duties. Third, some courses were too short and possibly too insensitive to overcome teachers' initial lack of confidence. Fourth, some courses focused only on technical aspects and gave little time to curricular or pedagogic matters. Indeed, even the basic task of familiarizing teachers with relevant software was sometimes ignored in favour of the teaching of programming. Fifth, it is now increasingly recognized that short courses need a period of school-based follow-up in order to have maximum effect. Unless the schools have the will and the capacity to do this much of this course is likely to be wasted. This problem is not necessarily solved by making courses school-based because teachers will still need individual support and coaching at the follow-up stage.

The lessons of this experience should be carefully noted. They point to a need for improved liaison between trainers and schools, for proper management of training and follow-up within the schools, for more relevant courses – and for greater attention to what is already known from research into educational innovation and in-service training (Bolam, 1987; Eraut, 1988).

The Vickers report (1987) also draws attention to another important problem, the extent to which the important pedagogic expertise, stressed in Section 3.5, is not readily available outside the classrooms of leading practitioners:

> It is the teachers themselves who are pioneering new approaches to practical pedagogy. What is needed is not just subject knowledge, but knowledge about how students might learn that subject in computer enhanced environments. Knowledge about how these environments work is only slowly being developed; it is being created at the classroom level by teachers who are acting as researchers, analysing the actual effects of different software packages, and experimenting with alternative ways of using them.

There is a major management problem in capturing this expertise for training purposes and continuing to develop and update it, without taking all the best teachers out of the classroom.

What, then, does the training of a subject teacher have to accomplish? First it has to overcome inhibitions about the hardware and achieve a degree of machine competence. Second, it has to establish sufficient familiarity with a range of software appropriate to the subject to give the teacher confidence in using it. Third, it has to enable the teacher to evaluate software critically in terms of its assumptions about knowledge and pedagogy, its implicit values and its impact on pupils (Johnston, 1987). Above all they need to become aware of a range of pedagogic strategies, to observe 'good practice' at first hand, to be able to experiment under guidance and to discuss the relative merits of different approaches. Such training will probably need to involve some formal sessions, and some guided visits and classroom experiment. While the former could be provided out-of-school, the latter will almost certainly require school-based support (Ellam and Wellington, 1987).

Such school-based support may be provided either by teachers within the school who have greater experience of NICT or by advisory teachers who visit the school and work alongside teachers in their classrooms. Both strategies are further discussed below. Another need is for teachers to have sufficient access to machines and in their own personal time for them to gain greater confidence as users and begin to explore new possibilities. The policy of New Hampshire, the American state, which has funded the purchase of computers for teachers' personal use, might seem unduly charitable, but it could be an excellent investment if accompanied by appropriate training.

So far this section has concentrated on the needs of secondary teachers, although most of the comments would also be pertinent at primary level. The differences will be greatest in those countries where primary teachers take a single class for all subjects. These teachers will need to be familiar with a wider range of software, but will nevertheless find that much of their experience can transfer across subjects. Primary teachers often have the opportunity to use computers more flexibly, but are likely to have fewer machines available.

While it is relatively easy to organize new computer studies courses within pre-service training, it is still difficult to meet subject-specific needs and to make such courses sufficiently relevant to classrooms. One reason is because the task of retraining subject-based teacher educators has not been seriously tackled in most countries. Another is that appropriate pedagogic expertise is scarce in teacher training institutions and it is difficult to find appropriate school experience for trainee teachers.

Training for school-based management of NICT

In Section 3.5, I briefly discussed the distinctive roles within schools of the 'system manager' and the 'NICT coordinator'. The system manager has responsibility for the purchase, distribution and maintenance of the equipment, and possibly also for the management of software. This requires a clear policy brief and close liaison with school management to ensure that the facility best serves the needs of the students. Administrative skills, and often technical expertise, are needed, although the technical side of the job will depend greatly on the help and advice available from outside the school and the quantity and quality of technician support inside the school. People with the appropriate skills for this task may not be well suited for the NICT coordinator role, yet they are essential for keeping the system running. Teachers abandon unreliable systems very quickly indeed, so attempting to innovate without a reliable facility is a total waste of time. System managers need: training that enhances their existing technical expertise and includes detailed study of the relevant administrative issues; access to information and advice from outside the school; opportunities to meet counterparts from other schools; and regular updating.

The NICT coordinator role is primarily concerned with curricular and pedagogical issues and NICT-related staff development. Such a person needs the same kind of basic training as the semi-specialist teachers of computer literacy, plus some knowledge and awareness of the more specialist needs of the various school subjects. As a coordinator he or she should not be expected to be the sole possessor of expertise, but rather to act as the channel through which it may be made available; for example, through organizing access to subject-specific training or a consultancy visit from an appropriate external expert. This requires good inter-personal and networking skills. The other kind of knowledge required by NICT coordinators relates to staff development, in-service training and the management of change. They have to assess staff development needs and find appropriate ways of meeting them, and to be a general source of pedagogic advice. They will also need to contribute to schools' policy for NICT and its impact not only on the curriculum, but also on teachers and pupils and the general school milieu. This kind of training is available in the UK on the more practice-oriented advanced post-experience courses, usually for masters degrees, but is less common in other European countries.

Finally, we should consider the headteacher, whose support, neutrality or opposition is crucial for introducing any innovation. Their training is now a recognized priority in many countries, but has not usually included familiarization with NICT. Apart from the need to become personal users, they need to be more aware of the educational issues, to be familiar with a range of possible school policies, and to be able to conceptualize what the proper management of NICT within a school involves. They will then be properly prepared to oversee the policy development process in their schools, to delegate the various NICT-related responsibilities to appropriate members of staff and to see that they get proper training to do their jobs well.

Training of out-of-school personnel

The main out-of-school roles to be considered are training and advisory work, administration and software development. As suggested earlier, the acute lack of suitably prepared trainers is a major barrier to rapid progress. Because curricular and pedagogic knowledge relating to NICT is still in its early development and largely created in schools, there has to be some kind of partnership between trainers and pioneering classroom teachers. But there also have to be limits on the recruitment of these teachers into training roles, if their creation of new pedagogic knowledge is to continue. Hence the initial build-up of a cadre of trainers is likely to be quite slow, although it will be possible to accelerate later. Subject knowledge of NICT is more widely available, though much in demand, outside teacher education. Finally, there is a danger of ignoring expertise in teacher education itself. People appointed as trainers have much to learn about the planning, design and delivery of courses, about how to provide advice or follow-up training, and about the knowledge and skills required by change agents. They will need to be familiar with the literature on the management of change and in-service education, and to develop an appropriate range of inter-personal skills. Thus training the trainers involves the communication of training knowledge and know-how in addition to the necessary subject knowledge and pedagogic expertise.

The long-term need, however, is not just for specialist trainers in NICT, but for the integration of a NICT component into all other forms of teacher training. Unless this is achieved fairly soon, the greater part of initial and re-experience teacher training will continue either without a NICT component or, more probably, with a NICT component that is purely technical and separated off from the other practical forms of training. This need applies not only to trainers of teachers but also to trainers of headteachers and administrators. In the short term, NICT specialists will be able to organize conferences and prepare special briefings for headteachers and administrators. In the medium term it may be possible to recruit at least one trainer who has some competence in NICT to each training team. Not many NICT specialists will be able to take on such a task, so the recruitment and preparation of suitable members of training teams will need to be carefully planned.

The planned development of teams is even more important for software development, where it is generally acknowledged that teams are needed – both to bring together a sufficient range of expertise and for the additional quality that their interaction is believed to stimulate. Earlier, I recommended that some software development should be embedded within a larger curriculum development brief, in order to tackle sizeable chunks of curriculum, to integrate computer-based and non-computer-based activities and to give greater attention to pedagogic issues. If this policy was accepted, then a wider range of expertise would be needed and teamwork would be even more important. All members of such a team should have some knowledge of NICT, though only some would need to be NICT specialists. Expertise would also be needed in curriculum development, instructional design and the appropriate subject pedagogy. Recruiting such teams and continuing to develop their expertise is an important function of any national policy for NICT in education.

RESEARCH AND EVALUATION

NICT is an area of rapid development and high investment. There is therefore considerable need for continuing research to see that the education sector both meets the challenge of NICT and derives maximum benefit from new developments. Alongside this research, ongoing evaluation of current developments must surely be prudent. Policies need to be continually adjusted in the light of evidence about how they are working out in practice. My main concerns in this area are three-fold:

1. Research on NICT in education must be sufficiently broadly based. There is a danger that it will focus too narrowly on hardware and software development. Such matters as the organization of NICT in schools, user interfaces and pedagogic strategies also need urgent attention. Curricular patterns need to be tried and evaluated in order to ascertain how best to incorporate NICT-related goals in the education system.

2. Evaluation projects need to be mounted to provide constructive feedback to developers, trainers and policy-makers. Innovation in NICT sometimes comes dangerously close to 'the blind leading the blind'.

3. More notice needs to be taken of previous research, particularly that relating to innovation and the management of change. The well-documented mistakes of the 1960s and 1970s are in danger of being repeated in the 1990s.

BIBLIOGRAPHY

Anderson, John S. (1987). Implementing information technology across the curriculum – what does it mean? In Moonen, J. and Plomp, T. (eds), pp. 649–56.

Baacke, D. (1980). *Kommunikation und Kompetenz. Grundlegung einer Didaktik der Kommunikation und ihrer Medien.* Munich: Deutsches Jugendinstitut; Weinheim: Juventa Verlag.

Ball, Derek *et al.* (eds) (1986). *Will mathematics count? Computers in mathematics education.* Hatfield, UK: AUCBE/MEP.

Becker, H.J. (1984). Computers in schools today: some basic considerations. *American Journal of Education*, **84** 22–39.

Berman, P. (1981). Towards an implementation paradigm. In *Improving schools: using what we know*, Lehming, R. and Kane, M. (eds). Beverly Hills, USA: Sage.

Bliss, Joan and Ogborn, Jon (1988). *Tools for exploratory learning.* ESRC InTER Programme Occasional Paper InTER/5/88, University of Lancaster, Dept of Psychology.

Bolam, Ray (1987). What is effective INSET? In *Professional development and INSET*, Proceedings of the 1987 NFER Members Conference. Slough, UK: NFER.

Boyer, Ernest (1983). *High school: a report on secondary education in America.* New York: Harper & Row.

Breckner, Ingrid and Frank, Herrath (1987). *Medienkonsum von Kindern und Jegendlichen (Materialien zum siebten Jugenbericht).* Weinheim: Juventa, Verlag.

British Film Institute (1989). *Primary media education – a curriculum statement.* Report of a BFI/DES National Working Party. London: BFI.

Broderick, C. and Trushell, J. (1985). Problems and processes – junior school children using word processors to produce an information leaflet. *English in Education*, **19** (2), 29–35.

Broudy, Harry S. (1986). Technology and citizenship. In Culbertson, J. and Cunningham, L. (eds), pp. 234–53.

Carter, Carolyn and Monaco, Jenny (1987). *Learning information technology skills.* Boston Spa: British Library and Information Research Report no. 54.

Cerych, L. and Jallade, J.-P. (1986). *The coming technological revolution in education*. Report for Netherlands Ministry of Education and Science on the potential and limitations of new media and information technologies in education. Paris: European Institute of Education and Social Policy.

Commission of the European Communities (CEC) (1987). *Developments in the introduction of new information technologies in education. Social Europe*, supplement 2/87. Brussels: CEC, DG for Employment, Social Affairs and Education.

Congress of the United States, Office of Technology Assessment (1988). *Power on! New tools for teaching and learning*. Report summary. Washington, DC: Office of Technology Assessment.

Culbertson, Jack A. and Cunningham, Luvern L. (1986). *Microcomputers and education: 85th Yearbook of the National Society for the Study of Education*. Chicago: University of Chicago.

Department of Education and Science (UK) (1987). *Aspects of the work of the Microelectronics Education Programme. Report by HM Inspectors*. London: DES.

Department of Education and Science (UK) (1988). *National Curriculum Design and Technology Working Group: interim report*. London: DES.

Department of Education and Science (UK) (1989). *Information technology 5–16*. Curriculum Matters 15. London: DES.

Deutsches Jugendinstitut (1988). *Medien im Alltag von Kindern und Jugendlichen*. Munich: Deutsches Jugendinstitut; Weinheim: Juventa Verlag.

Diem, R.A. (1986). Computers in a school environment: preliminary report of the social consequences. *Theory and Research in Social Education*, **14** (2), 163–70.

Dunstan, G.D. (1988). Word processing: an holistic language experience. University of East Anglia MEd thesis.

Ellam, Nigel and Wellington, Jerry (1987). *Computers in the primary curriculum*. Sheffield, UK: University of Sheffield Division of Education.

Ennals, Richard (1986). Artificial intelligence and educational computing. In Ennals *et al.* (eds), pp. 45–66.

225

Ennals, Richard *et al.* (eds) (1986). *IT and education: the changing school.* Chichester, UK: Ellis Horwood.

Eraut, Michael (1988). *Review of research on in-service education: a UK perspective.* Background paper for the Fifth All-European Conference of Directors of Educational Research Institutions, Triesenberg (Liechtenstein) 11–14 October 1988, organized by the UNESCO Institute for Education in Hamburg, the Council for Cultural Cooperation and the European Information Centre of the Charles University for Further Education of Teachers, Prague. Strasbourg: Council of Europe, DECS/Rech (88) 25.

Eraut, Michael (ed.) (1989). *International encyclopedia of educational technology.* Oxford: Pergamon.

Feurzeig, Wallace (1986). Algebra slaves and agents in a Logo–based mathematics curriculum. Reprinted in Jones, A. and Scrimshaw, P. (eds), pp. 323–47.

Friedrichs, Gunter and Schaff, Adam (1982). *Microelectronics and society: for better or for worse.* A report to the club of Rome. Oxford: Pergamon.

Fullan, Michael (1982). *The meaning of educational change.* New York: Teachers College Press.

Geoffrion, Leo (1983). Computer based approaches to overcoming language handicap. In Megarry, J. *et al.* (eds), pp. 215–29.

Goodson, Ivor (1983). *School subjects and curriculum change.* London: Croom Helm.

Govier, Heather (1988). *Microcomputers in primary education – a survey of recent research.* ESRC InTER Programme Occasional Paper ITE/28a/88. University of Lancaster, Dept of Psychology.

Graebner, Celia (1989). Microcomputers in adult education. In Eraut, M. (ed.) pp. 175–81.

Gross, N., Giacquinta, J. and Bernstein, M. (1971). *Implementing organizational innovations.* New York: Harper & Row.

Gwyn, Rhys (1986). *Teaching and learning with the new technologies.* Brussels: Association for Teacher Education in Europe.

Hall, G.E. and Loucks, S. (1978). Teachers' concerns as a basis for facilitating and personalizing staff development. *Teachers College Record,* **80**, 36–53.

Hall, J. and Rhodes, V. (1986). *Microcomputers in primary schools – some observations and recommendations for good practice.* London: King's College, Centre for Educational Studies, Educational Computing Unit.

Harris, Duncan (ed.) (1988). *Education for the new technologies: World yearbook of education 1988.* London: Kogan Page.

Hawkins, Jan and Sheingold, Karen (1986). The beginning of a story: computers and the organisation of learning in classrooms. In Culbertson, J. and Cunningham, L. (eds), pp. 40–58.

Hawkridge, David, Vincent, Tom and Hales, Gerald (1985). *New information technology in the education of disabled children and adults.* London: Croom Helm.

Heidt, E.V. (1985). Instructional design: media selection. In *International encyclopedia of education,* Vol. 5, Husen, T. and Postlethwaite, T.N. (eds), pp. 2548–53. Oxford, UK: Pergamon.

Heywood, G. and Norman, P. (1988). Problems of educational innovation: the primary teacher's response to using the microcomputer. *Journal of Computer Assisted Learning,* **4** (1), 34–43.

Hoyles, C. and Sutherland, R. (1989). *Logo mathematics in the classroom.* London: Routledge.

Hughes, M., Macleod, H. and Potts, C. (1985). Using Logo with infant school children. *Educational Psychology,* **5** (3,4), 287–301.

Hunter, Beverley (1986). Computer related learning in vocational education. In Culbertson, J. and Cunningham, L. (eds), pp. 59–80.

Ingenkamp, F.-D. (1984). *Neue Medien vor der Schultür. Was Lehrer, Eltern und Erzieher über Neue Medien wissen sollten.* Weinheim: J. Beltz.

Issing, Ludwig J. (ed.) (1987). *Medienpädagogik im Informationszeitalter.* Weinheim: Deutscher Studien Verlag.

Jallade, Jean-Pierre (1984). *New information technologies (NIT) and technical education.* A survey of trends and policy issues in three countries. The Hague: Organisatie voor Strategisch Arbeidsmarktonderzoek (OSA).

Jamieson, Ian and Tasker, Mary (1988). Schooling and the new technology: rhetoric and reality. In Harris, D. (ed.), pp. 11–27.

227

Johnston, Vivien M. (1985). Introducing the microcomputer into English. *British Journal of Educational Technology*, **16** (3), 188–218.

Johnston, Vivien M. (1987). The evaluation of microcomputer programs: an area of debate. *Journal of Computer Assisted Learning*, **3** (2), 40–50.

Jones, Ann and Scrimshaw, Peter (1988). *Computers in education 5–13*. Milton Keynes, UK: Open University.

Kent, A.W. (1986). *The use of computers in the teaching of geography*. University of London Institute of Education.

Kulik, James and Kulik, Chen-Lin C. (1987). Review of recent research literature on computer-based instruction. *Contemporary Educational Psychology*, **12**, 222–30.

Large, Peter and Bradbury, Neil (1989). Skills crisis in IT as computers go 'male'. *Guardian*, 17 February, p. 13.

Levie, W.H. (1985). Instructional design: media attributes. In *International encyclopedia of education, Vol. 5*, Husen, T. and Postlethwaite, T.N. (eds), pp. 2545–8. Oxford: Pergamon.

Levin, Harry W. (1986). Cost and cost effectiveness in computer assisted instruction. In Culbertson, J. and Cunningham, L. (eds), pp. 156–74.

Lewis, Bob (1988). *Learning through microworlds*. ESRC InTER Programme Occasional Paper ITE/26/88. University of Lancaster, Dept of Psychology.

Makrakis, Vasilios (1988). *Computers in school education: the cases of Sweden and Greece*. Stockholm: University of Stockholm Institute of International Education.

Marcus, Stephen (1984). Computers and the teaching of writing: prose and poetry. In Terry, C. (ed.), pp. 117–28.

Marland, Michael (ed.) (1981). *Information skills in the secondary school curriculum*. Schools Council Curriculum Bulletin 9. London: Methuen.

Masterman, Len (1986). *Impact of mass communication media on curriculum development and educational methods*. Paris: UNESCO.

Masterman, Len (1988). *The development of media education in Europe in the 1980s*. Strasbourg: Council of Europe, Council for Cultural Cooperation.

Megarry, Jacquetta *et al.* (eds) (1983). *Computers and education: world year book of education 1982/83.* London: Kogan Page.

Miller, Larry (1986). Computers and the language arts: theory and practice. *Journal of Curriculum Studies,* **18** (3), 285–97.

Moles, Abraham (1984). Media systems and educational systems. In *Media education,* pp. 17–43. Paris: UNESCO.

Moonen, Jef and Plomp, Tjeerd (eds), (1987). *EURIT 1986 – developments in educational software and courseware.* Proceedings of the first European conference on Education and IT. Oxford, UK: Pergamon.

Morocco, Catherine and Neuman, Susan (1986). Word processing and the acquisition of writing strategies. *Journal of Learning Disabilities,* **19** (4), 243–7.

Neuwirth, Erich (1986). Is it necessary to understand computers to use them sensibly? In Ennals, R. *et al.* (eds), pp. 23–8.

Olson, John and Eaton, Sandra (1986). *Case studies of microcomputers in the classroom. Questions for curriculum and teacher education.* Toronto: Ontario Ministry of Education. Available from The Ontario Institute for Studies in Education, 252 Bloor St West, Toronto, Ontario, Canada M5S 1V6.

Olson, John (1988). *School worlds, microworlds. Computers and the culture of the classroom.* Oxford, UK: Pergamon.

OECD/CERI (1986). *New information technologies: a challenge for education.* Paris: OECD.

OECD/CERI (1987a). *Information technologies and basic learning: reading, writing, science and mathematics.* Paris: OECD.

OECD/CERI (1987b). *The introduction of computers in schools: the Norwegian experience.* Examiners' report. Paris: OECD.

OECD/CERI (1988). *Human resources and corporate strategy. Technological change in banks and insurance companies.* Paris: OECD.

Papert, Seymour (1980). *Mindstorms: children, computers and powerful ideas.* Brighton, UK: Harvester.

Pea, Roy D. (1985). Beyond amplification: using the computer to reorganize mental functioning. *Educational Psychologist,* **20** (4), 167–82.

Pearson, Howard and Wilkinson, Andrew (1986). The use of the word processor in assisting children's writing development. *Educational*

Review, **38** (2), 169–87.

Peper, John B. (1986). Implementing computer-based education in Jefferson County, Colorado. In Culbertson, J. and Cunningham, L. (eds), pp. 132–55.

Petch, Rhiannon (1988). Crossing the divide. In Wild, M. (ed.), pp. 34–6.

Robert, Frederic (1984). *Possible uses of computers in primary education: the example of France.* Background paper for the Educational Research Workshop on Science in Primary Schools, Edinburgh, 3–6 September 1984. Strasbourg: Council of Europe, DECS/Rech (84) 32.

Salomon, Gavriel and Perkins, D.N. (1987). Transfer of cognitive skills from programming: when and how? *Journal of Educational Computing Research,* **3** (2), 149–69.

Saxer, U., Bonfadelli, H. and Hättenschwiler, W. (1980). *Die Massenmedien im Leben der Kinder und Jugendlichen (Zürcher Beiträge zur Medienpädagogik).* Zürich: Klett & Blamer.

Scottish Education Department (1987). *Learning and teaching in Scottish secondary schools: the use of microcomputers.* An HMI report. Edinburgh: Scottish Education Department.

Self, John (1987). IKBS in education. *Educational Review,* **39** (2), 147–54.

Sleeman, D. and Brown, J.S. (eds) (1982). *Intelligent tutoring systems.* London: Academic Press.

Sloan, Douglas (1984). *The computer in education: a critical perspective.* New York: Teachers College Press.

Smith, David (1989). Microcomputers in schools. In Eraut, M. (ed.) (1989), pp. 170–5.

Sturm, H., Holzheuer, K. and Helmreich, R. (1978). *Emotionale Wirkungen des Fernsehens – Jugendliche als Rezipienten (Internationales Zentralinstitut für das Jugend – und Bildungsfernsehen No. 10).* Munich: Saur.

Sturm, H. *et al.* (1979). Grundlagen einer Medienpädagogik. *Zürcher Beiträger zur Medienpädagogik.*

Taylor, William D. and Johnsen, Jane B. (1986). Resisting technological momentum. In Culbertson, J. and Cunningham, L. (eds), pp. 216–33.

Terry, Colin (1984). *Using computers in schools.* London: Croom Helm.

Turkle, S. (1984). *The second self: computers and the human spirit.* London: Granada.

UNESCO (1979). *Many voices, one world: communication and society today and tomorrow* (The MacBride Report). Paris: UNESCO.

UNESCO (1984). *Media education.* Paris: UNESCO.

van Weert, Tom (1984). *A model syllabus for literacy in information technology for all teachers.* Brussels: Association for Teacher Education in Europe. Reprinted as Chapter 5 in Ennals, R., Gwyn, R. and Zdravchev, L. (eds). *Information and technology: the changing school.* Chichester: Ellis Horwood.

Vickers, Margaret (ed.) (1987). *Microcomputers and secondary teaching: implications for teacher education.* Report on an International Seminar arranged by the Scottish Education Department in cooperation with the OECD. Edinburgh: Scottish Education Department.

Walker, Decker F. (1986). Computers and the curriculum. In Culbertson, J. and Cunningham, L. (eds), pp. 22–39.

Weir, Sylvia (1987). *Cultivating minds: a LOGO casebook.* New York: Harper & Row.

Wild, Martyn (1988). *Microcomputers in secondary educations – an annotated bibliography.* ESRC InTER Programme Occasional Paper ITE/28b – c/88. University of Lancaster, Dept of Psychology.

Wright, Ann (1987). The process of microtechnological innovation in two primary schools: a case study of teachers' thinking. *Educational Review*, **39** (2), 107–15.

PART 3

FIVE CASE STUDIES

CHAPTER 1

Denmark: Computer Conferencing in Distance Education

Since January 1988 Jutland Open University (JOU) has been using computer conferencing on an experimental basis. In December 1988 JOU, in collaboration with Aarhus Technical College, signed a study contract with IBM Denmark. The objective of this project is to develop, on the basis of strategic IBM products, a computer conferencing system for distance education/learning and to implement and test this system in specific open university courses.

So far we have tested the use of computer conferencing in distance education on five courses in 1988 and 1989. Before we describe the preliminary results, a short explanation of the educational model of JOU and the pedagogical motives for using computer conferencing is needed.

PEDAGOGICAL MOTIVES FOR USING COMPUTER CONFERENCING

The Jutland Open University is a joint venture between the Art Faculties of the University of Aarhus, the University of Aalborg and the University Centre of Southern Jutland.

The basic idea underlying adult education in Denmark has been that it should be available for all adults irrespective of

235

their educational qualifications and that the primary aim should be personal fulfilment. Therefore in Denmark no tradition of university-level correspondence courses has been developed and no degrees or university diplomas have been awarded within this framework.

JOU was established in 1982 to bridge the gap between the informal adult education system and the formal system, providing an opportunity for a university education to people without the formal entry qualifications. All the courses are developed by teachers from the universities involved. The teachers are in charge of the tutorials, the counselling and the exams. In other words there is no division of labour between course teams, tutors and counsellors. This means that JOU tutors are also scholars engaged in research parallel to their tutorial tasks in the JOU courses. In Danish universities there has been a close connection between research and education. University teachers have always devoted half their time to research projects. This model has been carried over into the pedagogical conception of JOU.

The group-oriented concept is another essential feature of JOU. This means that the students are organized in classes of 20–35 students. These classes meet five or six times a year, at weekend seminars and summer schools. All-in-all the students are given about 20 days of face-to-face tuition during a year. Within the class a number of smaller study-groups or project-groups may be organized to meet or communicate during the periods between the seminars. These groups may be organized on a local basis between students coming from the same area, or they may be organized on a more subject- or project-oriented basis, independently of where they live.

From an educational or pedagogical point of view we try to involve the students in the planning process and in the process of structuring the study material. In this way we hope to establish a higher degree of interactivity between the knowledge, experience and interests of the course teachers and those of the students. Technologically, this results in the need for open learning activities and processes characterized by multi-dimensional communication between teachers and students and between the students themselves. Therefore we needed to find media and develop media configurations which would enable geographically isolated students to communicate in groups and to get help and counselling from the teachers on a day-to-day basis.

We find that computer conferencing satisfies these needs in a lot of ways. It is one of the few pedagogical tools for promoting social integration and other interactive processes in an educational system where students are geographically isolated from each other, and where, consequently, the possibilities for close contact and cooperation are drastically limited compared to normal classroom teaching. At the same time computer conferencing is a democratic medium which allows authentic communication between participants. Perhaps most important of all, communication in computer conferencing takes place independently of time and place.

Until now we have used the Swedish PortaCOM computer conferencing system on an IBM mainframe and tested it through the teaching of three courses in 1988 and two in 1989. The computer conferencing facilities have been used for communication, group work, instruction and information retrieval in addition to the five seminars and normal telephone tutoring. Computer conferencing has been used as a supplement to help students in the periods between seminars – not as a substitute for face-to-face contact between students and teachers.

Different pedagogical models and different combinations of hardware have been tested. In 1988 two art foundation courses were taught in parallel. In one, all the students were equipped with a personal computer and a modem at home, whereas in the other course the students had to use the facilities of the nearest JOU study centre. A third course in archaeology also used the study centres.

The test period will end this year, so we have no final conclusions yet, but the preliminary results show that computer conferencing has been an efficient tool in distance education. The students with the home-based personal computers have found that computer conferencing has facilitated communication with the teachers and their fellow students. These students completed the art foundation course with better grades than on similar courses where computer conferencing had not been used. Their success rate was higher and there were considerably more activities between the students

237

and the teachers and between the students themselves.

For this group of students who had a microcomputer at home and very easy access to the conferencing facility, the conferencing system has been a very useful addition in distance education. However, there were problems with the use of the system. The students found that it placed a lot of attention on the system itself instead of on the actual learning process; the teachers were not trained efficiently for organizing subject-oriented communication on the system; the group of students who had access to the system only in the study centres did not use it very much; and there were problems inherent in the system itself. For instance, PortaCOM only handles 7-bit ASCII text files.

To test whether these problems can be overcome, a new approach has been implemented in 1989. The experiment on the arrt foundation course is being repeated with a new group of students equipped with home-based computers. We want to test the results of improved teacher training for computer conferencing (cf. Bodil Brander Christensen: *The Teacher and Computer Mediated Communication at Jutland Open University. A Case Study*) and the effect of placing responsibility for the technical introduction to computer conferencing within the JOU staff instead of the course. The new approach is also being used in a course in mass communication: 20 per cent of the students have home-based personal computers with modems; the rest are using the study centres.

COMPUTER CONFERENCING AND THE STUDY CENTRES

Originally five study centres were established: two in Aarhus connected to Aarhus University, one at Aalborg University, one at the University Centre of Southern Jutland and one in Holstebro, a city in the western part of Jutland. Each study centre is connected to the mainframe in Aarhus through a leased circuit (14.4 kbit/second) and is equipped with graphic terminals (IBM 3179), personal computers (IBM XT and PS/2 model 60), a scanner (IBM 3118) and a printer (IBM 4224).

The objective of our experiment with computer conferencing in connection with the study centres is to find out whether it will be a feasible solution in the future. At present such centres could be established all over Denmark so that every student would have to travel less than 50 km to find a study centre. It would be a cheap solution for the Open Universities and for the students compared to the alternative: for each student to have a home-based personal computer on a leasing contract. The study centres could be equipped and run by the city councils as a public service open for all sorts of educational functions. But the question is: will the students use the study centres?

So far our experience has not been very promising. It has been difficult to motivate the students without home-based personal computers to use computer conferencing. The students seem unwilling to leave their homes and go to the study centres for communication, when they can just as easily pick up the telephone or post a letter. The prospect of rewriting one's essays and comments on the conferencing system is not a productive one from the student's point of view.

The study centres have to be equipped with more facilities than just computer communication. The students must be able to work there for several hours. Therefore, the environment of the centres must be attractive, with rooms for group meetings among the students in the region, copying machines, television sets, video recorders, coffee machines, etc. A study centre has to be something between a laboratory and a library. Furthermore, the students have to be motivated for using computer conferencing. To most of them it is a completely new way of communicating and they have yet to discover its possibilities.

In the first couple of months of the mass communication course the teachers (Joergen Bang and Soeren Kolstrup) had the frustrating experience that very few students were using the computer conferencing system. The students did not use the telephone or the ordinary mail either, because they knew they were not supposed to. After two months the teachers decided to oblige the students to use the system. They designed a large-scale project in quantitative content research. Over a period of four days each student had to analyse a newspaper, a radio newscast or a television news programme. They had to register the main events on a prepared form in a conference, and give their comments on the genres and points of view in the different articles/elements. Later they had to write a small essay placing their news media in the context of the national news flow.

The experiment is still running, so we have no final conclusions. But the activities on the system have been enormous. It seems that the students can see the possibilities of computer conferencing in this situation. They are building a sort of database, instead of mailing an enormous number of letters. At the same time they gain access right away to all the information collected by their fellow students, and can use it when they need it.

In this case we have obliged the students both to use computer conferencing and to work through the study centres. They have had no alternative, if they wanted to continue with the course. Unfortunately, we think this is the only way to do it!

The economic argument is one reason why we are so keen on the use of study centres. Another is that the study centres are the only way in which we can give the students access to databases, graphics, etc. These facilities require fast connections (64 kbit/second) because huge masses of data have to be transferred, and rather sophisticated equipment, impossible using home-based microcomputers at a reasonable price, at least at this time. Within a few years it will be possible to establish slow scan video connection with all the study centres in Denmark using the Integrated Systems Digital Network (ISDN) service of the PTT. Integrated ISDN work stations consisting of a computer work station, an audio headset, a video monitor and a video camera will be available very soon. This will give the students opportunities for direct eye and ear contact with the teacher and fellow students as a further supplement to computer conferencing.

DEVELOPING AN IMPROVED SYSTEM

As mentioned above, the conferencing system itself had a great impact on the pattern of use. For trained computer users it was clearly an obstacle that PortaCOM is a command-driven system not like the systems they normally work on. For inexperienced users it was difficult to understand that only ASCII text could be put into the system and that it operated in line mode. That the system is only able to handle ASCII text was especially annoying in the phase where the students used the system for group-based production of their examination essays, as these typically had been produced off-line on a microcomputer using a word processor. These texts could not be put into the conferencing system itself, but had to be transferred on an additional file transfer system.

These restrictions – which are common in the conferencing systems commercially available for the moment (COSY, PAR-TICIPATE, CAUCUS, etc.) – have led JOU to the decision to start designing a new conferencing system which will be able to handle all sorts of data in the same integrated system. The system will be designed to run in full screen mode and be menu-driven.

It will be developed on the basis of commercially available products such as IBM's relational database program, SQL, a fourth generation programming language, CSP, and various help tools. This approach will enable the development to be finished within a short time. It is estimated that the system will be fully operational in December 1989 and that an alpha (test) version will be available in July 1989.

By designing the system in full screen mode it will be possible to work with pop-up windows and curtains and thereby to operate the system by the mouse and/or function keys. The design of the user interface will follow the standards now set by Apple and IBM. By following these standards the system will operate in much the same way as the systems that experienced users normally work on.

The design specifications stipulate that it must be possible to tailor the system for the specific needs of an institution or a specific course. In practice this will be done by blinding some of the available functions for the user and adding on new functions if needed. In the same way it will be possible to have a multilingual interface to the system.

By using the database program as the core of the system it will be possible to build into the conferencing system electronic libraries of CAL programs, spreadsheets, scanned-in pictures and texts. The texts can be either in the original format or transformed automatically into ASCII. The design specifications also stipulate that the system should be built in modules so that it will be possible to put part of the system (the reading and writing functions) on microcomputers integrated with the communication program, allowing automatic up- and downloading of news.

Once the system is available it is our hope that new ways of structuring distance education will emerge as teachers from different fields start using the system.

France: An Original Procedure for the Acquisition of Software in the French Education System – Joint Licences

COMPUTER STUDIES IN FRENCH SECONDARY SCHOOLS

To date, approximately 130 000 microcomputers have been installed in France in the 8000 general, technical and vocational state secondary schools. Most of these are PC-compatible computers and computers organized in mini-networks. The use of computers in the educational system is developing in three directions:

Informing and training future citizens. In addition to the need to make pupils aware of what will be a permanent aspect of their working lives, and indeed of their everyday lives, pupils should be taught to regard computer technology not just as an educational discipline – which is, in any case, studied only in higher education or as an optional subject in senior high schools – but above all as a series of applications, methods and approaches which make it possible to extend the boundaries of human thought and action.

Using computers for educational purposes. It was very quickly realized by teachers and educational administrators that computers could be used as a powerful instrument to improve the effectiveness of the transmission and absorption of knowledge. This involves using computers as educational equipment providing the opportunity to introduce modes of learning which were difficult, if not impossible, to apply using traditional resources.

Providing young people with training adapted to the requirements of the employment market. In order to give young people the qualifications they need to find employment there will need to be an unprecedented extension of the range of knowledge and skills taught. While it is easier to see the changes required in technical education (which are directly related to changes in the professions concerned), the fact remains that this process applies to all school disciplines.

These uses of computer technology in schools obviously depend on the existence and distribution of software through which the possibilities opened up by computers can be exploited to the full. The range of software available which corresponds to these requirements is vast and ranges from the specialized software used with certain classes preparing for the advanced vocational training certificate to tutorial programs via applications which have now become classic, such as word processing, spreadsheets, etc.

It was therefore necessary for the ministry to introduce purchase and distribution procedures which conformed to the main lines of its general policy. This report is intended to describe one of these, the procedure for the acquisition of user's rights in relation to software usually referred to as the 'joint licence procedure', which was introduced nearly two years ago. In addition to a technical study (stages of the procedure, 'philosophy' behind the contract, problems of implementation, etc.), the report will contain an initial assessment intended to analyse not only the impact of this operation but also its limits and potential pitfalls.

Before studying the procedure in detail, the report gives a brief account of the background to its adoption, since it formalizes relations between the private sector and schools which cannot be understood without a knowledge of the main policy options of the French education system on the one hand (decentralization and dispersal of resources, national policy on the introduction of computer technology into education, etc.), and problems arising directly from the enormous growth of the software market in the industrialized countries on the other (competition and legal questions, to mention only the most obvious). The attempt to give due consideration to these various questions is one of the original features of the procedure.

BRIEF CHRONOLOGICAL ACCOUNT OF THE PRODUCTION AND DISTRIBUTION OF SOFTWARE IN SCHOOLS

There have been three periods in the development of the use of computer technology in education, each of which had its own procedures for the production and distribution of software.

EXPERIMENTAL PHASE: DO-IT-YOURSELF PRODUCTION

Following the international colloquium organized in 1970 in Sèvres by the OECD, the so-called '58 lycées' experiment marked the beginning of the introduction of computer technology into French secondary education. As a result of this project approximately 500 teachers were given mainly technical training intended to enable them to decide how to make use of computer technology in their teaching. The educational programs created by these teachers were distributed free of charge to lycées by the Institut National de la Recherche Pédagogique (INRP) as they were produced. The operating system for the computers and the language (LSE), produced by the university sector, were delivered with the software. At this time there was no software industry in the proper sense of the term, i.e. a sector structured for the production and distribution of software.

The training and equipment aspects of the experiment were halted in 1976. The INRP continued to distribute the programs produced and an INRP research team was asked to assess them.

GRADUAL DEVELOPMENT PHASE: ESTABLISHMENT OF AN INDUSTRIAL AND COMMERCIAL SECTOR IN THE SOFTWARE FIELD

At the end of 1978 the government adopted a plan for the supply of 10 000 microcomputers; soon after, in 1983, as part of the ninth plan, this project was extended, becoming the operation known as '100 000 micros, 100 000 teachers trained'. The final stage of this process was the announcement by the Prime Minister in January 1985 of the 'computers for all' programme and the decision to equip all schools with computers.

In 1981 the Centre National de Documentation Pédagogique (National Centre for Educational Resources) was asked to coordinate the production of educational software and its distribution to schools. The principle adopted for this distribution was that the products would be free of charge, with the centre's regional branches being given responsibility for updating the products available. This public sector policy of ignoring the need for an immediate return on investment was calculated to create the conditions under which the educational quality of products could be guaranteed.

The same period saw the emergence of a commercial and industrial sector turning out professional products, thanks to the standardization of equipment and operating systems and the increasing computerization of society. This development raised a number of questions.

About the quantity and quality of the products available. As the Pair-Lecorre report pointed out as far back as 1981, 'one of the main obstacles to the introduction of computer technology in schools is the inadequate supply of high-quality educational software'.

About the relations between the public and private sectors. The production of both educational software and professional products requires more and more time, skill and development facilities; it must therefore be organized along industrial lines. The public sector cannot cope with the variety of necessary developments. The emergence of educational software produced by private

246

companies and based on the existence of an economic sector already specializing in the production of educational books and materials (school books, equipment for physics laboratories, etc.) raised the problem of relations between the ministry and private publishers. Consequently, it seemed more and more difficult to imagine the public sector in a monopoly situation without discouraging the development of a market in which the Ministry of Education would not be the only customer and the emergence of French products which would have to win their place in a European or even international market.

About the distribution of software to schools. Firstly, centralized distribution to schools by the Ministry of Education raised awkward management problems in view of the number of schools and the number of different products. Secondly, a legal problem was created by the practice adopted by many schools of making joint orders. This practice enabled each of the schools involved to acquire copies of the various software items received by the others, a method prohibited by the legislation of July 1985 on intellectual, literary and artistic property.

GENERALIZATION PHASE: STRUCTURING OF RELATIONS BETWEEN THE PRIVATE AND PUBLIC SECTORS IN THE PURCHASE OF SOFTWARE

The launch of the 'computers for all' programme may be regarded from one angle as the end of a centralized process for the introduction of computer technology into the various parts of the education system and from another angle as the beginning of a period of structuring and normalizing the relations between the public and private sectors.

The main policy options of the French educational system with regard to decentralization have naturally been applied to purchases of computer equipment. These are the responsibility of the local authorities (Conseil Général and Conseil Régional), with the exception of specific allocations, which remain centralized.

For the reasons mentioned above, the public authorities have decided that software should be produced by private sector publishers or computer software houses. Cooperative relations are beginning to be established through the educational innovations programme. Teachers participate in the design of teaching strategies which can be translated into educational software. Products which the private sector would not be able to publish (specific disciplines in which products would not be economically viable because of their limited distribution) are produced through co-publishing arrangements similar to those used for textbooks.

In dealing with this incipient market it is the responsibility of the Ministry of Education to specify its requirements clearly and to institute a purchasing policy; otherwise, educational software publishers will not continue to take the risk of publishing ambitious products which are expensive to develop. Moreover, and this applies to all types of products, the illegal copying of software in schools must be prevented by enforcement of legislation on breach of copyright.

The maintenance of adequate budgetary appropriations for the purchase of software from one financial year to the next is necessary to ensure that enough people are aware of the policy and to meet the growing demand for high-quality products. A substantial proportion of these appropriations is made available to schools directly so as not to restrict their freedom of choice.

THE JOINT LICENCE PROCEDURE: OBJECTIVES, PRINCIPLE AND 'PHILOSOPHY'

THE OBJECTIVES AND THE PRINCIPLE

The 'joint licence' procedure, which has been in use for two years, is intended to provide solutions to the problems raised by the developments described above. The objectives can be summed up as follows:

to avoid the need for teachers who wish or are compelled to use educational or professional software to resort to illegal practices;

to reduce the cost of these products, particularly for professional software, which is often very expensive;

to interest private publishers in developing and distributing high-quality educational software in a market which is still limited;

to encourage teachers to use products corresponding to ministerial guidelines;

to encourage schools to purchase high-quality software while respecting their freedom of choice in this field.

The principle of the 'joint licence' lies in the purchase by the Directorate of Senior High Schools and Lower Secondary Schools of the right to use for an unlimited period certain items of software previously selected for their educational and technical qualities. The software items concerned in these contracts are intended solely for educational use. Consequently, schools, initial and in-service teacher training institutions, and the information and guidance services responsible to the Directorate of Senior High Schools and Lower Secondary Schools can order these products directly from publishers, during a two-year period, at a price in keeping with the size of their budgets.

THE 'PHILOSOPHY'

The mechanism of the joint licence is apparently simple in principle, but the details are nevertheless fairly complex. The contracts concluded between the Ministry of Education and various publishers therefore have two aspects, which are related through the fact that, while the contracts are concluded between these two partners, the beneficiaries are the establishments concerned; they are contracts conferring a right on a third party.

The following considerations are intended as a description of the two types of relations which will be established: between the ministry and publishers on the one hand, and between publishers and schools on the other.

Relations between the Ministry of Education and publishers

The purpose of the licence is to enable schools to acquire software at a cost well below the usual market price. It does not replace all the contractual relations between publishers and schools; on the contrary, the latter will themselves purchase the software they regard as necessary for their requirements, but will simply do so at much more advantageous prices than those offered to the public as a whole or to the education service hitherto. The price in question is only marginally higher than the product's production costs plus postage.

This possibility of purchasing software at very low prices is not limited to a certain number of copies (for the whole of France or for individual establishments), even though the cost of the licence is initially assessed on the basis of an overall estimate of requirements. Such a limit would have been an irksome constraint, likely to lead to unfortunate consequences (as schools would need to hurry to buy in order to qualify for the special low price) and prejudice the success of the software concerned. It is therefore clear that when the number used for the initial estimate has been exceeded the producer will sell to schools at a price close to the cost of production, with no compensating adjustment to the overall cost of the licence: this is, in a sense, the price that has to be paid for the success of the operation.

If the opposite case occurs, i.e. if fewer orders for the product are received than were forecast, the Directorate of Senior High Schools and Lower Secondary Schools can order directly from the publisher on the same conditions as a school. Thus the central administration cannot make a financial loss.

The sum paid for the licence by the ministry takes into account not only an estimate of the numbers of compatible machines owned by schools but also the fact that selection of the software by the Ministry of Education gives a considerable boost to sales of the product. Although such selection is not intended as a seal of approval, that is nevertheless the function it serves.

The contract is concluded for a period of two years; only during this period can schools purchase the products under these favourable conditions. However, this period does not apply to user's rights in respect of the purchased products, which are valid for an unlimited period.

The product is defined by the name and version under which it is listed in the publisher's catalogue. It is identical with the version available commercially. It comes together with the relevant documentation (technical guide and teacher's notes). Nevertheless, in some circumstances, in view of economic requirements, it may be permissible not to include documentation with every set of software disks, e.g. documentation for four sets of disks, as in the case of professional products, which sometimes have bulky technical handbooks. On the other hand, more than one set of teacher's notes may be supplied for products intended for local networks, for example.

The contract specifies the types of machine with which the product can be used.

When products are updated during the term of validity of the contract, two different solutions may be adopted:

- The new version is substituted for the old version, with the agreement of the Ministry, without any change to the cost of the licence or the purchase price for the school. The publisher is not obliged to maintain supplies of the previous version. This was the case in 1988 when *Word* 4 took place of *Word* 3.

- The new version may be purchased by schools at a new price (but without change to the cost of the licence), in which case the publisher is obliged to maintain supplies of the previous version at its old price. It is then necessary to add a clause to the contract. This was the case in 1988 for four products: *Turbo Pascal*, *Turbo Graphics*, *VP Planner* and *Graph in the Box*.

If a company is wound-up or its assets are liquidated during the term of validity of the contract, the minister can take over responsibility for distribution of the products in order to meet orders from schools. To that end, the publisher is required, when the contract is signed, to deposit all materials needed for duplication of the product with an official depositary.

251

A copy of each official order form is sent to the central administration so that it can supervise the procedure. Thus it is possible to measure the distribution of each licenced product regularly.

Relations between schools and publishers

Schools themselves purchase the software they need from the publisher, either directly or through the latter's distribution network. This is therefore a second type of contract, established directly between schools and publishers, and formalized through the despatch of the official order form which schools are obliged to use to make their purchases.

The publisher undertakes to reply to any order made by an approved establishment within one month.

Use of the software is not tied to a particular machine or a particular place. As already pointed out, the right of use is valid for an unlimited period. In signing the order form, the school gives the publisher its express undertaking not to make any unauthorized copies of the software.

The publisher undertakes to correct as soon as possible any mistakes which might be detected in the software or accompanying documentation where such mistakes would prevent normal use.

IMPLEMENTATION OF THE PROCEDURE

The various phases of the procedure are as follows.

THE DEFINITION OF PRIORITIES

While the definition of requirements is relatively easy for professional software, it is much more difficult for educational software. It is therefore more important to define the objectives for each discipline; these will be specified in a document accompanying the consultation proposal which should enable publishers and software houses to decide whether their products can meet these requirements.

For this purpose the Directorate of Senior High Schools and Lower Secondary Schools coordinates the requests of the various boards of inspection and schools. Questions relating to budgetary possibilities may be submitted to arbitration.

IMPLEMENTATION

On the basis of the previously defined priority fields the Directorate of Senior High Schools and Lower Secondary Schools invites all publishers and software houses to take part in the consultation process, which is designed to give all publishers and companies developing software in the above-mentioned fields the opportunity to present their products and learn the details of the procedure. As a rough indication, in 1988 the Ministry of Education received 582 proposals for software or planned software through this consultation process.

ASSESSMENT AND SELECTION OF PRODUCTS

In order to examine these proposals and assess the educational value of the products concerned, the Director of Senior High Schools and Lower Secondary Schools has set up committees with responsibility for educational, technical and administrative details. These committees mainly cover particular disciplines, with the exception of committees specializing in the study of multi-purpose applications such as programming languages, authoring systems, expert systems, etc. The conditions under which this educational assessment is carried out guarantee the confidentiality of the information provided.

During the 1988 procedure a total of 111 persons participated directly in the work of 16 committees. The results of this work, which provide a detailed assessment of products currently available on the software market in relation to the requirements of the education system, are used as the basis for a series of reports. These reports specify which products have the appropriate educational and technical qualities. The purchasing procedures are implemented on the basis of these results.

The Directorate of Senior High Schools and Lower Secondary Schools then replies to all the publishers who have submitted proposals, informing them whether the products they have proposed during the consultation process are suitable for future purchase.

THE NEGOTIATION PHASES

The companies whose software has been selected are invited to the Directorate of Senior High Schools and Lower Secondary Schools to discuss their financial proposals. Negotiations are based on:

an assessment of the number of machines with which the product is likely to be used (planned area of use of the software, previous sales statistics, etc.);

consideration of the type of product: educational software (in particular items functioning only on mini networks) for which the only market is the education system is not subject to the same cost assessment criteria as professional type software.

Negotiations are concluded with the signature of the contract, which must specify the cost of the acquisition of user's rights and the licence holder's obligations, particularly his undertaking to reply to all orders made out by approved persons on an official form (appended to the contract) showing the unitary price of a single copy of the software in question.

PUBLICATION OF RESULTS AND INFORMATION

Information to schools about the products for which user's rights have been acquired is circulated through notices in the *Bulletin Officiel de l'Education Nationale*. A more detailed catalogue describing the products and specifying the conditions for their acquisition and use is sent to all secondary schools.

PRODUCTS AVAILABLE UNDER THE JOINT LICENCE PROCEDURE

To date, users' rights have been acquired for 55 items of software (21 in 1987 and 34 in 1988, including two CD-ROM titles). In 1988 priority was given to educational software and professional software corresponding to certain precise objectives of technological and vocational training. In 1987 the procedure was used more for programming languages (Pascal and Logo) and multi-purpose professional applications (spreadsheets, database management systems, word processing, graphics programs).

The procedure was given a very favourable reception by teachers and publishers. Orders from schools for 'licenced' products reflect the important role education tends to play in the field of the new information technologies (see Table 2); by 30 June 1988, i.e. scarcely a year after the signature of the first 21 contracts, 61 000 items had been ordered by schools. By that date, for example, 9518 copies of *Multiplan* had been ordered by senior high schools and lower secondary schools (out of 57 000 copies sold in Europe in 1987–88) and 8400 copies of *Word* (99 000 in Europe during the same period); the average for educational products was about 2000 copies.

Software coordinators in the local education authorities have conducted a large-scale information campaign on the types of products available, the arrangements for purchase and the conditions for use. The publishers of the products concerned have played a very active part in this campaign, proving, if proof were needed, that they regard the education sector not only as a market but also as an economic platform for the distribution of their products outside this sector.

CONCLUSION

The favourable reactions which met the initial implementation of this procedure seem to indicate that it meets the general requirements of secondary schools and that the use of computer technology in the various school disciplines is on the way to

Table 2 Total purchase by schools, at at 30 June 1988, of software made available under the 1987 joint licence procedure

Name of company	Title	No. of copies ordered as at 15 February 1988	No. of copies ordered as at 30 June 1988
ACL	Imagiciel	1240	1530
Act Informatique	Logo +	912	1400
Borland	Turbo Pascal	5496	8244
	Turbo Graphics	2630	3682
	Reflex	2018	2220
Commande	dBase III+	3195	3977
	Javelin	468	549
Fil	Tortue de Mer	1383	1647
	Valise Practi	1286	1644
Hatier	L'Ecrivain	1900	2550
Jeriko	Compolangues	2790	3550
Langage et			
Informatique	Apprenticiels	803	1250
Microsoft	Multiplan	6040	9518
	Word	5558	8439
	Windows	1102	1453
	Souris	1703	1720
Nathan	Euclide	1446	1855
	Cartax	1348	1838
Pi Soft	GMP2D	350	438
Softissimo	Graph in the Box	1559	2066
	VP Planner	1137	1588
Total		44 364	61 158

becoming common practice.

It should be noted that the procedure works well with completed products already on the market. However, educational software requires heavy investment in a relatively weak market and public institutions therefore need to intervene either in advance, through direct aid to production (as in the case of various European plans such as Delta or Comett and the policies of certain countries such as Canada), or through an undertaking to purchase completed products. The joint licence procedure belongs to this second type of intervention. It could be extended to products still at the development stage and this would help to encourage the emergence of promising products. It needs to be complemented by co-production agreements between the public and private sectors for software with a very limited potential market.

With regard to professional products, software publishers pay close attention to the Ministry's choices, in the hope that through the education system they will gain access to a faithful future market. As a result of this analysis the Ministry has begun to receive a growing number of proposals relating to products, services, discounts, etc. Processing of these proposals must not be allowed to slow down the procedure, or there will be a danger that the requirements initially expressed will not be satisfied in a field where changes are very rapid.

It is necessary to make sure that no monopoly is established with regard to a particular type of product. Schools have a duty to teach pupils the concepts behind software applications and give them experience of using the products based on them, but must ensure that there is no confusion between these concepts and the brand names of the products.

The 'joint licence' procedure obviously does not meet all the requirements of the educational system. For example, bulk purchase procedures are more suited to certain very specific requirements in technical education, where particular courses are run in only a few geographically scattered centres and the products are expensive and essential for the development of the disciplines involved. Similarly, the Ministry can acquire users' rights for only a limited number of software items; there is a risk that good products might not be ordered by schools because they have not been 'selected', even though schools are free to decide what to purchase. These problems would hinder the development of innovative educational practices. It is therefore very important to provide information to users and local decision-makers.

Finally, there has to be training in the use of the products concerned, and especially their use in the classroom; otherwise there is a strong danger that, however many items of software are acquired, their distribution will be measured only in quantitative rather than qualitative terms.

Italy: Schools and the Media, 1954-1987 – Social and Cultural Dimensions of Education Policies

INTRODUCTION

The purpose of this study is to highlight certain aspects of the relationship between the mass media and the school of which relatively little notice has so far been taken and which have not been studied in depth in Italy or elsewhere. These are the sociological and cultural questions underlying the technology, teaching methods and education policies themselves. This text is based on the results of several years of experimental research into the media, schools television and school–media relations; particular reference is made to a research programme which was centred during its first few years (from 1981 onwards) on the University of Naples, and for which the Department of Cultural Sociology of the Cesare Alfieri Faculty of Political Sciences of the University of Florence is now responsible. The nature and findings of the research programme are believed to be of potential general interest in a wider context than Italy. The two basic reasons for this interest are the methodology, which is linked to the research strategies adopted, and the fundamental nature of the research – the specific characteristics of the situation in Italy make it a fairly rich source of information for others who are conducting experiments, in both developed and developing countries.

As far as methodology is concerned, we shall highlight some original features of the research programme:

the intention to observe the education process in the long term, returning to the subject of the research on an annual basis;

a combination of quantitative data (objective and structural and the results of questionnaire-based surveys) and qualitative data (collected through ethno-anthropological observation in limited contexts);

comparative surveys involving the three social groups which together 'make' a school (pupils, teachers and parents);

a comparison between structural data and ideas (between 'objective' realities and the way in which these are represented, and between opinions and the respect with which society views them).

We have said that the Italian research is fundamental, and we shall now give some of the reasons which make it of particular interest to the international community and to administrators in other countries who are responsible for education policies.

Italy is, at the same time, unique and symbolic, sometimes being in advance and sometimes lagging behind; our tardiness (e.g. in the extension of compulsory schooling) and our progressiveness (e.g. in commercial television broadcasting) have not been the result of deliberate education policy decisions: the majority of the phenomena which are most significant from the point of view of this experiment, i.e. those which concern relations between the media and the school, have emerged 'spontaneously' out of the interaction or relationships, either symbolic or based on strength, within our society.

We shall cite three significant factors:

• The start of television broadcasting (1954), which reached a wide audience (1960) before schools and the other media did. Unlike most other highly developed countries, where television found its place at the end of a series of specific developments – education, the popular press, cinema and radio – Italy followed an unusual path, much more similar to that taken subsequently by other countries which only later, or recently, began the process of development.

- The first cycle of unified compulsory secondary education, for pupils up to the age of 14, was introduced in 1963. For just over 10 years, the nation had to cope with getting the mass of pupils to school, something which was largely done during a period upon which disputes and a generally anti-modern social atmosphere made a deep impression (1968–78), and which also saw a devaluation of training and education.

- American-style private commercial radio and television took root (to the point at which they won more than 50 per cent of the total audience) very rapidly (between 1979 and 1983), completely changing the relationship between the media system and both the economic and cultural worlds. Particular results of the expansion of commercial television were greater domestic demand, changes in young people's habits and an increased pace of community life. We are looking at three cultural and social processes that are highly important to the subject under discussion and that place Italy in a position which differs from that of the countries of Northern Europe, as they bring Italy's experience much closer to two realities which are themselves remote from each other: on the one hand the situation in America and, on the other, the experience of the countries in the Mediterranean area and, in general, of other countries which were late in starting down the development path.

In Italy, the outcome of the past 30 years of relations between schools and the media is a situation characterized by major changes, both structural (the industrialization and tertiarization of the economy and major population movements) and socio-cultural (the results of a variety of cultural influences from ethnic, traditional and ideological sources and major socio-political and socio-cultural conflicts), which have had some effect on these

261

relations, altering them in substance and in detail.

All these features of the situation in Italy mean that the lessons which can be learned have more general significance and importance and may be helpful for the structuring and management of education policies which aim to achieve beneficial cooperation between schools and the media.

TEACHERS' AND PUPILS' IMPRESSIONS OF THE MEDIA: DIAMETRICALLY OPPOSING VIEWS

Firstly, here is an amazing research finding. Questionnaires were distributed at higher secondary schools to a sample of final-year pupils (girls and boys aged between 17 and 19), their parents and all their teachers. They were asked to assess the influence (great, fairly great, little or non-existent) of seven major socializing factors (the family, the school, the media, the church, friends or peer groups, movements/associations and political parties) on young people in their formative years. While the replies from the three social groups (pupils, parents and teachers) were distributed in a fairly balanced manner – revealing substantial agreement – in respect of the role of five of these agents, the family (very influential), friends (fairly influential), the church, movements/associations and political parties (all three considered to have little influence), major differences emerged in respect to the school and the media.

Looking at the role of the school, the most negative view came from the teachers, followed by pupils and their families. In other words it is the teachers themselves, much more than the parents and even more than their pupils, who have a negative view of schools, as they consider that schools actually play an inadequate role in shaping the younger generations.

The result in respect of the media is even more amazing. It is the teachers who consider the media to have a great influence on young people in their formative years (a view held by between 52 and 67 per cent), while far fewer parents accredit so much influence to the media (between 20 and 30 per cent). The pupils' verdict is negative: the media have great influence in the opinion of between

5 and 18 per cent, depending on geographical location – the figure being higher among pupils from the southern regions.

In the following years the same questionnaire was given to other schools, with the same results.

To sum up, there is a clear contrast in Italy's higher secondary schools between teachers' and pupils' attitudes to the relations between the media and the school. The pupils have no strong feelings about the media, while teachers tend to believe that the media are their main rivals.

Useful information for the purposes of interpreting the research findings can be obtained from the replies given by teachers and pupils to the other subjects in the questionnaire, ethno-anthropological observation of their establishments and discussions with teachers and pupils.

It is important to point out that not only do teachers very clearly overestimate the part played by the media during young people's formative years, but they also view it in negative terms: they consider the influence of the media, particularly television, to be largely unfavourable. The role of the two major socializing factors recognized as being highly important – the family and the peer group – is regarded just as negatively. If we also bear in mind their lack of self-esteem and their view that the school has little influence on young people's formative years, we find ourselves looking at a rather disconcerting picture, which can be very briefly summed up as follows: the teachers at upper secondary schools believe that they are not carrying out their job satisfactorily, and lack motivation, as they feel that they are losing out to the greater attraction and influence on young people of three other socializing factors, namely, in order of importance, the media, the family and friends. In contrast, the pupils' attitude is very different. Not only do they attribute significantly less influence to the media than do their teachers, but they also hold a different view of the influence of the school, friends and the family. At the end of their schooling, although they do not have too rosy a view of their schools – indeed, their attitude is critical – they nevertheless reach a much more positive verdict than do their teachers. As far as their relationship with the media, in particular, is concerned, it emerges clearly from the replies to other specific items in the questionnaire that they maintain critical detachment from television, especially; and this attitude is all the more significant for the fact that the pupils are boys who attend grammar schools in the central northern regions which specialize in classical studies.

TIME AND SOCIO-CULTURAL FACTORS

Readers will not have failed to notice that the pupils questioned between 1982 and 1987 are members of the so-called 'television generation', since all of them were born at a time when almost every household had a TV set (and this, of course, in an era when a very high proportion of young people attend school); the replies therefore came from people who watch a lot of television, and who, generally speaking, know the media well. These research findings, which are very briefly summarized here, encouraged us to view the relationship between the media and the school in a different light from usual, particularly leading us to compare both the time and socio-cultural factors.

The research, which is still in an experimental phase and is intended to culminate in the setting-up of a real 'observation post' to monitor schools, focuses on numerous aspects of schools' practice, being based on the premise that the processes of cultural standardization activated by the media and by the school itself could acquire different shapes and meanings in different cultural contexts.

The research therefore concentrates on these contexts, centring on a number of towns and institutions (six towns and 62 institutions so far); this makes it possible to assess the influence of internal and external situations on the attitudes and behaviour of the three major social groups (pupils, parents and teachers) involved in the practical day-to-day running of schools. Hence variable elements play a part in the research, such as the organizational structure within each institution and the school's image in its town (society's view of schools in general and the image of the individual institution).

The adoption of this kind of research strategy has enabled us to cover aspects of schools' practice which had not previously been appropriately highlighted, such as the great variety of situations at local level. Despite the existence in Italy of a centralized uniform organization, the Ministry of Education, for teacher recruitment and career, curricula and assessment criteria, etc., there is a great variety of types of school (grammar schools and vocational establishments) and of institutions of the same type (traditional and experimental grammar schools). Furthermore, as the research continues over a period of time, it will be possible to take specific account of the time dimension.

THE ROLE OF THE MEDIA IN THE PROCESS OF EDUCATION

It is on the basis of this research experiment and the initial findings – which, we believe, provide ample food for thought and can be taken into account when education policies are implemented – that relations between the media and schools can be reconsidered in a different way.

Readers are bound to have been struck by the fact that all three social groups unanimously attribute considerable importance to the role of the family during young people's formative years. There is no doubt at all that the family is more important than experts and research workers believe – most of this group are accustomed to basing their thinking on even more general views or, on the other hand, on more variable opinions, such as the tendencies found in the large metropolitan areas or in intellectual circles.

The significance of the family, as revealed by the above-mentioned research and as compared with the role of the media, reflects the influence of cultural tradition as experienced and handed down by the family and local culture, and has some effect even on relationships between friends. In small and medium-sized towns, in particular (where the present research is concentrated), local cultural traditions remain as influential and as important as before, according to the subjects questioned, and this is not by chance. In view of this, it can be seen from the replies to the questionnaire and from the research findings that the socio-cultural situation is fairly complex and has specific features.

Young people find themselves within an educational context characterized by the strong presence of four major socializing factors. Two of them (family and friends) are influenced by local traditions and a network of social relationships (sociability, real relationships with emotional overtones). The other two (schools and the media) are of a broader nature and abstract in content, symbolically based on the written and spoken word and on pictures without strong emotional overtones.

Each of the two pairs is viewed by the adults involved (particularly the teachers and, to a lesser extent the parents) as being in mutual opposition: family against friends and schools against the media. The teachers, for example, are almost literally haunted by the thought that their influence on their pupils might be swamped by that of: the family (which they consider to be ignorant and protective); friends (regarded as a 'bad influence' who stir up trouble); and the media (viewed as vehicles of falsehood and inferior culture).

In contrast, the pupils, while they are able to understand these conflicts, tend to place the emphasis on what the four agents have in common, and their particular desire is to see all four working towards the same ends. We are very much simplifying the findings of complex research, which really need to be explained in more detail. We shall merely highlight one essential fact, which is the gap between the views of teachers and pupils: while the teachers feel relatively powerless in the face of the contrasting mixture of influences to which their pupils are exposed, and focus their attention on the media, which they make the scapegoat for all their difficulties, the pupils would like their teachers successfully to initiate interaction between the various socializing agents; they would also like to see their teachers skilfully stage-managing a combination of all four. What does this polarization indicate?

One possible answer calls for bold assumptions about the present situation of the education system in Italy, assumptions which would also relate to every situation in which there are various strong cultural influences, a situation found typically during transitional phases. This answer suggests that it is necessary, first and foremost, to alter teachers' cultural attitude and strengthen their motivation, so that they carry out their functions as educators differently, in a way which takes positive account of the role of the media (how they help pupils, rather than their bad influence). In other words, it is impossible to view the world of school culture as a consistent, finite universe – as if it provided a general, secondary means of preparing pupils for life in society as opposed to the primary, family course followed in private. The main reason for this is the presence of the media, which have brought deep changes in the cultural context beyond the school and family, providing a sort of 'almost natural' highly symbolic and abstract environment and infusing it with universal values and models which it is wrong to regard as being in opposition with the culture of the schools.

In other words, after several years on a country's cultural scene, television and the media can no longer be considered to be an additional and different agent, the negative role of which continues to be emphasized – something which was legitimate to some extent when television first appeared. The pupils in classes today are the children of their families, as well as being members of the 'TV generation'. In other words, television was and is a medium which provides a second or third way in which we can learn to describe objects and situations and derive concepts from them. In this respect, television and the media are on a wavelength which is not all that different from that of the school, although they partly reshape the relations between parents and their children and between children and their friends. If teachers' attitudes could be changed, the pupils' explicit objective of obtaining eclectic and, to some extent, syncretic education could be attained. It would be an education in which a balanced role may be played by both the school, which can consistently hand down the long-established cultural heritage, and the media, which can pass on the up-to-date, changing cultural heritage.

SOME CONCLUSIONS

Two aspects of the relations between the media and schools have been taken into account by education policy-makers: on the one hand, how could the media be used to provide educational back-up in schools; on the other hand, how was the role of the media in classroom activities to be viewed? (A not entirely dissimilar problem has been experienced in respect of computers in recent years.)

In the light of the reported findings of the research into the situation in Italy, we feel able to say that, as far as the first aspect is concerned – i.e. the use of the media in the sphere of education – significant advances have been made since the early stages (schools television, audio-visual equipment) thanks to the realization that the media may be used in a creative and beneficial way. The problem is a technico-cultural one:

inadequate numbers of audio and videocassettes suitable for use in schools are still being produced, although the types of products required by the market are fairly well-known;

there is not yet a sufficient number of teachers capable of using the audio-visual equipment.

In both these areas encouragement must be given to investment and to modernization policies intended to improve the situation. However, the situation in respect of the latter area is more dramatic: educational practitioners ought to take account of the existence of the media. The term 'take account' has always been interpreted in negative terms: the intention was to face up to the media and keep them in check. For a long time, this attitude had negative effects on the use of audio-visual equipment, which primarily served the purpose of exorcizing the media and competing with them. As the findings of the research mentioned above have shown, teachers still reject the media, predicting doom and citing intellectual grounds. Not only have they failed to change their attitude over the years, but they have used it to justify not so much their failures as teachers as their wish to have nothing to do with the media. This is particularly serious, as schools can only operate properly if they have highly motivated teachers.

If a useful conclusion is to be drawn from this analysis, it is the perhaps slightly paradoxical one that there is a need to promote in-service teacher training covering the role of the media in our society. It is not so much – or not only – pupils who need training relating to the media; their teachers' needs are greater. If teachers do not learn to live with the media, and to acquire a full understanding (better than that of their pupils) of what the media are and how they function, schools will be destined to perpetuate a schizophrenic educational atmosphere and will lose out in the long run, becoming less and less able to have any influence on the shaping of future generations.

NOTES ON THE RESEARCH

This report is based on the findings of research carried out by the 'observation post for culture in higher secondary education' at the Department of Cultural Sociology of the Cesare Alfieri Faculty of Political Sciences of the University of Florence.

The research started during the academic year 1981–82 and has so far involved direct sociological–anthropological observation in 62 higher secondary education establishments of every kind (varying from grammar schools to vocational institutions) in six small and medium-sized towns. Some 9000 respondents have been questioned, 4000 of them pupils, 3000 parents and 2000 teachers. The research has led to several publications on individual aspects: work is under way on an overall analysis and conclusions. This is the most extensive empirical sociological–anthropological research carried out in Italy.

The necessary funds were obtained from the Ministry of Education (60 per cent), the University of Naples, the University of Florence, the region of Basilicata and the region of Puglia.

CHAPTER 4

Spain: Introduction of New Information Technologies in the Spanish Educational System (Project Atenea)

HISTORICAL BACKGROUND

Computers began to be introduced in schools in various ways in the early 1980s. However diverse, all these attempts shared one common feature: it was teachers who took the initiative to carry them out. There were some channels open in the Ministry of Education and Science which allowed these enthusiastic, self-taught pioneers to carry out their projects for introducing computers in schools. These channels were:

1. Computer science could be taught in secondary schools (ages 14–17) as one of the optional subjects in EATP (technical and vocational education).
2. In second-level vocational training (ages 16–19) a need to update the means and methods used in branches such as administration and management was acknowledged, and therefore some training centres were allowed by the ministry to introduce computer science (data-processing equipment and computers in management) as a special optional subject.

270

Although the Ministry of Education and Science supported these initiatives, they were carried out only if teachers took the first steps and assumed a great deal of personal responsibility.

3. For general basic education (primary school, ages 6–14), the Ministry of Education and Science promoted the acquisition of computers through tenders for buying innovative material. Teachers took advantage of these offers by submitting voluntary experimental projects, a procedure that was necessary to obtain the materials. Here it would seem that the ministry showed more initiative in providing innovative resources connected with new information technologies; nevertheless, it by no means constituted a systematic plan for the introduction of this technology in educational centres.

In short, it may be argued that isolated and enthusiastic initiatives on the part of a large number of teachers created a favourable atmosphere for the introduction of microcomputers in schools, and that the experiments being carried out, and personal interest in the subject, allowed some teachers to become initiated in the use of microcomputers: these teachers are now the members of the first groups of teacher trainers and the first pedagogical teams of the Atenea Project.

In 1983, several non-educational sectors of the government (the Ministry of Industry and the Data Processing Centre of the Ministry of Education and Science) suggested that the Secretaria General Técnica (Technical Secretariat General) of the Ministry of Education and Science should create a working group whose task would be to elaborate a proposal for the rational introduction of new information technologies in primary and secondary education. The proposal was completed in April 1988, and established the following general objectives:

1. Promote basic knowledge of computer science and its applications, taking into account its influence upon all the factors that condition our social environment.
2. Improve the students' learning process.

3. Use computer science and its applications as a means of constant pedagogical updating for teachers.

Regarding the inclusion of computer science in the school curriculum, it was suggested that the subject matter should be considered from a two-fold point of view: general subjects, placing special emphasis on its cultural nature; and programming languages and programmes of application. It was suggested that computer science should be included in the later years of primary school and secondary school. This proposal included a budget which was rejected by the Ministry of Finance, owing to the amount of the investment involved.

The model established by this proposal was based upon three types of training, and general equipment. To a certain extent, in the elaboration of this model the Ministry of Education was only one decision-maker among many, and so the proposal was not drawn up solely from an educational perspective.

THE ATENEA PROJECT AS THE COORDINATION OF SEVERAL ADMINISTRATIVE UNITS

Despite the inconvenience caused by the rejection of the project's budget, the Ministry of Education and Science considered it urgent to start an experimental plan for the introduction of new information technologies, and thus started it, although in a much more modest form than had been originally planned. The money was obtained from the budgets for didactic material of the two Direcciones Generales (general directorates) in both educational levels, by redefining some of the didactic material modules traditionally sent to schools. At the same time, the Ministry of Education created the Comisión de Seguimiento y Coordinación del Proyecto Atenea (Follow-up and Coordination Commission for the Atenea Project) chaired by the Secretario General (vice-minister) of Education and made up of Subdirecciones Generales (general sub-directorates). These involved those of Secondary

Education, Primary Education, Teacher Training, Organization and Automation, and the National Centre of Educational Research and Documentation. This commission drew up the first call for applications from experimental centres to join the project. This call showed one of the most important characteristics of the Atenea Project: all centres taking part in the project do so voluntarily, through a group of teachers who draw up a pedagogical project approved by the Claustro (general meeting of staff) and the Consejo Escolar (school board). The Commission put the Direcciones Generales of primary and secondary education in charge of integrating these new technologies into their respective curricula and of following up the experiments carried out at their respective schools. Likewise, the Subdirección de Perfeccionamiento del Profesorado (Sub-directorate for Teacher Training), through the Institute of Educational Techniques, was put in charge of training. A technical coordination group formed by technical and educational advisors from each of the bodies involved was also created.

The money to start up the project and pay for materials and personnel came from the budgets approved for the programmes of the Direcciones Generales of both levels of education.

The first decisions were made about the sort of hardware schools were going to be equipped with, and compatible microcomputers were chosen. A choice of software was also made, which included programming languages such as Logo, BASIC and Pascal, an integrated package and an authoring language, Pilot, in order to facilitate the creation of educational programs by teachers.

All this was simultaneous to the creation of the Centros de Profesores, CEPs (teachers' centres), devised for the pedagogical and didactic improvement of teachers within a certain territorial area. These CEPs seemed to be the most suitable base for the teacher training infrastructure of the pedagogical teams in the Atenea Project, and they were therefore equipped with the same hardware that had been sent to experimental schools. At the same time the training of future teacher trainers began. They were to train the teachers of the pedagogical teams at the CEPs.

With the second call for the selection of experimental centres a booklet entitled *Proyecto Atenea* (consideration and annexes to guide plan-making in schools willing to take part in the project) was published and the Direcciones Provinciales (local educational authorities) distributed it to schools. This booklet was an important step towards defining what was intended to be experimented with in classrooms. At this stage, the project's profile was entirely educational and with the publishing of the previously mentioned annexes and the settling of a single two-level training model, its main features were definitely established in their present form.

The fact that the project was being directed by a coordinating board and financed by the different units under coordination often made decision-making not very quick or operational. In order to solve this problem, the then Secretario General de Educación decided to create a programme in which human and material resources would join under one single directorate.

AREA OF APPLICATION

The territorial scope of the Atenea Project covers only the 28 Spanish provinces directly under the administration of the Ministry of Education and Science. A third initiative was added to those two already being carried out in the Ministry of Education and Science in this field. The three initiatives were:

- The introduction of new information technologies in vocational education and in artistic education schools.
- The introduction of computer science as an optional subject in secondary schools.
- The Atenea Project. The objective of this project was to test the integration of new information technologies in different areas and subjects of the school curriculum. It includes the education of children with special needs.

CREATION OF THE PROGRAMA DE NUEVAS TECNOLOGÍAS DE LA INFORMACIÓN Y DE LA COMUNICACIÓN (NEW INFORMATION AND COMMUNICATION TECHNOLOGIES PROGRAMME)

In January 1987, the Ministry of Education and Science created the Programa de Nuevas Tecnologías de la Información y de la Comunicación (PNTIC) and gave to it its own budget. This programme included the experimental Atenea and Mercurio (introduction of video) Projects, and those connected with the introduction of computers and video in artistic education schools.

Important decisions have been made since then concerning both projects. First, they have been defined as innovation projects. Second, the functions of the teacher trainers and their own training have been adapted to those of agents of innovation. Third, follow-up and evaluation plans have been devised for both projects.

At the budget level, large amounts of money have been allocated for maintenance and didactic material for both schools and teachers' centres.

SUPPORT INFRASTRUCTURES

There are basically two support infrastructures: the headquarters of the PNTIC (New Technologies Programme) and the CEPs (teachers' centres). Both have their own staff formed by teachers devoted exclusively to this project.

The staff at headquarters are in charge of training the teacher trainers, acquiring equipment, developing prototypes, preparing software specifications, adapting strategies and establishing channels for sharing information between the various levels of experimentation. The training of teachers in the pedagogical teams of participating schools and the exchange of information and didactic experiences with other experimental centres, or with other groups of teachers working in given areas, is carried out

275

by the CEPs. These centres also serve as resource centres. We consider the creation of these human and material infrastructures, without which these activities could not be generalized throughout the school system, as one of the achievements of this project.

TEACHER TRAINING

Based upon the understanding that teachers are key elements for any innovation in a school, the general training model attempts to provide them with knowledge that will enable them to transform their way of teaching. The idea is to give teachers the theoretical and practical tools for analysing computer material and selecting those most appropriate for their environment and specific task. Teachers are to acquire a conceptual framework which will allow them to rationalize why, what for and how to use the new technologies. On the other hand, teachers are supposed to observe and analyse didactic experiences in which new information technologies are used. In short, the aim is to make teachers reflect upon their own use of the material and evaluate its results in the teaching–learning process.

Using this model as a basis, a two-level training programme was begun. The two levels were the plan for teacher trainers (the trainers working in the CEPs) and the plan for the training of teachers in pedagogical teams of schools taking part in the experiment. The main difference between the two is basically that the teacher trainers received a more specialized training not only in technical and didactic aspects but also in the design, planning and organization of training as well as the evaluation, diffusion and follow-up of experiences at schools, not to mention support for innovation processes.

The first 54 teacher trainers were selected by the CEPs mainly on the basis of their prior knowledge of computers. As a consequence of this, in a certain number of cases, the conversion of a computer enthusiast into a school-innovation-by-means-of-new-information-technologies enthusiast was difficult to achieve. These teacher trainers do not have to teach their normal classes to young students, they are staff members of the CEPs, and

276

are devoted exclusively to the Atenea Project. They receive no supplement to their salary for working on this project.

The pedagogical teams of the centres taking part in the experiment are formed by volunteers. They apply to join the project and agree to follow the training plan and carry out the experiments specified on the work schedule which they elaborate, with the help of their teacher trainer, once the initial training phase is completed. The training of pedagogical teams of participating schools is done outside normal working hours in the CEPs by the above-mentioned trainers. These teachers receive no monetary compensation for taking part in the project. Under these circumstances, the training of teachers in the pedagogical teams of participating schools is very difficult. It goes on thanks to enthusiasm and interest in learning to use new information technologies. Such a situation cannot be considered an adequate basis for extending the model to the entire school system.

SOFTWARE DEVELOPMENT STRATEGIES

The most significant aspect of an innovative educational project of the type we are describing is, perhaps, the material, non-existent at first, which must be used in the process. The very development process creates the materials and, at the same time, production and experimentation with the new materials cause the process to move forward. Teachers cannot order what they need if they do not understand the possibilities of these technologies, and they cannot get to know these unless they have a certain number of models with which to experiment. The increase in both will bring us to a critical mass of expertise which will make it possible to create these materials as easily as any other type of didactic material is drawn up today. But if this is to happen, not only do we need to have a number of models equivalent to this critical mass, but also the commercial firms of this sector must create and develop methods to introduce these materials into their usual development and planning processes. For these reasons the Atenea Project has developed certain strategies in order, on the one hand, to collect ideas and products from teachers who best understand the possibilities of the computer and, on the other, to encourage publishers and software designers to become interested in this aspect of production. These strategies include the following.

The agreement between the Ministry of Education, MINER and CDTI. This agreement was signed by the Ministry of Education, the Ministry of Industry and the Centro para el Desarrollo Tecnológico e Industrial (Centre for Technological and Industrial Development), CDTI. Its main features are: general prior specifications concerning CAI programmes in different areas; special projects on simulation backgrounds, special education, telematics, etc., drawn at the headquarters of the PNTIC (New Technologies Programme); environments, special education, telematics, etc.

The commercial firms submit projects based on the abovementioned specifications and those which are chosen receive partial subsidies and are supervised during the prototype development phase. Two calls for such commercial projects have been made so far and a significant increase in the number of companies taking part, along with a more active market, has been observed. Financing has been granted according to each case. Special education projects are 100 per cent subsidized. In general, subsidies represent some 33 per cent of the cost, low interest loans another 33 per cent, and the rest is paid by the company. The acquisition price for each copy paid by the Ministry of Education has proved difficult to negotiate, because the insufficient size of the potential market outside the ministry makes commercial firms hesitate.

The first call for projects has resulted in the development of approximately 50 programs related to mathematics, physics, chemistry, language, foreign language, logic and Logo for disabled children. There are 13 special projects being developed as a result of the second call for projects: acquisition of laboratory data, electronic bulletin board for school use, sets of special education programs based on concept keyboards and simulation environments and other programs for curriculum areas.

Translation of foreign programs. A special mention should be made here of the recent translation of a set of programs for solving physics problems.

Contests. These are organized by the PNTIC and the Centro de Investigación y Documentación) of the Ministry of Education and

Science, and aimed at teachers and commercial firms. Some 15 programs in different subjects have been obtained through these contests.

LESSONS LEARNED

Many lessons have been learned, and they have been hinted at throughout this short summary. To summarize even further, it may be said that the introduction of new information technologies into schools with the aim of integrating these into curriculum areas is slow, and that it must be carefully designed and generously planned. Moreover, special emphasis must be placed on the training of teachers who are to carry out this innovation, on the support these teachers need, and on strategies for the development and the testing of the teaching materials which must be produced.

CHAPTER 5

Turkey: Distance Education in Turkey

This case study aims to describe the Turkish distance education experience within its historical, social and educational setting. First, a brief historical perspective is given and then the main characteristics of Turkish distance education are presented.

BACKGROUND

The crucial year in Turkish distance education was 1982. In 1982, the new Constitution of the Republic was accepted, and in accordance with the Constitution, a new institution called the Council for Higher Education (CHE) was established to 'plan, organize, administer and supervise the education provided by institutions of higher education'.

The CHE immediately reorganized the existing universities and established new ones. There had been 19 universities, 19 academies and seven polytechnics before the establishment of the CHE. Through the CHE reorganization programme, these institutions of higher education were turned into 27 universities. Today, the number of universities has grown to 29 (including Bilkent, the first and only private university in Turkey).

In accordance with the new Higher Education Act that was passed in 1982, Anadolu University (formerly Eskisehir Academy of Economic and Commercial Sciences) was authorized to provide distance education in Turkey, on a national scale. The history of

Anadolu University, which has provided distance education at the faculty level since 1982, goes back to the Eskisehir Academy of Economics and Commercial Sciences established in 1958. The former Faculty of Communication Sciences of the Academy was turned into the Faculty of Open Education (FOE) of the newly established Anadolu University, because at that time (as today) it was the only institution that had experience in distance education techniques. The first educational television pilot project of Turkey was undertaken at that institution.

Although a distance education programme (Diffusion of Higher Education: referred to as Yay-Kur) was undertaken by the Ministry of Education between 1975 and 1978, this initiative had been a dramatic failure for various political, administrative, financial and even psychological reasons, which might be the subject of a separate case study. However, especially at the beginning of its own project, Anadolu University carefully evaluated and greatly benefited from the experience of Yay-Kur, and therefore the 1975–8 experience should not be taken as a total failure.

MAIN CHARACTERISTICS OF TURKISH DISTANCE EDUCATION

First of all, although the name of the faculty dealing with distance education in Turkey is Faculty of Open Education, the present system is not 'open' in the technical sense of the term. The system is not open to everybody unconditionally. The applicants should – at the least – be graduates of secondary schools and also have to take an entrance examination given by the Council of Higher Education. However, as Özgü (1988) has written, three major characteristics may justify the employment of the term 'open':

a. that a considerable part of the education is carried out through mass-communication media;
b. that students can participate regardless of their geographical and occupational status;

c. and a capacity such that, in practice, almost anybody who is academically qualified to become a student of higher education, has the chance to realize it.

MEDIA

Distance education in Turkey is based on the combination of three media: printed material; television and radio broadcasts; and academic counselling centres.

Printed material is prepared by the academic staff of various universities and edited by the faculty members of Anadolu University according to the principles and techniques of distance education. This material is sent to the students by regular postal channels. Students pay for these services at the beginning of every academic year.

Television and radio broadcasts are designed as supplementary to the printed material. As in the printed material, various university members work on TV and radio programmes, either as authors or as tutors (or both). More than 200 broadcasts are aired every year and every student can watch these programmes all over the country. Broadcasting services are carried out by the state-owned Turkish Radio and Television (TRT).

Academic counselling centres are located in 18 cities. At these centres, students receive advisory help provided by part-time instructors and academic advisers from the regional university members. One hour per week counselling services are provided for each course at these centres. Approximately 80 per cent of the students have a chance of regular access to these centres.

COURSES

Two types of programme are offered by the Faculty of Open Education (FOE): business administration and economics. Both are four-year degree programmes. In every academic year, each student has to take nine courses, including the history of the Turkish revolution and English. Diplomas given by the faculty are equivalent to the classical faculty diplomas.

STUDENT PROFILE

The distance education programme now serves more than 200 000 students in Turkey and abroad. According to McIsaac *et al.* (1988), 54 per cent of FOE students live in cities, 27 per cent in towns and 19 per cent in villages. Some 58 per cent are employed and 25 per cent are female. (The authors point out that 'suggestions have been made regarding the potential of the open education programme to improve the ratio of women who receive a higher education'.)

ACTIVITIES ABROAD

The Faculty of Open Education has started a new pilot project for 'training Turkish students abroad'. The main targets of this project are the Turkish migrant workers and their children living in various European countries, especially in the Federal Republic of Germany. (More than 2 million Turkish citizens live in European countries, 1.43 million of them in the Federal Republic of Germany.) Within that project, 'Anadolu University established a contact office in the city of Cologne . . . to offer the same distance education programmes as in Turkey to the eligible candidates who were settled in Western European countries' (Özgü, 1988, p. 5).

Besides these programmes, FOE also implemented a joint project with the Ministry of Education: 'Primary school teacher training project'. This project began in the 1986–87 academic year and covered 130 000 primary school teachers. Throughout this project, more than 100 000 teachers have received a degree, thus raising their professional status. This two-year programme also enabled the primary school teachers to enroll at the university for a faculty degree.

Table 3 Number of students matriculated in Turkish universities 1983–7

| Year | Other universities | | | Anadolu Univ. Faculty of Open Education | | | Total 2 as percentage of total 1 |
	Four-year degree programme	Two-year junior college	Total 1	Four-year degree	Two-year teacher INSET	Total 2	
1983	69 288	22 291	91 579	14 981	–	14 981	16
1984	74 894	27 955	102 849	47 999	–	47 999	47
1985	69 954	26 524	96 478	60 000	–	60 000	62
1986	69 404	23 891	93 295	68 911	48 774	117 685	126
1987	66 740	23 094	89 834	73 828	83 852	157 680	176

Source: Özgü (1988, p. 6).

284

EVALUATION

The statistics given in Table 3 show that within five years, the number of students in the higher education distance education programme has doubled. This quantitative success might be criticized from the qualitative point of view. However, a critical evaluation of the printed materials and broadcasts may well reveal success either by ('traditional') Turkish university standards or by foreign distance education standards, as indicated by McIsaac *et al.* (1988).

REFERENCES

McIsaac, M.S., Murphy, K.L. and Demiray, U. (1988). Examining distance education in Turkey. *Distance Education*, **9** (1), 106–14.

Özgü, T. (1988). *Distance education and its contribution to the solution of educational problems in a developing country (Turkey)*. Anadolu University, Cologne.

Index